KILTS ON THE COAST

KILTS
on the COAST
THE SCOTS WHO BUILT BC

JAN PETERSON

VICTORIA | VANCOUVER | CALGARY

Heritage House Publishing Company Ltd.
www.heritagehouse.ca

LIBRARY AND ARCHIVES CANADA CATALOGUING IN PUBLICATION
Peterson, Jan, 1937–
    Kilts on the coast: the Scots who built BC / Jan Peterson.

Includes bibliographical references and index.
Issued also in electronic format.
ISBN 978-1-927051-27-6

    1. Pioneers—British Columbia—Vancouver Island—Biography.
2. Scots—British Columbia—Vancouver Island—Biography.
3. Immigrants—British Columbia—Vancouver Island—Biography.
4. Miners—British Columbia—Vancouver Island—Biography.
5. Vancouver Island (B.C.)—Economic conditions—19th century.
6. Vancouver Island (B.C.)—History—19th century. 7. Vancouver Island (B.C.)—Biography. I. Title.

FC3844.3.A1P48 2012   971.1'2020922   C2011-907160-6

Edited by Karla Decker
Proofread by Lesley Cameron
Cover and interior design by Frances Hunter
Cover photos: The Charles Ross family in 1843 (photo F-05032 courtesy of Royal BC Museum, BC Archives); early sketch of Nanaimo Harbour (image 1998 032 M Prt 1 courtesy of Nanaimo Community Archives); tartan by Frances Hunter

MIX
Paper from
responsible sources
FSC
www.fsc.org   FSC® C016245

The interior of this book was produced on 100% post-consumer recycled paper, processed chlorine free and printed with vegetable-based inks.

Heritage House acknowledges the financial support for its publishing program from the Government of Canada through the Canada Book Fund (CBF), Canada Council for the Arts and the province of British Columbia through the British Columbia Arts Council and the Book Publishing Tax Credit.

  Canadian Heritage Patrimoine canadien   Canada Council for the Arts Conseil des Arts du Canada   BRITISH COLUMBIA ARTS COUNCIL

16 15 14 13 12 1 2 3 4 5

Printed in Canada

CONTENTS

ACKNOWLEDGEMENTS

I have many people to thank for help in writing this book. I am particularly grateful to family descendants for helping piece together the fabric of their ancestors' lives. Maureen Duffus, the great-granddaughter of James Yates, was a big help in filling in many blank spots in my research of the early days of Fort Victoria. I was also grateful to Alice Marwood, a descendant of William Isbister, the stonemason who laid many foundations and helped build early Nanaimo. My thanks also go to Mildred Simpson and her son Terry, who helped with information about the Adam Grant Horne family, and to Cathy Payne of San Francisco, who helped with the Sabiston brothers. I also appreciate those family members who researched their family tree and lodged the information in the archives for others like me to use.

Bruce Davies at Craigdarroch Castle is thanked for his help, as is the British Columbia Archives for its wonderful, easily accessible resources. Detailing the pioneer family histories was time-consuming but worthwhile. Hopefully, this work will add to the documentation already available.

My contacts in Scotland are not forgotten, especially my friend Bob Currie, of Strathaven, who never failed to supply information and offer encouragement, or to provide contacts for my research. Anne Geddes of Heritage Services in East Ayrshire, Bruce Morgan of the Dick Institute in Kilmarnock, David Roberts of the Paisley Museum, and Ian Macdonald of the Stewarton & District Museum all gave their time and energy to my questions.

The Hudson's Bay Company archives in Winnipeg contributed so much to the stories of these early settlers and the ships they sailed in. What a wonderful resource to have in Canada! I could not have written this book without their information and help.

This book would not have been possible without the Nanaimo Community Archives Society, its manager, Christine Meutzner, and her volunteers, Daphne Paterson and Jill Stannard. They all contributed so much to this project. Daphne was particularly helpful in suggesting new avenues of research that added greatly to the manuscript. Thanks also go to the Nanaimo Museum staff, who are always so supportive of my efforts. Having a family of positive people around really helps in a project of this size.

Thanks also to the Heritage House staff for bringing another of my manuscripts to life; also a special thanks to my editor, Karla Decker, for all her hard work, patience and expertise.

My own family continues to support my research and writing and has followed the trail of the early Scottish settlers along with me these past few years. Ray was always there when I needed him. Without his love and support along the way, this book might not have been possible.

PREFACE

Many of Vancouver Island's first settlers came from Scotland. Putting down roots in Victoria and Nanaimo, these hardy pioneers helped pave the way for future development.

Nanaimo is generally underrated in terms of its history, even though it was wealth from the coal industry that helped pay the bills in the early days of the new Colony of Vancouver Island. The most acknowledged personalities from the area were Robert Dunsmuir and his sons, James and Alexander. The family made its name in the coal-mining industry, building the Esquimalt and Nanaimo Railway (the E & N), and building castles in Victoria. Little physical evidence remains of their years in Nanaimo, perhaps due to the sour labour relations they left behind. There are no monuments to their contribution or their presence in the area so many years ago. The same can be said for those Ayrshire miners and their assistants who arrived before and with Dunsmuir, and the labourers from the Orkney Islands.

Victoria was different. Destined to be the centre of power in the new colony and later the seat of government in a new province, it was settled by Hudson's Bay Company employees, independent immigrants, businessmen and people from the upper-middle class of society. Governor James Douglas set the tone for the new British colony, made the rules and, though inexperienced in governing, managed to establish the first legislative assembly.

SCOTLAND

From the Orkney Islands to Inverness and the Isle of Skye, from Edinburgh to the Ayrshire mines, young Scots left their homeland to travel to an unknown land in the new world.

MAP COURTESY OF JOHN PETERSON

INTRODUCTION

From all over Scotland, young men open to new adventure and unforeseen difficulties signed on with the Hudson's Bay Company (HBC) for three to five years, first to man the Company's forts, then to mine coal and help colonize Vancouver Island. What they found on the Island was land and opportunity, a chance to build a life for themselves and generations to come. But they never forgot where they came from—such was the character of the Scottish pioneers. They kept old traditions alive: they celebrated Hogmanay on New Year's Eve by lighting bonfires, firing guns or banging pot lids; on Rabbie Burns's birthday, January 25, they ate haggis and recited the bard's poems; at family social events, they sang songs of their childhood and retold stories of their past to another generation. A simple lump of coal was a statement and a wish for a prosperous year ahead!

The HBC recognized the Orkney Islanders' steady work habits. Plus, the Islanders came cheap and were used to harsh weather and poor living conditions. Out of touch with their extended families in Scotland, some sought comfort from Native women. A local piper or fiddler occasionally dispelled feelings of isolation by keeping toes tapping in jigs, reels and quadrilles.

The polite Highlanders, from Inverness and west to the islands of Skye and the Outer Hebrides, were placed in positions of authority. Appointed as clerks and trained as fur traders, they moved up the hierarchy in the Company.

The Ayrshire recruits were Lowlanders who were skilled

miners used to working underground. They were just what James Douglas needed to justify the Company's exploration of the coal industry. The initial failure to mine coal at Fort Rupert, on northern Vancouver Island, was put aside when "black diamonds" were found in Nanaimo. It was revenue from this coalfield that kept the fledgling colony afloat in its early years of development.

With so few people in the colony, the Scots knew one another, and all identified with whichever HBC ship had brought them to the Island—the *Harpooner*, *Tory*, *Norman Morison* or the *Pekin*. Each person had a story to tell of the horrific voyage across the Atlantic, around treacherous Cape Horn and up the Pacific coast to Fort Victoria. For six months they suffered harsh shipboard conditions in steerage, food shortages, stern taskmasters and terrible storms that tossed the ship around like a plaything in a bathtub. They witnessed the occasional death followed by burial at sea. But the rough voyage did little to prepare them for the wilderness that was then Vancouver Island.

Some completed their contracts with the HBC and returned to Scotland. Some renewed for a few more years and put down roots, while others deserted to the California goldfields. Each arrival who remained inched the British new colony forward, giving birth to a more stable economy and, eventually, the new province of British Columbia. Generations to come benefited from their sacrifices.

CHAPTER I

From Scotland to Vancouver Island

The Last Frontier

Split off from the mainland like a broken piece of viridian glass, Vancouver Island was rugged and inhospitable to the early settlers. Shards formed a multitude of small islands within the Strait of Georgia. White-capped mountains ran the length of the Island, with mile-long sandy beaches edging the Pacific Ocean on the west coast. Elsewhere on the coast, rivers, inlets and sounds gouged like fingers into the land, draining and pulling the soil into the ocean. Howling winter gales and cold turbulent waters battered against rocky shores, while on the east coast of the Island, lush river deltas offered meadows of flat agricultural land. The east-coast ecosystem supported the only evergreen broadleaf tree—the magnificent arbutus—and the Garry oak, the only oak native to the west coast. The interior part of the Island had tranquil lakes and lush rainforests of towering, magnificent cedars and Douglas-fir trees hundreds of years old.

For thousands of years, Native people had made their home here. They fished and hunted without impediment, collecting sea molluscs and wild vegetation for food. Their traditions were

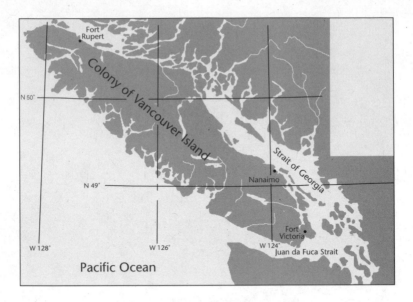

Fort Rupert

Colony of Vancouver Island

N 50°

N 49°

Nanaimo

Strait of Georgia

Fort Victoria

W 128°   W 126°   W 124°
Juan da Fuca Strait

Pacific Ocean

THE COLONY OF VANCOUVER ISLAND

Broken off from the mainland of New Caledonia, Vancouver Island remained undisturbed for thousands of years until the Hudson's Bay Company made its headquarters at Fort Victoria. MAP COURTESY OF JOHN PETERSON

strong and their cultures rich and diverse. Stories and historical events were passed down from generation to generation through an oral tradition, for they had not developed a written language. They had survived and developed different ways of managing the available resources. Boundaries were clearly defined, and social patterns were based on kinship and lineage. They traded with each other, developing strong connections. The sea was their highway.

The Songhees of the Victoria area were part of the larger Coast Salish group, whose territory stretched along the east coast of the island from Victoria north to Comox. The Cowichans of Duncan, the Chemainus, and the Snuneymuxw of Nanaimo were all branches of the Coast Salish and shared some language ties. The Nootka, or Nuu-chah-nulth, lived along the west coast. Fort Rupert and the north end of the Island was home to the Kwakiutl people.

The Pacific Northwest was the last place in the world to be

explored by Europeans. Bounded on the west by the largest of oceans and to the east by a high range of mountains, it was a great distance from Europe. To the north lay the Arctic ice cap. Any approach from the Atlantic could only be made after sailing down the entire coast of South America, around Cape Horn, and then north for thousands of miles. No one suspected the region was rich in natural resources, so the incentive to explore the area was absent. (Preoccupation with other matters probably contributed too: between 1741 and 1825, Russia, Spain, France, the United States and Britain were all busy competing for the maritime fur trade with the indigenous people of the Pacific Northwest.)

The earliest encounters between Native people and Europeans occurred on the west coast of Vancouver Island at Nootka Sound, when Spanish explorers sought to expand their territory. The first arrival was the Spanish ship *Santiago*. It entered Nootka Sound on August 8, 1774, making the Spanish the first Europeans to see Vancouver Island (although, at that time, it was thought to be part of the mainland). Some trading was done with the Natives, who were happy to exchange furs for goods. The Spanish placed wooden crosses along the shore, with statements of possession placed in sealed bottles to document the expedition. The Spanish explorers left their mark on maps and charts of Vancouver Island, along with drawings of the indigenous people and documentation of their way of life, and the flora and fauna. Many of the islands were named after Spanish explorers.

British representative Captain James Cook was also known to have anchored near Nootka on March 7, 1778, and traded for sea otter pelts. As he sailed up the coast, he noted that the nearby mainland (as he thought it, though it was in fact Vancouver Island) was "covered to a considerable breadth with high straight trees, that formed a beautiful prospect, as of one vast forest."[1]

Cook's father, also named James, was a Scottish farm labourer. His son James, born in 1728, spent his early years tending livestock on the farm where his father was employed. At 17, the young man first apprenticed to a grocer in the village of Staithes, England, then later apprenticed to shipowners in Whitby, England. In his spare time he studied mathematics and navigation, before enlisting in the Royal Navy in 1755.[2] Cook's exploration into unknown waters over the next 24 years made history, opening up uncharted waters and new lands. He met a violent end on February 14, 1779, in Hawaii after a scuffle with Natives.

Others made voyages to Nootka in the ensuing years to trade for sea otter pelts, but Cook and his crew were the first fur traders.

The names of ship-captain explorers of Vancouver Island are reflected in present-day place names and street names such as Cook, Quadra, Meares, Barkley, Martinez, Vancouver, Galiano and Valdez, to name only a few.

On October 28, 1790, Spain and Britain signed the Nootka Convention, giving each the power to trade in the Pacific Northwest with neither side having sovereignty. It took years for the Convention to be implemented, and in the interim, Spain withdrew from Nootka, leaving Britain the sole presence.

The Hudson's Bay Company

To newcomers, Vancouver Island may have seemed uninhabited, certainly by white people, but it had sustained a quality of life for Native people for thousands of years. Half a world away, steps were being taken to colonize, or settle, Vancouver Island. Great Britain's Queen Victoria signed a grant on January 13, 1849, making the Hudson's Bay Company "the true and absolute lords and Proprietors" of Vancouver's Island, enjoying "all royalties of the Seas upon the Coasts within the limits aforesaid and all mines royal thereto belonging."[3]

The British Crown granted the Company the exclusive trading right over the Island for a period of 10 years, after which the Crown could repurchase the right if it chose to. In return, the Company was required to develop and sell land at a reasonable price to anyone wishing to settle. The HBC obviously thought that the most desirable settler would be a British gentleman of substantial means. Land would be offered at one pound sterling per acre, and a settler could bring out one labourer for every 20 acres purchased.

For three centuries, the HBC men had used the upper half of North America as their personal domain, exploiting the land, lording over their forts and posts and seducing Native women, whom Sir George Simpson lightheartedly called their "bits of brown."[4] Fur was their goal and economic engine. When it was discovered that beaver pelts were perfect for making men's hats, the fur trade was born. When wide-brimmed felt hats became all the rage in Europe, the fur trade grew.

This grand enterprise of Canadian history created its own agenda and hierarchy, even its own military force. The early traders faced an untamed land, traversing raging rivers, rugged mountains and prairie lands, and making it all their own. The Company, or "The Bay," as it became known, was a world unto itself. The governors of the Company ran the enterprise from London's financial district, never having set foot on the land or even knowing what a beaver looked like. Their responsibility was only to a small group of British shareholders, all influential men with close political ties.

The white men who ventured into this remote part of the world were primarily interested in trading for furs. Until 1843, when the HBC came to Vancouver Island, they came only as visitors, seldom coming ashore. They had no interest in settling in the region. Even with the establishment of the North West Company forts in the Interior, beginning at Fort McLeod in 1805, and the HBC forts on the coast, beginning with Fort Vancouver in 1824, and Fort Langley in 1827, their prime concerns were their own commerce and safety; there was no administration, and only the beginning of missionary activity. Adventurers like Sir Alexander Mackenzie, who crossed the Rocky Mountains and reached the Pacific in 1793, Simon Fraser, who in 1808 followed the Fraser River to the sea, and David Thompson, who in 1811 explored the Columbia River by following it to its mouth, opened up the west coast to new opportunities.

The Hudson's Bay Company's Fort Vancouver was situated on the northern bank of Oregon's Columbia River in present-day Vancouver, Washington, near Portland, Oregon. The fort was then under the command of Dr. John McLoughlin, a striking figure with a shock of shoulder-length white hair. From his headquarters at Fort Vancouver, McLoughlin ruled for two decades, from 1824 to 1845, and was so effective he was called the "Father of Oregon." The fort was built as the Company headquarters for the entire Pacific area.

The hope was that when the time came to divide American and British territory, the boundary would be the Columbia River. When it was decided by the Oregon treaty of 1846 that the boundary would be the 49th parallel and Fort Vancouver would be in American territory and subject to customs duties, Sir George Simpson ordered the construction of Fort Victoria on Vancouver Island. This became the new administrative centre.

Several forts were established during this time in New Caledonia, as the HBC trading district was then known. Fort Simpson, built in 1831 on the coast between the Nass and Skeena rivers, north of Prince Rupert, was later relocated to the Skeena River. Fort McLoughlin was built in 1833 on Milbanke Sound near Bella Bella. There were other forts situated on rivers or lakes in the interior and north of the province that provisioned fur-trade routes.

The HBC forts were safe havens for traders and were also used for storage of furs before shipment. Company recruits arrived as apprentices and then were promoted to clerks in charge of the stores. After a suitable period of field experience they became traders, continuing to rise to the posts of factor and chief factor.

Life at the forts was not easy. Sunday was the only day of rest, and boredom was a constant problem. News was eagerly anticipated. Men would often marry Native women, or bring out a wife from their hometowns. Schools were established for children in the larger forts.

At the forts, furs were packed in bales and kept in storage, then taken to larger depots, where they were then carried by pack train or taken by boat down rivers and inlets to the sea to await shipping to world markets. Pack trains were amazing sights, with about 400 horses, 16 per section with two men in charge, and each horse carrying two 90-pound bales of furs.

Within the Company, the Scottish influence was everywhere. Nearly all the notable people in its history were born, grew up or were educated in Scotland. Sir James Douglas, Sir George Simpson and Andrew Colville were only a few of the familiar names in the higher echelon of the early days of Vancouver's Island.

Manning the Forts

"If England can not furnish you with men, Scotland can, for that countrie is a hard country to live in and poore-mens wages is cheap. They are hardy people both to endure hunger, and could, and are subject to obedience, and I am sure that they will serve for six pound pr years and be better content with their dyet than Englishmen."[5]

For decades, from at least as early as the 1700s, the HBC had been recruiting men from the Orkney Islands to work at its trading posts. Orkney is an archipelago of 67 islands situated off the north coast of Scotland. The largest is Mainland, where the two largest communities, the capital city of Kirkwall and the small harbour town of Stromness, are located. Company ships called in at Stromness to fill up with fresh water and supplies before the trans-Atlantic crossing. The most important item on a sailing ship was fresh water, and this was the last item placed aboard the ship in order to ensure its freshness.

MAJOR FORTS OF THE HUDSON'S BAY COMPANY

The area west of the Rocky Mountains opened up new opportunities for the Hudson's Bay Company. A series of forts were built along the new fur-trade route to the Pacific Ocean. MAP COURTESY OF HANCOCK HOUSE PUBLISHERS

Stromness, on the southwest tip of Mainland Island, provided an excellent, deep anchorage that was sheltered in all directions. The arrival of a Company ship here was one of the great events of the year. Generally a ship would stay for a couple of weeks in order to pick up all the young men who had been hired under contract for service with the Company. All were expected to gather there prior to the arrival of the ships. The men came from across the Highlands and the islands of Orkney, Shetland and Lewis. The Company always secured their men from these areas, as they had proved to be the best for service in North America.

Each man had to pass a very tough medical examination before he was engaged, and only those found physically fit under severe tests were accepted. They had to be between the ages of 18 and 25 years, and were classified as clerks, carpenters, boat builders, blacksmiths, coopers, tinsmiths and labourers. All had a chance of promotion in the service in accordance with their demonstrated capacity and ability in the service.[6]

All the ships took on cargo, including parcels or boxes from parents or friends of the men who had gone out previously. The captains and officers held a carnival during their stay, with dinner parties on board and ashore, and dancing every night. Yet, despite all the gaiety and cheer, there were many salt tears shed by fathers, mothers, sisters, brothers and sweethearts when it was time to depart; many knew they were leaving forever. The whole population gathered on the shore and cheered farewell as a salute was fired.

Stromness prospered as the English Channel became increasingly unsafe because of wars with Holland and France. The first recorded ship visiting Stromness was in 1702, when Captain Michael Grimington called, searching for 12 suitable men.[7] Richard Glover wrote about the islanders:

> The Orcadian was the perpetual migrant. Women went into domestic service in Edinburgh, Newcastle, and London. Men found outlets in the Iceland or Greenland fisheries and also

turned to the Hudson's Bay Company, for even the wilderness of North America offered them a higher standard of living and a better chance of saving money than a labouring life at home.[8]

The Orcadians were more than ready to seek opportunities away from the harshness of the islands. Economic conditions in Europe in the 18th century were extremely difficult, with harvest failures, malnutrition and starvation due to climate conditions that were much harsher than today. Local ocean temperatures were five degrees Celsius cooler than at present around the Orkney Islands, and the cod fishery was virtually eliminated. Scottish mountains had permanent snow on top, and this included the Cairngorms. One odd result of this climate anomaly was that several dead Inuit who had been hunting seals along the edge of the pack ice in Labrador and other locations were washed ashore, still sealed into their kayaks, on the Orkney Islands between 1690 and 1728.[9]

The Company began hiring Orcadians to work in their flourishing outpost at York Factory, located halfway up the west coast of Hudson Bay. This was the Company's first permanent trading station in 1684 and was named for the governor, the Duke of York. Over the next two centuries, almost all of the goods and furs traded by the Company moved in or out of York Factory. In addition to being used to harsh conditions, the Orkney Islanders were either farmers or fishermen and were good on both land and water. They also brought with them basic literacy and simple recordkeeping skills, which they had learned in their parish schools.

The Orkney Islands share the same latitude as Hudson Bay, less than eight degrees south of the Arctic Circle. The Islands' main cash crop was kelp. Seaweed found washed up on the shore was burned to make an alkaline sludge used to make glass, soap and dyes. Orkney kelp was of good quality and had a reputation with glassmakers; it was said to make the best window glass.

The Orcadians also had an uncomplaining attitude, and their steady work habits made them good employees—and they were cheaper to hire than Englishmen or Irishmen. "Of the 530 employees on the Company's overseas payroll in 1799, 416 were Orcadians. Stromness had a population of 1,400 at the time."[10] The men were offered salaries of six pounds sterling a year, with small increases at the end of each five-year indentured period. They also received room and board, but had no place to spend their money and so looked forward to returning home to Orkney with enough savings to buy a boat or a farm. The Company had agents on the Islands recruiting prospective workers from 1771 to 1867. The last agent was Edward Clouston, who held the post from 1836 to 1867. His job likely ended when the Dominion of Canada was established and control over immigration was transferred to the new country.

The Scottish migration to Vancouver Island between 1848 and 1854 resulted in entire families arriving in Fort Victoria indentured to the HBC for three to five years. Some were miners or worked in related industries; others were labourers and farm workers. The Company viewed these new arrivals as necessary to fulfill its agreement with Great Britain to settle the new Colony of Vancouver Island, so labourers, carpenters and farmers, and their families, were welcomed. The face of Vancouver Island was changed forever with the arrival of the HBC.

The Ayrshire Coalfield

The HBC began looking for experienced miners for its coal operation at Fort Rupert on northern Vancouver Island and found them in the Ayrshire coal mines, in towns like Kilmarnock.

Today, Ayrshire is one of the most agriculturally fertile regions of Scotland. The county's principal towns include Ayr, the capital city, Kilmarnock and Irvine. Many avid golfers know the areas of Troon and Turnberry for the magnificent golf courses located there. Others are more familiar with the county described so well in the work of Scottish poet Robert Burns.

It is hard to imagine the spectre of the coal mines that once dotted the landscape, when the area was heavily industrialized—not just with coal mines, but also with steel mills and manufacturing. While the story of the HBC's Ayrshire miners is rooted in this beautiful area, their lives were not easy, and many looked to the New World to find their dream on Vancouver Island.

The coal industry in Ayrshire was busy and prosperous. Coal was found in 33 of the 44 Ayrshire parishes, from Kilbirnie in the north to Dailly in the south, from Muirkirk in the east to Tarbolton in the west. Mines were clustered around towns like Kilmarnock, Riccarton, Irvine and Muirkirk. In the 19th century, Ayrshire had 14,000 coal miners producing 4 million tons annually for household use, factories, blast furnaces and locomotives.

The Ayrshire coalfield was completely separate from other coalfields in Scotland. The lucrative industry rested squarely on the shoulders of the miners, who worked in the semi-darkness of lamp-lit tunnels. Whole families were sometimes employed, including wives and children who were hired to carry the coal to the pithead. For most, the only way to survive was to have the whole family involved. Mine owners knew the benefits of employing members of a family: because the families wanted to keep the money they earned within the family, the owners paid them less than they would have had to pay an equivalent number of unrelated individuals. It was not unusual to have male children start work in the mines at the age of 10 and continue working their way up the ladder to full collier. They worked 10- or 11-hour days, 6 days a week, for a daily wage of between 2 shillings and sixpence, and 3 shillings and sixpence. Older boys helped their families, particularly their fathers, to cut the coal, while younger boys helped their mothers and sisters haul their intolerably heavy burdens to the surface. Although girls and boys under 10 years of age were eventually forbidden by law to work underground in 1842, the reality was that the family could not afford to live without undertaking this work. The law was widely ignored as late as the 1870s for women. Compulsory school attendance was introduced for children in the Education Act of 1872.

Managers worked similar hours but received a wage of about 70 pounds a year. Miners' homes were the property of the mine owners and were usually row houses located near the pit. Some of the miners' rows were of stone and built almost a century earlier. Most were one or two rooms, in a style often referred to as "but and ben." Set-in beds were common, crowded conditions the norm. Several families shared the outdoor toilets and washed in tin tubs indoors on brick tile floors. Most of the towns had a good supply of piped water, obtained from streetside wells.[11] Many workers kept animals and grew vegetables.

Scottish miners were politically active. Colliers from 27 pits around Kilmarnock founded the first Scottish miners' union on October 25, 1824. This same year, 1,400 Ayrshire miners were on strike for over two months. The following decade saw the formation of a number of small-scale unions. In 1837 the first large strike in Scotland took place, brought on by the hiring of cheaper Irish labour and out-of-work handloom weavers. A commission was established to look into working conditions for children and recommend improvements, but ended up investigating all workers' conditions. It recommended that no child under 10, or any women, be employed underground; that wages were not to be paid near drinking establishments; and that mines be inspected regularly. The Miners' Association of Great Britain and Ireland was formed in the early 1840s, but later dissolved in the 1850s, during a low period in mining union activity.[12]

When the HBC began recruiting, some Scottish miners were ready to sign as indentured workers. Ayrshire miners had been accustomed to short-term contracts of only two weeks, a month or, in rare cases, a year, but the HBC wanted to sign them for three to five years. The longer contracts offered security but also curtailed their freedom.

In Scotland the miners would not have been able to afford land or gain access to political and social prestige. They were working-class people, struggling like thousands of others to gain a foothold on respectability. They wanted a life of greater ease for their children, if not for themselves. On Vancouver Island, they could own more land than imaginable in Scotland, at a price they could afford. Even with as little as 20 acres, they could vote and participate in the political and social life of the community. The Ayrshire miners became some of the first settlers on Vancouver Island and also the first to open up the Nanaimo area to coal-mining activity.

The Little Emperor: Sir George Simpson

After Sir George Simpson, the HBC's overseas governor, was knighted in 1841, he went on a world tour. He attended a civic dinner in Christiania [Oslo], Norway, where he was toasted as "head of the most extended dominion in the known world."[13] This statement showed the extent and domination of one of the world's largest trading companies at that time.

Simpson was born out of wedlock to an unknown mother and the son of a Calvinist minister and was raised mainly by his aunt Mary in Dingwall, a small port town in the northern county of Ross-shire in the western Highlands. Showing great promise in mathematics at school, he was offered an apprenticeship by his uncle, Geddes Mackenzie Simpson, at his London sugar broker-age house of Graham & Simpson, a partnership that expanded in 1812 to include Andrew Colville.[14] In 1820, in his early 30s, he was appointed acting governor-in-chief of Rupert's Land after being nominated by Colville. In a letter to Colville from York Factory dated September 8, 1821, Simpson conveyed his sincere thanks to him for having obtained for him the position of governor of Rupert's Land, and adds the following sentence:

To you I feel that I am solely indebted for my advancement in life and it will ever be my study to show that your good offices have not been misapplied.[15]

This was the beginning of a lifelong alliance between the two men. Being Scottish and London-trained were important credentials, and it didn't matter that Simpson had no experience in the fur trade, as long as he could deal effectively with proud Highlanders.

For four decades this Scot dominated the HBC. He ruled an empire so large that he was likened to the "Little Emperor" (Napoleon). Although small in stature, with hair curling around the nape of his neck, he looked and acted tough and was ruthless, petty and chauvinistic. But he was the right man at the right time in the right place. Like a stereotypical Scot, he could hold a grudge. He held grievances against anyone brave enough to question his will. And he was a master politician, using people to advance Company interests, playing one off against another. When he was knighted, a newspaper editor asked for personal information for publication. Simpson gave them only his name, position and address, the response of a savvy politician.

He liked to travel with an entourage. With flags flying, cannon blasting and his piper leading the way, Simpson stepped ashore in his theatrical Royal Stuart tartan cloak with a collar of soft Genoa velvet. The piper's music was an emotional way to reach the hearts and souls of his men in these lonely outposts. Simpson's piper was Colin Fraser, who arrived in 1827 at York Factory from Kirkton, Sutherlandshire, in northern Scotland. To win the 30-pound-sterling-a-year job, Fraser had to walk in front of a carriage 20 miles to the point of embarkation, playing all the way. Fraser was the only one of three candidates who made it.

The Natives might have been a bit bewildered by the Scottish kilt and the wailing bagpipes. One Cree who heard Fraser play at Norway House described the dress to his chief:

One white man was dressed like a woman, in a skirt of funny color. He had whiskers growing from his belt and fancy leggings. He carried a black swan which had many legs with ribbons tied to them. The swan's body he put under his arm upside down; then he put its head in his mouth and bit it. At the same time he pinched its neck with his fingers and squeezed the body under his arm until it made a terrible noise.[16]

During his 40 years with the Company, Simpson made at least one major journey a year. When he went on one of his grand tours, he noted, "It is strange that all my ailments vanish as soon as I seat myself in a canoe."[17]

Simpson has sometimes been called the "father of the fur trade," but it was said with a nudge and a wink. One historian claimed that he had fathered 70 sons between the Red River and the Rocky Mountains. But who was counting? And even if it was possible, Simpson did spend 10 years in the fur country and certainly made the most of being a bachelor. When he decided to marry a white woman, he disrupted the accepted norm of his officers. He disliked the "country wife" who exerted influence over the decisions of her husband, even though he also had such an arrangement. After 1823, HBC husbands had to sign marriage contracts, and whenever they left their country wives, besides supporting their children, they were obliged to find other suitable providers for them.

Before leaving for England, where he planned to find a wife, Simpson sent his then-pregnant country wife Margaret Taylor to visit her sister, who was married to Chief Factor John Stuart at Bas-de-la-Rivière, at the mouth of the Winnipeg River. The sister was also pregnant. Simpson had told them nothing of his plan, and by the time he got a letter from Stuart telling him about the birth of his son, the governor was about to marry his cousin Frances, 26 years younger than him. Frances was the daughter of Geddes Mackenzie Simpson, the man who gave Simpson his first job, with his London sugar company. Margaret was placed with an HBC employee named Amable Hogue.[18]

The Simpsons settled first at Lower Fort Garry, where he built one of the finest mansions in the territory, the Stone Fort, now a National Historic Park. No expense was spared. Their first child died at seven months old, an event that traumatized both parents. Adding to this, Frances was unhappy in that remote location, so Simpson moved management operations to Lachine, Quebec, and Frances returned to England. This arrangement seemed to suit the couple well; she saw her husband occasionally, and over 12 years she raised 4 children before returning to Lachine in 1845. Frances continued to long for London, and endured their relationship with grace but no enthusiasm. Simpson and Frances are buried in Mount Royal Cemetery in Montreal.

The Intellect: Andrew Colville

Andrew Colville was a successful London sugar broker and an intellectual with a lively sense of resolve when he joined the HBC governing committee in 1809. At the age of 34, in 1814, he took the surname Colville because his mother, Isabella, was the great-grandniece and heir to the last Lord Colville of Ochiltree. Andrew's ancestral home was Craigflower House, at Torryburn, Fifeshire, in Scotland.

Andrew's sister Jean married the Scottish nobleman Thomas Douglas, the fifth Earl of Selkirk and the founder of the Red River Settlement—the forerunner of the province of Manitoba. Andrew had two brothers, Peter and James.[19]

In 1802, Andrew married Elizabeth Susannah Wedderburn. This marriage lasted only a year, as Elizabeth died in 1803. His second marriage was in 1806 to the Honourable Louisa Mary Eden, fifth daughter of William Eden, First Lord Auckland. They had two sons, James William and Eden Colville, who was given his mother's maiden name.

Andrew purchased shares in the HBC and assumed a position of power almost immediately. He cut the final deal in the amalgamation of the North West Company and the Hudson's Bay Company in 1821, and served as deputy governor from 1839 to 1852, and as governor from 1852 to 1856. When son Eden graduated from Eton and Cambridge, he was appointed associate governor of Rupert's Land in 1849. The Colvilles, father and son, spent almost 79 years directing HBC affairs.

Andrew Colville died on February 3, 1856. Several places in Canada honour him: Fort Wedderburn, on Lake Athabaska; Colville House, at the junction of Peace River with Loon River; Colville River and Fort Colville, near the junction with the Columbia in Washington State; and, for a brief period of time, Colvilletown on Vancouver Island, now known as Nanaimo.

CHAPTER 2

The Scots of
Fort Victoria

The Governor: James Douglas

James Douglas, known as the "Father of British Columbia," was the most influential man in the history of the colony. Within the fur trade, he was known as a "Scotch West Indian." He was born out of wedlock in 1803 in Demerara, British Guiana. His father, John, and his three brothers in Glasgow held interests in sugar plantations there. John Douglas entered a union with James's mother, Martha Ritchie, the daughter of a black freewoman in Barbados. Martha and her three children, Alexander, James and Cecilia, were left behind when John Douglas returned to Scotland. In 1809, John married Jessie Hamilton, the daughter of John Hamilton, a Greenock merchant. He returned to Martha in 1811 and made arrangements to take his sons, James and Alexander, back to Scotland the next year. His daughter, Cecilia, was left behind with her mother. The boys were then aged 11 and 9.[1]

Douglas and his elder brother, Alexander, did not live with their father and his new wife, Jessie. The circumstances of the boys' births to a coloured mistress probably played a part in this decision, and John and Jessie now also had four children of their own. Instead, the boys were sent to nearby Lanark Grammar School, one of the oldest schools in Scotland, founded in 1183. They boarded at the home of Mrs. Glendenning, a woman who accommodated a number of young pupils at the school. James was a good student and seemed to thrive in the country environment. It has been said that the landscape helped shape his lifelong love of nature. Lanark is close to the Falls of Clyde, a very picturesque and fertile part of Lanarkshire in southern Scotland.

When Alexander was 17, he was indentured to the North West Company in the fur-trade business. James stayed behind and spent a year at boarding school in England, where he studied French before joining his brother as an apprentice.

Douglas was assigned to Fort St. James in 1825, to the HBC New Caledonia Department, where he clerked under Chief Factor William Connolly. During this time, Douglas was discouraged by the isolation, the lack of companionship and of good books, the hostility of the Natives, and the danger of starvation after the salmon run failed, and he thought of retiring from the fur trade, since he was at the end of his three-year contract. However, when the Company increased his salary from 60 pounds to 100 pounds, he renewed his contract. Alexander returned home in 1924 after completing his six-year contract.

Douglas was attracted to Connolly's mixed-blood, 16-year-old daughter, Amelia, whom he married on April 27, 1828. Her father officiated at their wedding. Connolly's wife, Suzanne, was a Cree Indian; their marriage lasted almost 30 years. Connolly eventually left Suzanne and legally married a white woman, Julia Woolrich, a circumstance that was a great blow to Amelia, who was now considered illegitimate. It was not until 1869 that the Supreme Court of Canada declared her father's first marriage to her mother valid, thus freeing Amelia from her illegitimate status.

Douglas's posting at Fort St. James was not without incident; in fact, it could have been his last. While attempting to apprehend a Dakelh (Carrier) Native who had killed two HBC men at nearby

Fort George, Douglas was stabbed with an arrow. The man was hanged on the spot. When the Dakelh chief heard what had happened, he headed a war party to Fort St. James, where Douglas was caught and pinned down on a table with a knife held at his throat. Amelia, who had been hiding in a storeroom, started throwing tobacco, blankets and other goods at their feet and begging for her husband's life. The chief accepted her pleas and retreated.

Amelia may have been more fortunate than most of the women in mixed marriages, for Douglas officially remarried her in 1837 before Reverend Beaver, an Anglican minister, at Fort Vancouver. Douglas had been transferred several years earlier to Fort Vancouver, where extensive coastal trading and farming operations were under way. In 1830 he became an accountant under Dr. John McLoughlin, then superintendent of the vast Columbia Department. Amelia and James had 13 children, of whom only 6 survived into adulthood: Cecilia, Jane, Agnes, Alice, James and Martha. Sir George Simpson gave his opinion of the young clerk in 1833: He said Douglas was:

> a stout powerful man of good conduct and respectable abilities—tolerably well educated, expresses himself clearly on paper, understands our Counting House business and is an excellent trader. Well qualified for any service requiring bodily exertion, firmness of mind and the exercise of sound judgment but furiously violent when roused.[2]

Four years later, Douglas was promoted to chief trader, and in 1839 to chief factor. By 1840, when it became apparent that the fort might become part of the United States as thousands of American immigrants moved west over the Oregon Trail to settle in the nearby Willamette Valley, Simpson decided a new headquarters for the region had to be found and gave Douglas orders to explore Vancouver Island. Simpson knew of negotiations under way to try to resolve the problem of defining a boundary separating British and American territories in the Oregon Country. A letter from Douglas described this stressful period:

> A much greater number is expected this year, so that the country will soon be overrun with—people of a class, hostile to British interests. What is our Government about? When will the boundary be settled? It must be soon, if we wish to keep the Columbia.[3]

Captain William McNeill, master of the *Beaver*, first examined the coast of Vancouver Island and found "an excellent harbour of easy access with good anchorage, surrounded by a plain of several miles in extent, of an excellent soil."[4] Douglas explored the site in 1842 on the *Cadboro* and took a liking to what he called "Camosack," a Native term meaning "gorge," known today as Victoria Harbour. Douglas seemed quite enthusiastic about his choice when he wrote to a friend in 1842:

> The place itself appears a perfect "Eden" in the midst of the dreary wilderness of the Northwest coast...one might be pardoned for supposing it had dropped from the clouds into its present position.[5]

On March 1, 1843, Douglas left Fort Vancouver with a party of 15 men and arrived at Fort Nisqually on the southern end of Puget Sound on March 9. They left Fort Nisqually aboard the *Beaver* on March 13, arriving the next day off Clover Point, Vancouver Island. He examined the woods of the north shore of the harbour, but thought the wood on the south shore was of better quality. On March 16, six men were put to work digging a well, while six others squared timber for building. He spoke to the Songhees and informed them of his intention to build there, and noted that this appeared to please them. They offered their services in getting pickets for the fort. Douglas promised to pay them a blanket for every 40 pickets of 22 feet by 36 inches each. He lent them several axes to be returned when the job was finished. Chief Trader

Charles Ross was put in charge of the construction of the new post, which was named Fort Victoria.[6]

In October 1843, horses and cattle were transported from Fort Nisqually on the *Beaver* to Fort Victoria, and five acres of wheat were seeded. By the fall of 1844, the HBC ship *Vancouver* was directed to sail directly from London to Fort Victoria. It arrived in the spring of 1845, and returned to London in December 1846 carrying the first shipment of the Columbia Department's furs from Fort Victoria.[7]

The Oregon Boundary Treaty was signed on June 15, 1846, with the border to be drawn along the 49th parallel all the way from the Rockies to the Pacific, where it bisected Juan de Fuca Strait, leaving Vancouver Island entirely in British hands. Some small islands lay on either side of the line. Douglas was pleased that the British had managed to keep the whole of Vancouver Island. According to the treaty, since the HBC was not the British government, it retained its right to trade south of the border. However, when the US began raising tariff rates and other taxes, the Company worried about its future and the trail to Fort Vancouver.

On January 12, 1849, the Company accepted a royal grant to Vancouver Island for 10 years. A colony was to be set up within five years, and Douglas expected to be chosen governor. The conditions under which Vancouver Island was granted to the HBC were clearly stated in a letter to Douglas from Sir John Henry Pelly, governor of the HBC in London:

> You will have seen by a grant from the Crown Vancouver Island is the property of the Hudson's Bay Company but with the condition to sell to any British subject such part as emigrants may be disposed to purchase for the purpose of settling thereon. The condition on which those purchases may be made has been sent you; you will see that the Hudson's Bay Company are little more than agents for the sale of the lands, mines, etc.,

retaining to themselves one-tenth of all the sales may produce, and trustees for the other nine-tenths to be expended in public purposes for the Colony—that the Government is exclusively in the Crown, who appoint a Governor and Council, and ultimately a House of Assembly to be elected.[8]

The Company began administering the new colony. Douglas was instructed to keep a register of all grants of lands, receive survey reports and appoint people to perform duties as required, and for these services he would be paid 200 pounds a year.

Fort Victoria, first named Fort Camosun, was a small but important outpost for the HBC and eventually became the western headquarters for the Company. The fort, officially named after young Queen Victoria, had water and a good harbour, and was well positioned for a naval depot, with enough green space to grow crops. However, not everyone was impressed. When the Honourable John Gordon, brother of the Earl of Aberdeen, the British Foreign Secretary, arrived as captain of HMS *America*, he looked around and declared that he would "not give one of the bleakest knolls of all the bleak hills of Scotland for 20 islands like this arrayed in barbaric splendor."[9]

On March 11, 1850, the first appointed governor of the colony, Richard Blanshard, arrived. Seventeen guns were fired in honour of the new appointee, while the welcoming committee stood in a foot of snow. The cool weather might have been a signal of the frosty welcome he would receive from Douglas.

Blanshard, a tall man with a large moustache, was not an HBC employee and had no affiliation with the Company. An Oxford-educated lawyer who lacked experience as an administrator, he was hired without a salary but promised 1,000 acres of land. Upon arrival, he soon found out it would be Douglas who would be doing the governing. Douglas did everything he could to discourage Blanshard, who resigned within a year. Douglas then took his place and worked in the dual capacity of governor and chief factor.

For the next 10 years, the HBC was lord and proprietor of the Island.

Douglas and Amelia moved to Fort Victoria in 1849 and purchased land to build the colony's first private residence. The home, within sight of the fort, was built on the south shore of James Bay, which was named for Douglas. Located where the Royal British Columbia Museum now stands, the house was the biggest and grandest in the colony for some time.

The Douglases moved into their new home in 1852. Amelia, a shy, retiring woman who had lived in her husband's shadow for many years, took pride in her Native heritage and enjoyed relating legends to her children and grandchildren. She once invited a Songhees chief for a visit. She must also have been proud of her new home, where she gave birth to the couple's 13th child, Martha, in 1854. When Douglas was knighted in 1863, Amelia was already an accepted member of Victoria's high society.

A description of a celebratory day in Beacon Hill Park illustrates the central role the Douglas family played in early Victoria:

> June 1st, 1853 was a festive day for Fort Victoria, with Governor Douglas providing a magnificent picnic at Beacon Hill to celebrate his son James Jr.'s second birthday. The Royal Navy officers, the HBC officers, the local population and hundreds of Natives turned out for the occasion. After a hearty lunch there was horseracing. Then old John Tod got out his fiddle and "the most respectable of the party" danced a quadrille on the green. Meanwhile, in another part of the grounds, "the Scotch Piper in full costume was playing the pipes to a party of Scotch mechanics and labourers who are in the Company's service. The latter were kicking away at Scotch reels with great energy." A couple of prizefight rings were set up where the opponents smashed at each other "most desperately."
>
> Towards sunset the Douglas family, the naval officers and "the most respectable part of the residents" withdrew to

Government House for tea followed by quadrilles, polkas and waltzes—and the homely music of the fiddle and the bagpipes gave way to the most cultured tones of the pianoforte. The party broke up about 11 o'clock.[10]

Douglas ran the fort like a military operation. Company officers, who were mostly Scots, were separated from the labouring class of French Canadians, Metis and a few Kanakas, who were recruited in the Hawaiian Islands. Only officers dined at the chief factor's house. Young officers had their own quarters in the Bachelors' Hall, where they congregated for smokes or a drink.

The division of classes was something Douglas faced daily as he took control of the Colony of Vancouver Island. There were those Scottish HBC men who were well educated, but there were other Scots who scorned his rise to fame, and disagreed with his marriage to a Native woman. One of these was Annie Deans, the wife of George Deans, who was hired to work at Craigflower Farm. She wrote home to Scotland:

> The Governor of Vancouver Island has been in the Company out here ever since he was a Boy about 15 year and now is a Man upwards of 60 now—so you may say he has been all his life among North American Indians and has got one of them for a wife so how can it be expected that he can know anything at all about Governing one of England's last Colony's in North America.[11]

When Annie wrote this letter home, Douglas had already been married to Amelia for many years and had formalized their union.

Douglas is seldom considered an explorer, although he did cross the Rockies for the first time in 1826 to take charge of Fort St. James. That same year, he saw the Pacific for the first time. Seven times he crossed the Rockies, proving he could travel with the best of the North West Company men, and later with their equals in the HBC.

His canoe trip in 1853 from Fort Victoria to the site of the coal discovery in Nanaimo was an important milestone in the history of the Island. After that trip to Wentuhuysen Inlet (Nanaimo Harbour), Douglas wrote about his experience:

> I returned last night from an exploratory excursion through the Canal de Arro and along the east coast...undertaken for the purpose of examining the beds of coal reported to exist in that quarter, and I rejoice to say that our journey has been productive of very satisfactory results; as we have had abundant evidence to prove that the mineral wealth of Vancouver's Island has not been over rated...This discovery has afforded me more satisfaction that I can express...[12]

Proving the success of the coal discovery in Nanaimo was important to Douglas, for this was his chance to blot out the failure to mine coal in Fort Rupert, where he had first attempted it. Coal was important to the colony—as a cheap source of fuel, and as a commodity to sell to visiting ships or export to San Francisco.

There are varying opinions about Douglas's views of First Nations people, but to his credit, he negotiated 14 treaties on Vancouver Island. Eleven were in Fort Victoria and the Saanich Peninsula, one in Nanaimo and two at Fort Rupert. The Natives were paid in goods, mostly HBC blankets. He perhaps mistakenly believed that the Natives would willingly abandon their villages and culture for European ways, so there was no need to extinguish title to their traditional lands. Nearing the end of his tenure, he gave instructions that First Nations were to have "as much land as they wished, and in no case to lay off a reserve under 100 acres."

Douglas experienced resentment from colonists who accused him of nepotism when he appointed his brother-in-law David Cameron as judge, and others accused him of neglecting the fur trade. Simpson began to question Douglas's loyalty to the Company when he heard adverse reports from Company men. Douglas trod a fine line between his association with the

Company, his own place in it and the needs of the colonists. The power over the colony was clearly in his hands, and he must have expected a clash of interests because of his acting in dual roles as governor and chief factor. Complaints about Douglas were heard in London, and he was ordered to establish a legislative assembly.

Elections for the first assembly were held in 1856. Two years later, on his advice, Parliament converted the territory of New Caledonia into the Crown Colony of British Columbia. He was offered the governorship of the new colony, with a salary of 1,800 pounds as dual governor of the colonies of Vancouver Island and British Columbia, on condition that he sever his connection with the HBC. On November 19, 1858, he took the oath of office as governor of British Columbia. He then divided his time between the two colonies until he announced his retirement in 1864, when two new governors were appointed: Arthur Kennedy on Vancouver Island and Frederick Seymour in British Columbia. Douglas was angry when Queen Victoria gave royal assent to the British Columbia Act on November 19, 1866, amalgamating the two colonies. In 1867, Victoria became the capital city.

Douglas left personal notebooks, diaries and scrapbooks that show his interests in nature: cyclones and earthquakes, tidal waves and unusual rainfalls fascinated him. He was fond of astronomy and read about science, and he was preoccupied with baldness. When he discovered the Natives of the Northwest Coast used a certain root for medicinal purposes, he recorded: "It prevents baldness and produces a new growth of hair." Dr. John Sebastian Helmcken, who became Douglas's son-in-law, told the story of how Douglas asked Dr. Alfred Benson why so many HBC men were bald. He expected a medical answer, but instead Benson jokingly replied, "They send their furs home!" Perhaps Douglas feared he might lose his hair as he grew older. This did not happen; he kept his hair to the end.

Much has been written about James Douglas, including how he was obsessed with ritual, a penny-pincher and a dangerous

Born in British Guiana and educated in Scotland, Sir James Douglas, seen here around 1863, is widely known as "the Father of British Columbia." IMAGE A-01228 COURTESY OF ROYAL BC MUSEUM, BC ARCHIVES

adversary should someone disobey his commands. However, he was also literate and seldom spent a night without opening his prized leather-bound 45-volume set of English classics, and occasionally he was poetic. Later in life, in 1869, he relived a journey from Fort Vancouver to York Factory in a journal entry he wrote:

> A day highly suggestive of the past, of fresh scenes, of perilous travel, of fatigues, excitement and of adventures by mountain and flood; the retrospect is full of charms; images of the morning breezes, the bright sky, the glowing sunrise, the rushing waters, the roaring cataract—the dark forest, the flowery plains, the impressive mountains in their pure white covering of snow, rise before me, at this moment, as vividly as ever and old as I am, my heart bounds at the bare recollection of scenes I loved so well...I can recall nothing more delightful than our bivouac on a clear moonlit May night, near the Punch Bowls— the highest point of the Jasper Pass. The atmosphere was bright, sharp and bracing, the sunset in gorgeous splendour, bringing out the towering peaks and fantastic pinnacles dressed in purest white, into bold relief. Our camp was laid and our fire built, on the firm hard snow which was about 20 feet deep. As the daylight faded away, and the shades of night gathered over the Pass, a milder light shot up from behind the nearest Peak, with gradually encreasing brilliancy until at last the full-orbed moon rose in silent majesty from the mass of mountains shedding a mild radiance over the whole valley beneath.[13]

Douglas was a man who knew the internal politics of the Company and skirted around them. Like Simpson, he liked pomp and ceremony; he enjoyed wearing gold-braided military uniforms, perhaps as a display of power, and was often accompanied by a sword-bearing bodyguard. From the moment he decided on the site for Fort Victoria, he was forever linked to the future of Vancouver Island. For all his traits, both good and bad, he helped guide the fledgling colony in its early days to take its place in the Canadian confederacy. In October 1863, Queen Victoria made him a Knight Commander of the Bath. He was now Sir James Douglas, KCB.

In 1864, Douglas returned home to Scotland and visited his sickly son James, who was sent home for his

This obelisk honouring Sir James Douglas sits in front of the Legislative Buildings in Victoria. IMAGE COURTESY OF JAN PETERSON

education, and also his daughter Jane (wife of Alexander Grant Dallas), who now lived there. He also visited his half-sisters and other family relatives. Then he went on a grand tour of Europe before returning to Victoria.

Douglas lived out his remaining years in Victoria. He died of a heart attack on August 2, 1877. A public funeral was held, and throughout the province there was a great outpouring of grief and affection for the man who became known as "the Father of British Columbia."

The Shepherd Incident: Peter Brown

On November 5, 1852, at the Christmas Hill sheep station north of Victoria, Company worker James Skea found the body of shepherd Peter Brown, who had been shot several times in the chest. The young man was only weeks away from his 22nd birthday. The murderers were identified as Siamasit, the son of a Snuneymuxw chief, and an unknown Cowichan companion. Both young men had fled to their homes. It was reported that the shooting happened after Brown "had insulted the squaws of the Indians."[14]

Peter Brown was born in Harray in Orkney on November 27, 1831. He had signed on with the Company in 1851 and had come out with other Orcadians travelling in steerage aboard the *Norman Morison* and arriving in Fort Victoria June 12, 1852. Brown was hired as a labourer and was put to work as a shepherd at the Company sheep farm.

Douglas's reaction to his murder was immediate: he informed the Company that he planned to capture the suspects. He may have been afraid of an attack on Fort Victoria, so immediately stopped the sale of gunpowder and suspended all trade with the Cowichans of Cowichan Bay until the situation was resolved.

Sitting at anchor in Esquimalt Harbour on New Year's Day of 1853 was the fully armed HMS *Thetis*, which would play a pivotal role in the search for and arrest of the young men. An armada of armed forces was assembled. Douglas boarded the *Beaver* along with 20 marines from the *Thetis* and 10 of the Victoria Voltigeurs, a small French-Canadian paramilitary constabulary. They had in tow a second vessel, the *Recovery*, carrying 4 naval officers and 80 bluejackets, with the *Thetis* carrying artillery.

This odd little armada left on January 7 for Cowichan Bay, where Douglas arranged a parley and landed his forces. He pitched a tent, sat down on a stool in front of his troops and lit his pipe. Nearby he had assembled presents for the tribe, should the need arise. Before long a flotilla of canoes, filled with warring Cowichans wearing war paint and beating drums, appeared around a bend of the river. Douglas sat patiently and kept on smoking. They landed below his post, and then a large number rushed up the hill. Douglas ordered his men not to fire, and sat there stolidly. The warriors were baffled by his indifference.

Speaking in Chinook, Douglas told them that just as a white man was punished for killing a Native, so too should a Native be punished for killing a white man. He told them, "Give up the murderer, and let there be peace between the peoples, or I will burn your lodges and trample out your tribes!"[15] A young brave was surrendered, but he was not the person who had killed Peter Brown. He was a slave who had been substituted as compensation. Douglas, knowing of the deception, accepted the exchange in order to avoid hostilities with the Cowichans. He promised them a fair hearing.

In Nanaimo, Joseph William McKay, officer-in-charge, had a visit from the accused on December 6, asking him to act on his behalf. McKay did not want to get involved. He wrote:

> The Nanaimo murderer waited on me accompanied by a party of Nanaimo braves for the purpose of exculpating himself from the accusation of being concerned of the murder of Peter Brown. I told him that I had no right to examine depositions on such subject and referred him to the legal authorities at Victoria.[16]

Douglas's expedition arrived in Wentuhuysen Inlet, Nanaimo, where Douglas opened negotiations with the Snuneymuxw for the delivery of Siamasit. The chiefs offered to pay indemnity, according to their custom, but when this was refused, Tchewhetum, the boy's father, was arrested and held by a pledge for delivery of his son into custody.

A posse of voyageurs, sailors and some miners began searching for Siamasit, following him up a small stream, today known as Chase River after the infamous chase. He had hidden in a hollow tree trunk, and since it was snowing, he remained there, thinking he might have escaped because the snow had obliterated his footprints. However, when he saw his pursuers approach, he tried to shoot one. A flake of snow fell on the firing-pin of his musket, dampening the priming charge. He was detected and captured.

This historic event was later documented in the "Reminiscences of the historic Steamer *Beaver*":

> Both Indians were taken on board the *Beaver* and tried by Grand Jury, our friend Captain Sabiston served on the Grand

Jury. Both men were found guilty and were sentenced to be hanged by the judges Sir James Douglas and the 1st Lieutenant of the *Thetis*. Captain Sabiston and a fellow sailor John Spence, with the assistance of others, rigged up the gallows on Protection Point close to where the new shaft is, and there the Indians were hanged by a marine in disguise. The dead bodies of the murderers were delivered over to their friends, who took them to Cameron Island where they were kept for years in the hope that they may return to life. After the hanging, the *Beaver* returned to Victoria, leaving the *Recovery* behind as a guide ship.[17]

Cameron Island was the burial ground for the Snuneymuxw before the coal wharves were built. The Nanaimo HBC Daybook recorded the sequence of events in 1853:

January 15: The Nanaimo murderer was today captured near the mouth of the Nanaimo River and put into safe custody on board the *Beaver*.

January 17: Two men were tried for the murder of Peter Brown. They were found guilty, condemned and executed at Tide Staff Point.

The trial of the two young men aboard the *Beaver* was the first trial by judge and jury under English law in the colony. The Snuneymuxw mourned the death of their young man. The tribe viewed his hanging as a great injustice. His widow was nicknamed the "Gallows Widow," and after a suitable period of mourning, she married her husband's brother, a practice of levirate that was common among the Coast Salish people.[18]

This was an early turning point in Douglas's relationship with the Natives. He wanted to show strength, and be seen as a forceful person who would not stand for the wilful murder of a company employee. Douglas was happy with the outcome and wrote to the London office of his encounter with the tribes:

I am happy to report that I found both the Cowegin and Nanaimo Tribes more amenable to reason than was supposed; the objects of the Expedition having, under Providence, been satisfactorily attained, as much through the influence of the Hudson's Bay Company's name, as by the effect of intimidation. The surrender of a criminal, as in the case of the Cowegin murderer, without bloodshed, by the most numerous and warlike of the Native Tribes on Vancouver's Island, at the demand of the Civil powers may be considered, as an epoch, in the history of our Indian relations, which augers well for the future peace and prosperity of the Colony. That object however could not have been effected without the exhibition of a powerful force.[19]

The expedition did succeed in allaying the fears of white colonists and reinforced the power of British military force.

Not much is known about shepherd Peter Brown. The young man had been in the colony only a few months when his murder occurred. Two letters addressed to him, held in the HBC Archives in Winnipeg, Manitoba, shed some light on his family. They were addressed to Peter Brown, Fort Victoria, Vancouver Island, Columbia.[20] Both letters appear to be written by the same hand, and were probably dictated to a correspondent; one is from his father, the other from a friend, James Brown. Both are dated Harray, 19th 1852. (The month is absent.)

Dear Son: I take the opportunity of writing you these few lines to let you know that we are all well at present. Thank God for it, hoping this finds you the same. We got two letters from you all at one time on 2 of June, and was glad to hear of your welfare. Dear son I hear of no person going to Columbia as yet. I will said [will let you know] it if I hear of anyone. I received a letter from James on Feb. 11 and he is well: [He is] driving stones to the rail road at $3 a day. He likes it well...I have not much news to tell you but plenty [getting] married and plenty dying. I will tell you all of that; first married then died.

His father proceeds to list the people who were married or who died; it is a list of people from the young man's community. Then he tells him of those friends leaving Orkney for America and Australia, including his cousin William Brown. He notes that plenty of others had gone to Australia. Then he gives some fatherly advice: if he wants a wife, he will have to bring her home to meet him.

The other letter, from his friend James Brown, gives directions on how to contact his brother James, "care of Andrew Grant, innkeeper, Hameltown (Hamilton), Canada West, N. America."

The letters were never received. Peter Brown was dead, his young life cut short by two bullets, his passing now just a footnote in the history of Vancouver Island. This would have been devastating news for his family back in Harrah. It is not known if he was buried in Victoria, or if his remains were returned to Orkney.

A Man of Leisure: Alexander Grant Dallas

Alexander Grant Dallas was born in Berbice, British Guiana, on July 25, 1817. His father, Murdoch Dallas, a medical doctor from Inverness, died soon after the boy was born. His grandfather John Dallas was a merchant in Inverness. His mother, Helena Grant, also Scottish, returned to Scotland with the children after her husband died, and Dallas was educated at Inverness Academy, where he won a gold medal. About 1842 he began his professional career in China with the powerful trading house Jardine, Matheson & Company, travelling the world in their employ. He spent some time in the Far East, where he almost died of yellow fever, then returned to Scotland and purchased the estate of Dunain, near Inverness.

Dallas was canny enough to use his money wisely. By the time he was 30 years old, he was wealthy enough to retire as a man of leisure, but he continued to be involved in business and investments. While in London, he spent considerable time sitting on various boards and held many corporate directorships, one with the HBC. At the age of 40, he had almost everything in life he could have wanted, except for a wife.[21]

Jane Douglas was 19 when her father, Governor James Douglas, led her down the aisle of Victoria District Church on March 9, 1858, to marry Alexander Grant Dallas. She was a beautiful bride. With a dark complexion and straight black hair, she was one of the prettiest of the Douglas daughters, according to Dr. Helmcken. She was also talented; she spoke fluent French and she played the piano, a must for entertaining in Fort Victoria in its early days. She was also a fair horse rider. The young couple lived with the Douglases at their home, James Bay House, until their home, on Humboldt Street across the bay from the Douglases' home, was completed in June 1859. Their home became a centre of social activity in Fort Victoria.

Dallas had been hired by the Company to come to Fort Victoria to conduct an investigation into the operations of the Puget Sound Agricultural Company (PSAC). Prior to this appointment, he had spent five years as president of Vancouver Island's council.[22] He only intended to stay for a year after his work was completed, but then he met Jane and his plans changed. He had left an estate in Scotland and had a busy business life that required attention. After much discussion, the newlyweds decided to take a cross-country journey to eastern Canada. Dallas wrote to a friend that Jane was "young, strong & a capital rider & her father sees no difficulty whatsoever."[23] Jane kept the Scottish tradition alive: wherever she travelled, a maid and a piper always accompanied her.

The young couple's plans changed. Their journey to eastern Canada was postponed when gold was discovered in the Cariboo and Britain stepped in to solidify its position on the west coast by declaring the mainland the new Colony of British Columbia. When James Douglas was sworn in as governor of both colonies, the position came with the condition that he sever all association with the HBC and the PSAC, as he was now in a conflict-of-interest position. He had to break with the Company and dispose of his shares in the PSAC, and Dallas was appointed head of the HBC Western Department.

Dallas's marriage to Jane did not win him any favours from her father. Their association was sometimes stormy but always respectful. He thought nothing of suing his father-in-law in his capacity as HBC representative, claiming certain land for the Company that Douglas claimed for the government. Such was the case with Beacon Hill Park. Dallas said it belonged to the HBC, and that Douglas had no right to give it away. It was clear where Douglas's loyalties lay when he tried to hang onto power until the bitter end, May 30, 1859, which was the date that the HBC's charter of Vancouver Island was due to expire. One has to wonder what Douglas thought when he received a letter from the governor of the HBC with instructions "to hand over to Mr. Dallas all documents, papers and accounts connected with the company's affairs hitherto under your charge."[24] The Company trading licence, or Royal Grant of Vancouver Island, took years to sort out, especially over land ownership.

Dallas never shared Douglas's enthusiasm for the coal-mining operation at Nanaimo. He also instituted a new management style. The two men who had managed the coal mines left their positions, and Dallas hired Charles S. Nicol, a new manager without any Company or coal-mining experience. Nicol was a retired engineer trained as a land surveyor, and it was his recommendation that a British-owned joint stock company be formed specifically to purchase the Nanaimo mines and town. This proved to be a wise decision. He successfully conducted the sale while at the same time keeping his job as manager, even though he was clearly in a conflict-of-interest position.

The Nanaimo mining operation was sold to a British company, the Vancouver Coal Mining and Land Company, in 1862. Dallas became a shareholder in the new company. By this time, the British Crown had taken back from the HBC all rights over

Vancouver Island. Dallas never believed the Company should be in the coal business, for he thought it could never make a profit. He suggested the future of the Company lay in commercial ventures, not coal. Perhaps he paved the way for the successful HBC retailer known today. Despite Dallas's feelings about the Nanaimo coal operation, the town proudly named its main square Dallas Square in his honour.

Dallas was well regarded by the hierarchy of the Company. When Sir George Simpson became ill, he suggested Dallas be offered his position. By this time, Dallas was tired of Victoria and wanted to leave Vancouver Island. His prospective one-year stay had turned into years. Late in the fall of 1860, Dallas accepted the top position with the Company as governor of Rupert's Land.

Dallas and Jane, who originally had thought of travelling overland to eastern Canada, instead now made preparations to return to England in 1861 before going to Fort Garry to take up Dallas's new position—only this time, they decided to go by sea, by the less strenuous Isthmus of Panama, as Jane was three months pregnant. As the steamer left Victoria Harbour, a band played "Auld Lang Syne," a sad farewell for Jane as she said goodbye to her parents and family. On her finger was a ring given to her by her mother as a parting gift. Mother and daughter never saw each other again. When the Dallases left Victoria, their home and lot were sold at auction to Dugald McTavish for $4,050.[25]

The couple stayed in Britain long enough for Jane to have her baby daughter, Mary Jane. In March 1862, they sailed to New York and then travelled by train to Montreal, then west to St. Paul, Minnesota. They continued on horseback to Georgetown, Minnesota, where they caught up with Robert McMicking and a group known as the Overlanders, who were on their way to the Cariboo, where gold had been discovered.

Dallas spent time with the men, who had saluted him, and he gave them information about British Columbia. Dallas always seemed to have an opinion about the west coast. Earlier he wrote about the type of immigrant needed for the colony of Vancouver Island:

> It [the colony] is not the country for broken-down gentlemen or "swells." Washing costs 72 cents per dozen. You cannot get your boots brushed under a shilling: servants' wages are five to eight pounds per month. This is enough to dismay a professional man with a family, but it is good news for the washerwoman, the shoe-black and the servant of all work. Single men can generally rough it out, and the restaurants, generally kept by Frenchmen, are far better than they are in London.
>
> The miner is not very particular—"plain, fat, and 50" even would not be objected to; while good looking girls would be the nuggets and prized accordingly... Permit me to draw attention to a crying evil—the want of women. I believe there is not one to every 100 men at the mines; without them the male population will never settle in this country, and innumerable evils are the consequence.[26]

Robert McMicking, brother of Thomas, wrote in his diary about this meeting. He was one of "the 70 Cariboo boys" who crossed the prairies and travelled through the Rocky Mountains to British Columbia. The "rousing congratulatory impromptu parade and salute was quickly put together by the men who marched to Dallas's residence in double file." After the salute into the air:

> The Captain (Thomas McMicking) then introduced himself and the Company. The Governor then thanked the Company & Introduced a Hiland piper who played two or three tunes. The Co. then gave three cheers for the Governor, Three for her Majesty & for the President of the U.S. Three for the piper, and again three for the Governor & three for His Lady. The Co. then Marched back to Camp Singing God Save the Queene. The piper went to the camp and gave us another tune there.[27]

In May 1862, Jane and Dallas arrived at Fort Garry, where Jane got an opportunity to visit her grandmother, Miyo Nipiy, in St. Boniface, across the river from Fort Garry. Shortly after the two women met, Miyo died at 74 years of age. Perhaps thinking of her parents, Jane wanted to go to Fort Victoria for a visit, but another pregnancy ended that possibility. Son Rupert David Dallas was born in 1863. The young boy saw little of his father, for he was travelling throughout the Company territory during the next two years. Dallas had been governor for only two years when he and Jane decided to return to Britain. They left Fort Garry in May 1864 with their two children. For Dallas, the world of business and commerce beckoned, as did his estate at Dunain, where he enjoyed his pastimes of riding and hunting. He was also an accomplished watercolour artist.

The family remained in Britain. Of their nine children, seven survived childhood; only their first-born child, Helena Amelia, was buried in Victoria. Alexander Grant Dallas died in 1882 and Jane Douglas Dallas in 1909.

An Unhappy Man: Charles Ross

Charles Ross is credited with being the first man to begin building Fort Victoria. Before he arrived on Vancouver Island, he had already amassed a knowledge of forts and outposts from his time with the North West Company and the HBC. His employment record reads like a travel log of early Canada. His experiences in the fur-trading business and with First Nations made him a valuable employee.

Ross was born in 1794 in Kingcraig, Inverness, Scotland, to a well-educated family. His brother Walter was a physician who settled in British Guiana and accumulated a fortune before he died in 1832, leaving Charles with a bequest of 500 pounds sterling. Another brother, John, a Presbyterian minister in Edinburgh, was lost at sea, leaving behind a wife and several children. There were three sisters. Kate married Walter Young, the editor of the *London Sun* from 1820 to 1862. Another sister, Elizabeth, or Elspat, married Joseph Macdonald; the third sister's name is unknown.

Ross joined the HBC in 1818. He arrived on October 6 at Norway House, near the foot of Lake Winnipeg, having travelled from York Factory on Hudson Bay. Norway House was so named when in 1814, eight Norwegian axemen were brought in to cut a winter road to York Factory. After Fort William was downgraded on Lake Superior, Norway House became the main inland distribution depot and base camp for the Athabasca Region, one of the world's most lucrative fur farms. Ross was clerk at Norway House for a year before becoming clerk at Lac la Pluie.

In 1820, the North West Company and the HBC amalgamated their 173 posts under the name and dominance of the HBC, giving it control of more than 3 million square miles of land. Ross was transferred to New Caledonia in 1824, where he clerked for the next eight years. New Caledonia stretched from the Gulf of California to the southern edge of Alaska. It was so named by explorer Simon Fraser because the landscape reminded him of Scotland. (The name "Scotland" was first used in the 11th century. The Romans had called the country "Caledonia." Scots kept establishing "New Caledonias" wherever they went.)

Ross's next move was to Fort Babine, where he remained for two years between 1825 and 1827. When trade there declined, Chief Factor William Connolly charged Ross with mismanagement. He was exonerated of these charges, and then took charge of Bears Lake Post. In 1828 he moved to Fort George (now Prince George), was in Fort Connolly from 1829 to 1831, and in 1832 moved to Fort McLeod, the first permanent white establishment between Alaska and California.

Ross married Isabella, a Native woman from Michilimackinac, Lake Superior, in 1822. They had nine children. In a letter to his sister Elspat, he described Isabella:

She is not, indeed exactly fitted to shine at the head of a nobleman's table, but she suits the sphere (in which) she has to move much better than any such toy—she is a Native of the country, and as to beauty quite as comely as her husband.[28]

He told Elspat about his children and how his chief regret was that they were growing up in the wild without a proper education and "my means too slender to send them where they can get either." As soon as he received word he had been made chief trader, he sent John, 20, Walter, 16, and Elizabeth, 14, to London to be educated.

From his letters Ross does not appear to have been a happy man. He wrote about the remote posts as a "dreary wilderness being dark and insipid." The HBC posts were positioned great distances apart with little communication between them. Once a year, staff met to exchange cargoes of furs. "There is no society that a person must direct himself the best way he can with his own thoughts."

In 1835, while stationed at Fort McLeod, he visited his sister Kate in London, and together they travelled to Edinburgh to visit with his brother John's wife and children. John was the clergyman who was lost at sea. Ross reported back to Elspat that all were in excellent health and grown men and women. They did not go north to their home in Inverness because, he said, "I could find nothing there, but painful recollections."

Ross was high on the ladder of employment progression within the HBC when he was transferred from Fort McLoughlin to build the new fort on Vancouver Island. The fort was constructed using only primitive tools such as saws, chisels and axes. In another letter, this time to Donald Ross (no relation), he wrote about his work there and the environment:

> We landed June 4, when Douglas started for Vancouver leaving myself and Mr. R. Finlayson with a body of 40 men to carry on operations at this place...we have since been hard at it—fortifying—building, farming, etc. etc. Finlayson and myself are

doing the best we can save for the annoyance occasionally given us by the Natives who have been about us in great numbers ever since our arrival. The landscape is beautiful and strongly reminds one of some of the noble domains at home. Such is Camosun, alias Fort Albert, alias Fort Victoria. Immense numbers of whalers have been on the coast this last summer, some say as many as 300 sail.[29]

Ross did not have the disposition to work in a lonely and isolated place, and he occasionally became deeply depressed. He wrote of the sudden transition from the seclusion of Fort McLoughlin to "this place, has been sufficiently trying to myself. In fact, I never before was in such a turmoil in my life, building, farming, etc." He may have been a bit overwhelmed by what was expected of him.

A disgruntled Ross didn't think much of the fur-trade possibilities on the island. He reported to Sir George Simpson: "Trade here does not seem to augur anything very propitious. We have as yet collected little beyond 400 skins, beaver and land otter."[30]

Simpson was not concerned; he thought the fort was well positioned for the fishing industry, or supplying American whalers. His reply to Ross, dated June 20, 1844, arrived too late, for Ross had died the week before. Simpson acknowledged the difficult state Ross had been in when they last met. "I am really glad that you got over the nervous state." He went on to give an optimistic view of the future of Fort Victoria:

> I think Fort Victoria is likely to become a place of much resort to strangers, especially so if American whalers continue to frequent the Northern Pacific and that a profitable business may be made by sale of provisions and supplies to those vessels.[31]

Simpson seemed surprised to learn that Ross had sent three of his children to England to be educated: "Considering the state of your finances, you must be a very bold man." He suggested it

Charles Ross with his wife, Isabella, and children. Ross, an HBC trader, began building Fort Victoria in 1843. PHOTOGRAPHER: RICHARD MAYNARD. IMAGE F-05032 COURTESY OF ROYAL BC MUSEUM, BC ARCHIVES

would have been better to send the children to Red River School. When next in London, he promised to look up Ross's brother-in-law Walter Ross, the editor of the *London Sun*.

In a letter dated January 11, 1844, to Dr. William Fraser Tolmie, who was in charge at Fort Nisqually, Washington Territory, Ross asked for advice about a recurring medical complaint. Tolmie was also from Inverness and was a graduate of Glasgow University. Ross described the ailment as "coldness & irregularity of the Bowels." Tolmie prescribed early rising and vigorous exercise. Not one to miss a Scottish Hogmanay, New Year's Eve, Ross reported back to the good doctor that he "tried to dance my complaint 'down the wind,' but...I rather made things worse."[32]

Ross died a painful death in June 1844. His wife, Isabella, outlived her husband by 41 years. Using money from his estate, she purchased 100 acres near Fort Victoria and became the first woman to own property in the colony.

Twenty-six-year-old Roderick Finlayson took over command of the fort. He had been with the company for only six years but was determined to finish Ross's work.

Clerk-in-charge: Roderick Finlayson

Work continued on construction of the fort under clerk Roderick Finlayson. Being in control must have been a daunting task for the young Scot, who was born on March 16, 1818, in the Kyle of Lochalsh, Ross-shire, to Mary Morrison and Alexander Finlayson, a sheep and stock farmer.

He emigrated to New York in July 1837 and, through the influence of a relative there, received an appointment as apprentice clerk with the HBC at its head office in Lachine in Lower Canada. The Company already employed two of his uncles. Finlayson worked for a time at Fort Coulonge, on the Ottawa River, where he learned about trading and forestry. The next year he served at Fort William, and in 1839 was assigned to the Columbia district under Dr. John McLoughlin. He had gained experience in various posts and quickly moved up the ladder from apprentice clerk to chief trader and then chief factor. From 1839 to 1843, he had served at Fort Stikine (now in Alaska) and Fort Simpson (now in northern British Columbia) before being appointed to the "Straits of de Fuca" post. In 1843 he became second in command at Fort Victoria.[33]

Fort Victoria was described by a correspondent in *The Times*, London, dated May 4, 1849:

> The fort is an oblong stockade, sunk four feet in the ground and eighteen feet above it, with a blockhouse at the opposite corners with a few guns in each. There is a house for the head man, one for the two next in rank, three for the men. The people are now kept up late as it is harvest time and they dare not carry the wheat away in the day, it being so dry that all the grain falls out, so they wait till a little dew has fallen, and then go to work until past twelve at night.[34]

In Fort Victoria's first year of existence, the Company supplied food. Thereafter, the fort's residents were expected to be self-sufficient. In this regard, two dairies were established, each with a herd of cows supplied from Fort Nisqually. By 1847 the Company farm, initiated by Finlayson and located in what is now James Bay, was growing more than 300 acres in wheat, peas and potatoes.

In addition to his work at the fort, Finlayson was involved in the formation of Vancouver's Island Steam Saw Mill Company at Esquimalt. He earned the respect of Douglas, who said of him:

> He is not a man of display, but there is a degree of energy, perseverance, method and sound judgement in all his arrangements... He is besides a young man of great probity and high moral worth.[35]

In 1849, James Douglas took over the fort and became chief factor and trader-in-charge of operations. Finlayson was appointed chief accountant, a position similar to that held by Douglas under McLoughlin at Fort Vancouver.

That same year, Finlayson married Sarah Work, one of John Work's daughters, on December 14. Work, an Irishman, was married to Josette Legace, the daughter of a French-Canadian voyageur and a Spokane Native woman. The Works' Hillside Farm was a bit of a social centre for all the young people in the community. The trader's children, with their mixture of Scottish and Indian blood were, as one Englishman quipped, "improved Scots."[36] After 25 years of living together, John and Josette Work decided to legitimize their union. They were married before Reverend Staines on November 6, 1849, five weeks before Sarah married Finlayson and three months before Jane married Dr. Tolmie.

The Reverend Robert John Staines and his wife, Emma, had arrived in Fort Victoria in March 1849 and resided in the fort. Staines, a newly ordained Church of England chaplain, fulfilled the Company's need to have someone capable of teaching and administering the gospel. Finlayson thought the man was a snob and a prig. While they lived at the fort, Finlayson was forced to lay planks in advance of Emma's progress so that her skirts would be kept out of the mud.

Staines died tragically in a shipwreck in 1854 when returning to London. After missing the ship he had booked passage on, he instead boarded a lumber ship that overturned in rough weather off Cape Flattery. Trapped underneath, he managed to cut his way through but died clinging to the wreckage just before rescuers arrived. Emma Staines and the children returned to England, having been granted free passage home by the Company.[37]

After their marriage, Finlayson and Sarah moved into rooms attached to his office in the fort. The couple later purchased 100 acres south of John Work's land, the first of his extensive real-estate dealings, which over the years made Finlayson one of the largest property owners in Victoria.[38] His status within the community was reflected in his promotion to chief trader in 1850. Two years later he was appointed to the Council of Vancouver Island, on which he served as treasurer until 1863.

Douglas and Finlayson were associated with the 1859 founding of the St. Andrew's Society, a Scottish benevolent association that became the St. Andrews and Caledonian Society. The first Highland games were jointly organized by the St. Andrew's Society and the Sir William Wallace Society and were held in 1864 at the old Caledonian Grounds on Cook Street.

In 1861, Finlayson became chief factor of the western district, and that year he visited Scotland on furlough. On his return, he was appointed chief factor of "Interior B.C." (but with headquarters in Victoria) for the period 1871 to 1872.[39] On June 1, 1872, after 44 years with the Company, Finlayson resigned his position. He was elected mayor of Victoria in 1878, and, during his tenure, Victoria's city hall was built.

Finlayson was not without means; the income from his leases made him one of the city's wealthiest and most prominent citizens. Finlayson died on January 20, 1892.[40]

Doctor, Botanist, Climber and Librarian: William Fraser Tolmie

Chief Factor Dr. William Fraser Tolmie began service with the HBC in 1832. He was born in Inverness on February 3, 1812, the eldest son of Alexander Tolmie and Marjory Fraser. His mother died when he was three, and an aunt raised him. His early education was at Inverness Academy, Perth Grammar School and private schools in Edinburgh. An uncle encouraged his interest in medicine and helped finance his studies from 1829 to 1831 at the University of Glasgow's medical school. Although often referred to as Dr. Tolmie, he did not have an MD degree. He studied as a licentiate of the Faculty of Physicians and Surgeons of Glasgow, a body independent of the university. He received his diploma in the spring of 1831. A near-fatal illness prevented him from undertaking further studies in Paris.

In 1832, when a cholera epidemic devastated Scotland, he worked in an emergency cholera hospital organized in Glasgow. In the summer of that year, the HBC was looking for two medical officers for the Columbia District, and Tolmie was one who was recommended for the post. On September 12 he signed a five-year contract to serve in the dual capacity of clerk and surgeon for the Columbia District. Three days later he sailed from Gravesend on the ship *Ganymede*. He celebrated his 21st birthday on board.[41]

The *Ganymede* travelled by way of Cape Horn and the Sandwich Islands (now Hawaii) and arrived at Fort George (also known as Fort Astoria) at the mouth of the Columbia River on May 1, 1833. The voyage had taken more than eight months. Three days later, Tolmie reached Fort Vancouver and reported to Dr. John McLoughlin, the chief factor.

Tolmie began work immediately as medical officer. He was assigned temporarily to the new post at Nisqually, on Puget Sound, and would then move to Fort McLoughlin, a new post built in the spring of that year at Milbanke Sound. He arrived at Fort Nisqually on May 30, after what he termed "a pleasant journey of 12 days." While he was there, a man was seriously injured and needed long-term skilled medical attention, so it was decided that Tolmie would remain there for the time being. He wrote in his diary on June 23 after he was out riding:

> Recollected as I scampered along that the past week was my second anniversary of my trip to the Trossochs [*sic*], (and) last year at this time I was officiating at the Cholera Hospital, and this year am commander of a trading post in a remote part of the New World with only a force of six effective men in the midst of treacherous, bloodthirsty savages, with whom murder is familiar.[42]

The Trossachs is a picturesque countryside of hills, forests and lakes and a prime recreational area between Loch Achray and Loch Katrine, north of Glasgow, in Stirlingshire.

Tolmie was an enthusiastic botanist who collected and recorded many new plants, some that would bear his name. He sent some of the specimens to his friend, Sir William Hooker, a celebrated naturalist at Kew Gardens, England.

Tolmie was also a climber, and was the first white man to climb in the Mount Rainier area, making observations of living glaciers within what is now the United States. He set out on August 29, 1833, and on September 2 reached the summit of what is now known as Tolmie Peak.

He left Nisqually on December 12, 1833, on the *Cadboro*, for Fort McLoughlin, arriving there on December 23. After celebrating Christmas Day with friends Alexander Caulfield Anderson and Donald Manson, he wrote: "Passed the evening very agreeably. Sang several old Scotch ditties and the other gentlemen also tuned their pipes." Manson came from Thurso, in Caithness, and was clerk-in-charge at Fort McLoughlin from 1834 to 1838.

Tolmie loved to read, and during his stay at Fort McLoughlin, he and Donald Manson conceived the idea of establishing a circulating library among the HBC officers. The officers subscribed, and then ordered books and periodicals from the Company's agent in London. The library was kept at Fort Vancouver, and books were sent out to all the forts and posts. This was the first circulating library on the Pacific coast and was in operation from 1833 to 1843.

Tolmie also studied Native languages and, with Dr. George M. Dawson, compiled a dictionary of the Aboriginal languages in British Columbia.

In 1835, while Tolmie was stationed at Fort McLoughlin, a number of Natives from the north end of Vancouver Island came to trade. The blacksmith was working at his forge, and when he put more coal on the fire, the Natives were curious. They asked the blacksmith where the coal came from, and was told it took six months to bring it by ship from Wales. He noticed they were amused by this and asked what was so funny. The Natives told him that it seemed funny that men should carry this soft black stone so far when it could be had without expense close at hand. The blacksmith called Tolmie, and the Natives told him where he could get all the black stones he wanted on Vancouver Island. Tolmie notified McLoughlin, at Fort Vancouver, who ordered the crew of the *Beaver* to stop on the next voyage at the place the Natives had described. The result was the discovery of the coalfield at Beaver Harbour and the founding of Fort Rupert several years later. This was the first important coal discovery in British Columbia, and it was this deposit that brought many Scottish miners to Vancouver Island.

In 1841, Tolmie was granted permission to visit his homeland. He travelled across the country from the Pacific to the Atlantic, by canoe and horseback, he commented, "without taking a single drink of alcohol." A record for any Scot! In addition to visiting Scotland, he went to France, where he took a postgraduate degree in medicine and even acquired a knowledge of Spanish, having in mind a possible appointment to the HBC post at Yerba Buena (San Francisco). However, on his return, he was stationed back to Fort Nisqually and directed to organize the Puget Sound Agricultural Company (PSAC) as a subsidiary of the HBC. The PSAC was a large operation with more than 8,000 sheep, 3,180 cattle and 300 horses. As early as 1841, the company's farmers were milking 200 cows and making cheese and butter to supply the forts and sell to the Russians in Alaska. Hides, horns, tallow and wool were exported to Great Britain. Tolmie once drove more than 3,000 sheep to the Willamette Valley, going as far south as Eugene, Oregon.

He began to feel that his association with the PSAC stood in the way of his advancement in the Company and that any promotions would probably go to those serving the parent company. It was not until March 1847 that he was promoted to chief trader, an appointment he felt was long overdue. Eight years later he became chief factor.

Hubert Howe Bancroft described Tolmie as "rather below medium height, broad-shouldered and stout... high forehead, coarse features, round deep-set eyes glittering from under shaggy brows, large round ruby nose." Others admired his capacity to

Dr. William Fraser Tolmie and his family at their Victoria home, Cloverdale, in 1878. Dr. Tolmie studied medicine in Glasgow before coming to Vancouver Island. IMAGE G-04990 COURTESY OF ROYAL BC MUSEUM, BC ARCHIVES

endure "irritations with calmness and courage," and that he was a "solemn man who could turn almost anything into hard work for his conscience."[43]

Rather than return to Scotland after his retirement from the Company, he decided to remain in Fort Victoria, where he married Jane Work in 1850. Earlier in his life, he had agonized over a decision never to marry an Indian woman.[44] Jane was of mixed blood and one of 11 children born to John and Josette Work.

Tolmie was a man with some influence. When Great Britain had the opportunity to purchase the Alaska Panhandle from Russia, it consulted HBC men in the field, one being Tolmie at Fort Victoria. Up until this time the panhandle had been leased, and negotiations by the Company to pay for a renewal were deadlocked, leaving Britain in a bit of a quandary. Tolmie had the foresight to see the opportunity this presented, and he urged that the Russian offer to sell be accepted.[45] By the time his letter reached

London, however, the Company had renewed the lease for another two years. The US purchased Alaska in 1867 for $7,200,000. Britain did not seem interested in acquiring more empire on the other side of the world.

Tolmie purchased farmland near Work's Hillside Farm, and by 1859 had cultivated 1,100 acres and constructed his home, named Cloverdale, on Lovat Avenue. It was the first stone dwelling house in what is now the province of British Columbia. By any standard, it was a grand mansion, built in three stages with sandstone from Salt Spring Island and redwood from San Francisco, walls two-feet thick constructed of stone quarried on the farm, and logs salvaged from the old Company buildings being dismantled within the fort.[46] The thriving farm had everything, including imported purebred stock. Sadly, the house was demolished in 1963.

The Tolmies had five daughters and seven sons. Their seventh son, Simon Fraser Tolmie, was born in Victoria and served as premier of the province from 1928 to 1933.

In 1860, Tolmie was elected to the first House of Assembly of Vancouver Island and was a member from 1860 through 1866. He retired from the HBC in 1871. After the union of the crown colonies in 1866, he was elected to represent Victoria in a by-election necessitated by the resignation of Amor de Cosmos. He served from 1874 to 1878, when he retired from politics.

One of the legislative measures Tolmie introduced was *An Act to prevent the Spread of Thistles*. His interests in plant life continued throughout his life. He died on December 8, 1886.

Several landmarks in Victoria commemorate Tolmie, including Mount Tolmie and Cloverdale Elementary School.

Victoria's First Retiree: John Tod

"I have long since given up the thoughts of going to lay my bones in the land of my Fathers. I must seek out some retired spot, where my savage habits & mode of life will be less under the eye of ceremonial observance, and where my liberty is not likely to be hemmed by Game laws."

John Tod had been around HBC forts and outposts for most of his life. He was born in Dumbartonshire, Scotland, in October 1794. He worked in a cotton warehouse in Glasgow before signing on with the Company. In 1811 he came out on the ship *Edward and Ann* to York Factory, near Lake Winnipeg, where he worked as a writer/clerk.[47] After a remarkable career he shared with four wives, Tod had the distinction of being the first HBC man to retire to Victoria in 1850. At that time, he was the oldest resident in the colony.

His first wife, Catherine Birstone, gave birth to their son, James, in 1818 at Lake Winnipeg. Five years later Tod was transferred to Fort George, New Caledonia, and he left behind Catherine and James. In his absence, Catherine became involved with another trader, and, in 1826, Tod found himself a new companion to enliven his evenings by singing while he played his flute. This union also produced a child, a daughter, but she too was left behind when Tod returned to Scotland to take a leave of absence in 1834 because of ill health. On the way there, he met Eliza Waugh, a Welshwoman who was returning home after working in the Red River for five years as a lady's maid. The couple married in London. Eliza returned with him, and in 1835 gave birth to their daughter, Emmeline Jean.

Perhaps unknown to Tod at the time of marriage, Eliza was mentally unstable. Other traders suggested he had married a "half Cracked Brainid Chamber Maid."[48] This would have been a rough time for Eliza, living in isolation with a new baby. In 1837, Tod took a leave of absence and took Eliza home to Wales to be with her mother. She was placed in an asylum after being diagnosed as "a confirmed lunatic."

Tod's fourth wife entered his life sometime between 1843 and 1844, when he was stationed at Thompson River (now Kamloops).

She was Sophia Lolo, a Native woman 30 years younger than him, in her late teens. She was the daughter of John Baptiste Lolo, a respected interpreter of the Company at Fort Kamloops. After they retired to Victoria, Sophia gave birth to five children. Eliza died in 1857, leaving Tod free to marry Sophia, but he postponed his marriage until 1863, just before his daughter Mary was about to marry. Then Catherine, his first companion, showed up in Victoria, saying she wanted to be closer to their son, James, who was now married and settled on a farm. Life in Victoria became a little uncomfortable for all concerned. However, Tod did the right thing by marrying Sophia, thereby legitimizing his daughter and confirming the identity of his current wife, Mrs. Tod.

The Colony of Vancouver Island, with its mild winters, warm, dry summers, few mosquitoes and no blackflies, was a dream location for retirees from the Company. In 1848, when Tod retired from the fur trade, he spent 100 pounds sterling to purchase land at the Company's Oak Bay Estate, an easy walk to Fort Victoria. There he built what today is known as Tod House, on Heron Street, near Willows Beach. Tod received a letter from Governor George Simpson, dated June 20, 1850, commending him on deciding on retiring to Vancouver Island:

> Your determination to settle upon British Territory rather than follow the example of so many of your friends who have become United States Citizens, manifests both good taste and sound judgement—Vancouver's Island seems to be a very eligible situation for the Company's officers to retire to. There can be little doubt that, in due time, it will become the seat of a very extensive commerce, its position in reference to the British, United States & Russian possessions on the N.W. Coast being superior to that of any other place possessed by either of the latter powers; while its coal mines, fisheries, good harbours, &c. give it a decided preference over all other settlements on the coast.[49]

In 1851, one of Governor Richard Blanshard's last accomplishments before resigning was to appoint a provisional council of Vancouver Island to arrange for the election of a general assembly. He appointed HBC retiree John Tod, free settler Captain James Cooper and James Douglas, chief factor, to the council.

Tod lived out his days in his modest comfortable house on Oak Bay. Although his sight was failing, his mind was as sharp as ever, and his love of music seemed as intense as when he had entertained at the second birthday party for Douglas's son, James Jr.

From Cloth Merchant to Chief Justice: David Cameron

James Douglas, searching for a suitable candidate for chief justice of Vancouver Island, selected his brother-in-law, David Cameron, husband to Douglas's sister, Cecilla Cowan, from Demerara in British Guiana. Granted, there were not many qualified people to fill the post in Fort Victoria, but still, Cameron's background did not suggest a man with legal experience. There were cries of foul at the apparent patronage of a family connection. A petition was sent to the Queen calling for an investigation into the appointment.

David Cameron, born in 1804 in Perthshire, Scotland, spent his early life in Perth. Relatives there financed him as a cloth merchant in 1824, but he was "too liberal in giving credit" and the business failed. He declared bankruptcy, and, after settling his affairs, he emigrated to Demerera, where he worked as manager of a sugar plantation. He purchased a small plantation and married Cecilia, a free coloured girl from a privileged minority in the colony. This was her second marriage; her first husband had deserted her. She had a daughter named Cecilia Eliza from her first marriage.

Douglas did not have a close relationship with his sister or her husband, although they had kept in touch periodically. They had not met since his father took him to Scotland to attend school. Nevertheless, Douglas intervened with Andrew Colville in presenting an offer of employment to Cameron as bookkeeper, or clerk, for the Nanaimo coal mines, at 150 pounds per year plus board. Cameron accepted the position principally because his wife's failing health required a more temperate climate. Now, after 41 years, Douglas was reunited with Cecilia and introduced to her husband, David Cameron, and their daughter, Edith Rebecca, now 12. They arrived in Fort Victoria on July 16, 1853.

Cameron was given the title of superintendent. He never actually lived in Nanaimo, but had the Company books forwarded to him in Victoria. However, it was his second job that had the colony abuzz. "Family nepotism," cried his opponents when Douglas offered Cameron a second job as the first judge of the recently organized Supreme Court of Vancouver Island. The oath of allegiance was duly administered to Judge David Cameron on December 2, 1853. Douglas readily admitted he wanted someone who would not oppose him. The editor of *The Colonist*, Amor de Cosmos, used his newspaper to vent against family appointments.

Settlers in the colony now raised their voices. Ninety people signed a petition protesting the establishment of the Supreme Court and Cameron's appointment to it. Not everyone agreed with this; another 54 freeholders protested against the petition, urging Douglas not to comply with the wishes of those who had "little or no vested interest in the island." However, on February 4, at a public meeting chaired by independent settler James Cooper, $480 was collected to send the Reverend Staines to England to take the petition to Queen Victoria and to request an inquiry into the establishment of the court and Cameron's appointment, noting his lack of legal training and his family ties to Douglas. Staines died in a shipwreck, but the petition was duly sent to England in April 1854.

Douglas received a letter from London asking for a report. In his reply he staunchly defended both the establishment of the court and Cameron's appointment, and concluded that the petitioners' "grievances were less real than imaginary." And there the matter rested until April 4, 1856, when the Supreme Court of Civil Justice of the Colony of Vancouver's Island was established by order-in-council. On April 25, Cameron was confirmed as chief justice without jurisdiction in criminal cases. Soon afterwards he resigned his position with the Company, but he continued to receive his Company salary until 1860, when the legislative assembly awarded him 800 pounds annually from colony land revenues.

Chief Justice Cameron presided over the swearing in of the first legislative council of Vancouver Island on August 12, 1856, and the installation of the first government of British Columbia at Fort Langley on November 19, 1858.

Amor de Cosmos introduced a motion before the legislative assembly on February 4, 1864, requesting the governor to pension Cameron, who was being replaced as chief justice by a qualified barrister from England. The motion passed, with Cameron's pension set at 500 pounds yearly. In March, after the arrival of his successor, Joseph Needham, Cameron tendered his resignation to Governor Arthur Edward Kennedy, effective October 1865.

Proving all his detractors wrong, Cameron proved to be a good judge, and to everyone's amazement held tight to his position even though his judgments were often questioned and criticized. He handed out sentences based on common sense until his retirement as chief justice in 1865.[50] Cameron was appointed justice of the peace in 1867, a position he held until January 1871.

The Camerons continued to reside at their home *Belmont*, entertaining family and friends at dinner parties. Cecilia's death in 1858 was a terrible loss for Cameron. When he died on May 14, 1872, *The Colonist*, which had been so against his appointment as judge, praised his accomplishments and declared he had acquitted himself to the best of his ability.

The family name lives on in Cameron Lake, near Port Alberni, and Cameron Island in downtown Nanaimo; also in Victoria, at

Belmont Point and Belmont Road, the street that bears the same name as their Colwood home, and at Edith Point on Mayne Island, named for their daughter.

The First Senator: William John Macdonald

William John Macdonald was one of the first three senators appointed from British Columbia in 1871—and the first from Vancouver Island—when the colony entered Confederation, becoming the sixth province in the new Dominion of Canada. He served twice as mayor of Victoria, and was also a member of the legislative assembly and the council of the colonies of Vancouver Island and British Columbia.

Macdonald was born on November 29, 1832, to Captain Alexander Macdonald of North Uist, and Glendale, Isle of Skye, and his wife, Flora McRae of Kintail. At this time, much of Scotland was in an economic depression. Two successive failures in potato and grain crops pushed people to the edge of starvation and made them vulnerable to disease. Educated by private tutors, Macdonald began working in 1847 with his father, who was in charge of relief work during the potato famine, employing men to build roads and women to knit stockings.

In the mid-19th century, crofters in the Highlands were dependent on potatoes as a source of food because they had been deprived of access to most of the land they had worked in previous centuries and were expected to subsist on small patches, generally of poor quality and in exposed coastal locations. Crofters were not simply given their oatmeal rations; they were expected to work for them, eight hours a day, six days a week. Relief programs produced projects with little real value, and their administration was very bureaucratic, employing legions of clerks to ensure compliance with a complex set of rules.

Some landlords worked to lessen the effects of the famine on their crofter tenants. Others, rather than accept any responsibility for their plight, resorted to eviction. One even hired a fleet of ships and forcibly transported his crofters to Canada. During the 10 years following 1847, throughout the Highlands, more than 16,000 crofters were shipped overseas to Canada and Australia.

In 1849 the Honourable Edward Ellice, MP, a director with the HBC, offered Macdonald a commission in the Company's service as apprentice clerk on Vancouver Island. He left Scotland for London to prepare to take up his appointment. The Company had booked a room for him at the George and Vulture Hotel, and he went shopping for an outfit for the long voyage ahead. Before he boarded the *Tory*, he met Captain William Mitchell, a passenger also on his way to Fort Victoria to take command of the *Beaver*. The previous skipper of the *Beaver*, Captain William Henry McNeill, had been appointed officer-in-charge at Fort Rupert. Macdonald also met John Work, who was travelling to Fort Victoria as well.

When the *Tory* left England at the end of November 1850, there were 21 passengers in the first cabin and 30 in the second, and 90 labourers and families in steerage. Miss Cameron, James Douglas's niece, fresh from school, was on board. Captain Duncan, the ship's captain, had brought along his wife; she had a piano with her, so this provided some entertainment on the long voyage. Macdonald also had a number of interesting travelling companions who would make their mark on Vancouver Island: Captain James Cooper and his wife, who became the second settler; Dr. George Johnstone, who was the surgeon on board; Charles Bayley, the ship's schoolmaster and his family; Richard Colledge, who became secretary to James Douglas; John Humphrey, who would become the first farmer in the Cowichan Valley; Captain Edward Edwards Langford, his wife and five daughters; and two engineers, Andrew Hunter and John Henry Johnson. These were only a few of the pioneer notables. Others on board were destined for the coal mine at Fort Rupert. The voyage around Cape Horn was as difficult and eventful as the other long voyages encountered by early settlers.

Historians are thankful today for a diary Macdonald kept of his years with the Company from 1850 to 1858, and for recording the early life of Victoria. He wrote in the preface: "The events of my early life will not be of much interest to strangers, and perhaps no part will be."[51] Of his voyage, Macdonald wrote:

> After getting into the Pacific Ocean our voyage was uneventful, no ships met, no land sighted. Our food, by this time three months out, became bad and scarce, cheese and biscuits full of weevils, water scarce and putrid part of the time. Very monotonous sailing week after week without seeing any signs of life beside some birds and porpoises.[52]

Passengers had lasting impressions of their voyage to the Colony of Vancouver Island. In his old age, Macdonald remembered the mountainous green seas crashing down on the little ship. Cooper thought it was a "very boisterous and unfavourable passage." Charles Bayley remembered the end of the journey, "The entrance to the Straits of Juan de Fuca was a welcome sight after such a long passage ... the scene that presented itself was grand. Mountains on the mainland capped with snow ... around us verdure most luxuriant." Dr. Johnstone wrote to the HBC in London: "I have great pleasure in being able to say after a voyage of 27 weeks in a small vessel with 127 passengers I landed one more than I received in London."[53]

The *Tory* arrived at Fort Victoria on May 14, 1851. After such a long journey, Macdonald, aged 19, felt reluctant to leave the ship and the friends he had made, but the next day, George Simpson, in a large canoe manned by Natives, arrived to take him ashore. He was welcomed at the fort by James Douglas and Roderick Finlayson. They had dinner together, and Macdonald enjoyed the change of food, especially the fresh vegetables, mutton and grouse.

A sketch of the barque *Tory*. One of its passengers on the voyage that left England bound for Victoria in 1850 via turbulent Cape Horn described it as a "very boisterous and unfavourable passage."

IMAGE Q-125 COURTESY OF NANAIMO MUSEUM

Afterwards John Ogilvy, a young HBC clerk, brought two horses to the mess hall and together they went riding around Beacon Hill and Clover Point. "Wild clover over those parts a foot high. Milk and butter in abundance, the Company having a dairy of 100 cows in the hill."[54]

After a few days' rest, he began work in the Company's office with Chief Factor Finlayson. "At this time there were no houses outside the Fort, all the officers and men, about 70 in all, lived inside the Fort, gates locked every night and watchmen set."

In June, Macdonald was sent to one of the San Juan Islands to establish a salmon fishery. He canoed there accompanied by Joseph W. McKay, chief trader and pilot of the expedition, plus four French-Canadian workers and a Native crew. They selected a small sheltered bay and erected a rough shed for salting, packing and canning salmon. As the year had a short run of fish, only 60 barrels of salmon were cured. Macdonald described his primitive living conditions:

> The first month on this Island I lived under a very primitive, rough shelter—four posts stuck in the ground with a cedar bark roof—and wolves used to prowl round us all night. My men soon built a house for me of rough logs, with bedstead and table of the same, and as the Hudson's Bay Company always furnished plenty of blankets, I had a very comfortable bed. Soon the old schooner *Cadboro*, Captain Dixon, came into our little bay with different kinds of supplies. I removed my quarters to her, and after a month we came back to Victoria and I went back to office work.[55]

Among the many tasks asked of Macdonald was to train and organize a militia of 50 men to guard the coast from northern Natives. He and the militia accompanied Douglas when he sailed to Cowichan and Nanaimo in 1853 to arrest and punish the two Natives accused of murdering Peter Brown, a shepherd at Christmas Hill, near Victoria.

The Company's young men of Fort Victoria mounted an amateur dramatic play entitled *The Rivals* by Richard Brinsley Sheridan. Macdonald played *Captain Absolute*, and Joseph William McKay played *Sir Anthony Absolute*. Other cast members included the two surveyors, Joseph Despard Pemberton and Benjamin William Pearse, and Richard Colledge, Douglas's secretary. The play was originally planned for the New Year's festivities, but was delayed until January 14, 1857. Their excuse for the delay was that "professional duties kept them from getting together earlier." Macdonald considered the play a small respite from the more serious duties of the colony.

This same year, Macdonald married Catherine Balfour Reid, the second daughter of Captain James Murray Reid. Reid was in command of the brigantine *Vancouver*. He arrived in Fort Victoria

William John Macdonald, seen here with sons Reginald and Douglas, was
one of the first three senators appointed from British Columbia in 1871, when
the colony joined Canada.

IMAGE B-00080 COURTESY OF ROYAL BC MUSEUM, BC ARCHIVES

in 1852 with his wife and three daughters. On a voyage to Fort Simpson in August 1854, Reid took the outside route around the Queen Charlotte Islands to Fort Simpson. Carrying a valuable cargo and barrels of rum, the ship was wrecked on Rose Spit. When Natives began pillaging, Reid burned the ship. This so enraged the Natives that they threatened the lives of the white men, but on a promise of compensation, they reached an amiable settlement. Reid had now lost his ship, had no pay, and had a wife and family to support and a home to build, but he never lost hope and decided to start his own business.

Macdonald and Catherine built a home they named Glendale Cottage. He said it cost him about $5,000. The couple would have five children: Regy, Willie, Flora, Edythe and Tiny.

During his eight years of service with the HBC, Macdonald performed many jobs. He was a veritable jack of all trades: collector of customs duties, postmaster, gold commissioner, road commissioner, captain of the militia, magistrate and issuer of mining licences. His wife, Catherine, and her sister, Mary Ann, assisted him with the clerical work. Douglas eventually relieved him of the position of collector of customs, giving the position to Dr. Tolmie's friend, Alexander Caulfield Anderson.

Perhaps Macdonald's most important appointment came in 1871, when he was appointed to the Senate of the newly formed Dominion of Canada. After a visit from Sir Hector Langevin, from Ottawa, "to look me over," his commission arrived at the end of the year.

In 1872, Glendale Cottage was leased for a year while Macdonald and his family went to Ottawa. Catherine and the children continued on to Great Britain, while Macdonald attended Parliament. In his memoir, he makes no mention of the work being done in the Senate, except to say of the 1894-96 session, "The same old routine; nothing important going on." Between sessions, he travelled back and forth to London, occasionally travelling north to his home on Skye. In 1889 he visited his father's grave at

Kilmuir. Later he visited Miss McLeod at Dunvegan Castle, the seat of the McLeod clan, and she gave him a tour of the castle. On his return to Canada, he travelled across the country by the new Canadian Pacific Railway.

In 1907, Catherine and Tiny accompanied him to Ottawa, and after the session they sailed to England on the steamer *Empress of Britain*. In London, they were invited to Windsor Castle. "All the first class carriages in London were engaged to convey guests to Windsor." He met and had a long talk with King Edward VII, proudly telling him that his three sons were in the King's service.

Travelling back and forth to Ottawa for Senate sessions took a toll on his health. Catherine died in 1913, and Macdonald wasn't well enough to attend the Senate. He sold their home and moved into a rented house in Oak Bay.

Macdonald served the HBC, the city of Victoria and Canada with dedication and distinction. He died in Oak Bay on October 25, 1916, at age 84. Albert Edward Planta, a former mayor of Nanaimo, succeeded him in the Senate in 1917.

CHAPTER 3

The Independent Settlers

The Wakefield Experiment

The Wakefield experiment was a theory concerning the economic planning of colonization that was proposed by Englishman Edward Gibbon Wakefield. While serving a three-year prison sentence for abducting and marrying an underage heiress, Wakefield studied social problems and poverty, and their possible solutions; this study led him to examine colonization in general.

He found that colonies had plenty of land but lacked sufficient free labour to cultivate it. Great Britain, on the other hand, had a surplus of labour, which led to high unemployment and poverty but not enough land in proportion to the population. Emigration would be the solution, but it was expensive and only people with money could consider it. After his release from prison in 1830, he started a campaign to put his theory into practice. His idea caught on with the British government. There were early experiments in South Australia and New Zealand and, in 1849, when the Colony of Vancouver Island came into being, the Wakefield system gathered momentum.

The system he proposed was similar to one common in Great Britain at the time. Rich gentlemen landowners would pay five pounds an acre for vast tracts of land, go out to the colonies with their own labourers, millers, bakers and blacksmiths, and their families, and set up self-sufficient communities.

Britain feared the west coast was in danger of falling to American interests and therefore wanted to secure its territory. In theory, the Wakefield system sounded good, but in fact there was no lineup of independent settlers in Britain willing to part with their money for 100 acres, plus pay passage for themselves, their families, and their workers and their families, to travel to an unknown colony on the other side of the world. There were no maps or surveys of land beyond the Rocky Mountains to influence their decision.

When the HBC leased the new Colony of Vancouver Island for 10 shillings a year, the Colonial Office in London and the HBC directors came to an arrangement. Part of the deal was to encourage settlers, even if they had to lure them out as employees of the Company and have their passage paid by gentry on Company sailing ships. Douglas tried to warn the Colonial Office that farming on Vancouver Island would not be profitable for years and that the land was covered with forest, much of it rocky and all of it unfenced, not at all like the cultivated farms in Britain. Even the first governor, Richard Blanshard, did not think the Wakefield system would work, "A mere theory, sure to fail in practice."[1]

Two men came to Vancouver Island as independent settlers: Captain Walter Colquhoun Grant and Captain James Cooper. The latter came out on the *Tory*, bringing with him an iron ship knocked down in sections, intended for trading between the Island, California and Hawaii. He purchased 300 acres at Metchosin and hired an Australian stockman, Thomas Blinkhorn, to manage the farm. Cooper had an entrepreneurial spirit; one of his schemes was to export barrels of cranberries from the Fraser Valley to San Francisco. However, the barrels made by the HBC were priced so high that he could not afford to purchase them. The Company took over his idea and initiated the California trade in cranberries.

In the end, none of the men made money in agriculture, but they did set the stage for settlement.

An Independent Man:
Walter Colquhoun Grant

Captain Walter Colquhoun Grant was Vancouver Island's first independent settler and was considered the founder of Sooke, near Victoria. He was born on May 27, 1822, in Edinburgh, Scotland, to Colquhoun and Margaret (née Brodie) Grant. Colquhoun Grant had been the Duke of Wellington's chief intelligence officer at the Battle of Waterloo. Grandfather Duncan Grant, the last owner of Mullachard, a small estate near Duthel, on the River Spey about 10 miles west of Granton-on-Spey, was the provost (mayor) of Forres. Duncan married Jean, the daughter of Robert Grant of Kyliemore, with whom he had nine sons and three daughters. Seven of the sons lived to maturity, each distinguishing himself in his chosen career.

The eighth son, Walter Grant's father, Colquhoun, was born in 1780 and had a notable military career. He was made Commander of the Bath for his services. Grant's mother, Margaret, accompanied her husband to India when he went there on military service. On her voyage home, she died aboard ship near St. Helena and was buried there. Colquhoun Grant died in 1829. Walter was their only son.

There is no information about who raised young Walter, but it is presumed it was one of his aunts. With a strong military tradition in his family, he turned to the army for a career. At the age of 24, he was the youngest captain in the British Army when he reached that rank in the 2nd Dragoons (Scots Greys). A bank failure amounting to 75,000 pounds swept away his estate, and that loss of income made it impossible for him to maintain his rank in the army. As a result, he resigned his commission and decided to emigrate to the colonies.[2]

Grant's uncle, Sir Lewis Grant, gave him money to buy 200 acres on Vancouver Island, where land was being offered by the HBC at one pound per acre. As a deterrent to absentee landowners, for every 100 acres acquired, the purchaser, at his own expense, had to send out five single men or three married couples. The Company hired the 26-year-old as colonial surveyor at an annual salary of 100 pounds.

Grant had the idea of establishing a Scottish colony on Vancouver Island. Perhaps he had heard of the Earl of Selkirk's settlements in Nova Scotia and the Red River, or was familiar with the Wakefield system. He arranged for Highlands schoolmaster Alexander Macfarlane to join him in order to teach Gaelic in the school he hoped to establish. He also requested passage for Thomas Poustie, his wife, his sister-in-law, Mrs. Susan Poustie, and their three children, all less than six years of age. Thomas Poustie was hired as Grant's *grieve* (farm overseer). Grant requested that the cost of these passages be deducted from his future salary as a surveyor. This request did not sit well with the HBC. The Company advised that the expense of transporting the men and their families must be borne by him.

His grand plan for a Scottish settlement did not materialize. The schoolmaster and the Thomas Poustie family could not travel on the *Harpooner*. However, the names of the eight men he hired did appear on the passenger list. They were James Rose (blacksmith and engineer), William McDonald (joiner and house builder), Thomas Tolmie (carpenter and house builder), Thomas Munro (gardener), James Morrison (farmer and labourer), William Fraser (farmer and labourer), William McDonald (farmer and labourer) and John McLeod (labourer).

Alexander McFarlane, the schoolteacher, sailed on the *Norman Morison* from Gravesend on October 20, 1849. Sadly, he died on January 21, 1850, of cancer before the ship reached Fort Victoria. Dr. Helmcken, the doctor on board, noted the elderly Scot had been in "declining health" on his arrival on board. He wrote:

In the Pacific a schoolmaster who was going out to teach Gaelic to Capt. Grant's settlement at Sooke died of cancer. He was a very quiet worthy old Highlander, always ailing of course. When dying he gave me his fishing rod, with which he had hoped to catch salmon in the River of Sooke. I kept this rod for years—my boys destroyed it. Poor Dominie [schoolmaster]— peace be with you.[3]

He was buried at sea. There is no indication of what happened to the Poustie family.

The *Harpooner* docked at Fort Victoria in June 1849 with the eight workers, who had to wait there until August 11, when Grant finally arrived by canoe from Fort Nisqually on Puget Sound. His men were decidedly unhappy about having had to wait two months for his arrival. Grant had taken the Panama railway route to save himself the long voyage around Cape Horn, but the time saved was evidently not enough to get him to his destination on time.

Grant's financial difficulties plagued him during his stay on Vancouver Island. When he had arrived in Panama on March 29, 1849, he was flat broke and so applied to the HBC to advance his second year's salary. He also asked his uncles, Sir James Grant and Sir Lewis Grant, for their help. Uncle James told him to look elsewhere for money, but Uncle Lewis gave him assistance—for the last time, he said. Grant had alienated himself from his uncles as far as money was concerned.

When he arrived in San Francisco he was again broke, and once again the HBC advanced enough money to get him to Fort Victoria. Grant felt confident enough that he would soon retire his debt and become the well-to-do person he envisioned. He may not have been as confident in his role as surveyor.

After a few days' rest, James Douglas helped him select 200 acres about 25 miles from the fort, in the Sooke area, where there was a good water supply and an adequate forestry resource. It might as well have been in the wilderness as far as Grant was concerned. Douglas had made sure he was far enough away from the Fur Trade Reserve, the prized agricultural land he wished to retain for the HBC. Douglas gave him cattle, oxen and horses to stock his farm.

The young ambitious Scot brought with him a remarkable assortment of equipment including harnesses and horse carriages (to a countryside without roads), plus 170 gallons of whisky and a cricket set. The whisky, he claimed, was for the use of his men and not to barter with Natives or others. Undaunted, he began clearing land and building a home of squared logs, roofed with cedar shakes. As a show of strength, he placed two cannons between two rocky knolls. Perhaps this was to ward off the inquisitive Natives in the area. He named his homestead after Mullachard, his ancestral Scottish home on the River Spey.

In 1850 he installed a small water-powered sawmill at the mouth of a stream at the northeast end of the Sooke Basin. Trying to be self-sufficient, he started a small farm, but his life was far from idyllic. He was not a happy man, and his workers were disgruntled. He dismissed a few for incompetence, and some deserted.

Grant wrote to a friend in Britain that, of his eight men, "They are all except three now established on the island—of these three, one was drowned, one died of cholera, and the other is now working in Oregon."[4]

James Rose had entered Grant's service on May 27, 1837, and was from Garinin, Parish of Lochs, County Ross.[5] His mother Margaret, his grandmother, and two brothers and a sister all lived in the Inverness area. Rose left for Oregon City in the spring of 1850. John McLeod deserted, and his whereabouts were unknown. Thomas Tolmie appears in the 1854 Nanaimo Daybook, where he is noted as building houses and doing day labour. Thomas Munro leased Grant's farm when the captain went south to search for gold.

Sometime after he was settled, Grant decided to walk to Fort Victoria alone but lost his way in the countryside at the back of Albert Head. Word reached the fort that he was on his way, but nothing had been heard from him, so a search party of rangers was sent to look for him. Grant was discovered in a very debilitated condition, having been nearly five days without food. This episode did not provide the best credentials for a potential surveyor.

Sooner or later Grant had to try surveying, the job he had been hired to do. He had requested some men to help him, but none were offered. It wasn't long before Douglas noticed that the rudiments of surveying taught to Grant at the Royal Military College in Sandhurst, England, really didn't qualify him as a competent surveyor. Grant did some surveying of the HBC's Fur Trade Reserve, an area of about 20 square miles of good land around the fort, but never got the job completed. Those surveys he did complete were notable for their lack of accuracy. After finding some discrepancies, the HBC hired an expert surveyor, Joseph Despard Pemberton, who came with qualifications as a civil engineer and had served as a professor of surveying. He arrived in Fort Victoria in June 1851.

In October 1850, Grant sailed for Hawaii on the American schooner *Dart* with the hope of finding a market for his lumber there. While he was in Honolulu, the British consul presented him with some broom seeds. On his return to Sooke, Grant planted the seeds outside his home. Little did he know that this would be his permanent legacy! Now, years later, masses of bright, chrome-yellow Scotch broom (*Cytisus scoparius*) continue to multiply along the roadways and uncultivated fields of the Pacific coast. The weedy species is not unlike the gorse hedges that are prevalent in Scotland; though the gorse is spinier, the flowers are similar in colour. After Grant sold his property to John Muir Sr. before returning to Scotland, the Muirs found the broom plants still growing. The men wanted to pull out the plants, but Ann Muir said the plant reminded her of home and demanded they be left.[6] Grant returned home from Hawaii in February 1851. Seeking company, he was a frequent visitor to Fort Victoria. He enjoyed a wee nip of Scotch whisky before he joined in the high jinx with the young men in the Bachelors' Hall.

Grant had reached the end of his colonial experience financially, and decided to go south in search of gold. He leased his farm to Thomas Munro, one of the workers he had hired as a gardener, and set off for Oregon and the Klamath gold mines in July.

Little more is heard about Grant until September 16, 1853, when Martha Ella (née Cheney), of Metchosin, wrote in her diary about accommodating four men overnight, including Captain Grant and Captain Cooper. Grant had wound up in San Francisco, again broke, but had found work at the city docks. He managed to get enough money to buy passage back to Vancouver Island, arriving just about the time of Martha's entry in her diary.[7]

Grant now held out little hope for his Sooke property. He wanted to sell it for the best price before returning to Scotland. He found a ready buyer in John Muir Sr., a miner from Ayrshire, who had come with his family to mine coal at Fort Rupert. Muir paid Grant $4,000 for the property, and Grant left Victoria in November.

In a letter dated August 8, 1857, written from Oregon City to a Scottish family friend, Brodie of Brodie, Grant asked Brodie to use his influence with Lord Fife to find him another position. The Brodie estate and castle are east of Inverness and north of Grant's home in Strathspey. Grant wrote about his unhappy experience on Vancouver Island:

> Until this year I was entirely alone as a settler, but within the last few months 3 old servants of the Hudson's Bay Coy, have taken claims of land, though none of them have as yet paid anything for the land or brought out men to cultivate it. The Hudson's Bay Coy, having claimed 40 sqe. miles in the neighborhood of Victoria; although I had paid for my land in England with the understanding that I was to have free choice

on the island, I was obliged to go 25 miles off, where I have been living a totally solitary life ever since. I soon got tired of my own society & except when a stray ship came along the coast, never saw a creature save my own men and a few rascally Indians. I got quite weary of my existence, and if it had not been for the episode of a 2 months trip down to the Sandwich Islands last winter, I really believe I should have committed suicide, by hanging drowning or otherwise.

I returned from the Islands with fresh vigour, but soon got disgusted again, seeing that no other bona fide settlers were coming out to enliven my solitude, I therefore was glad enough to let my place, which I did on a lease of 5 years for 70 pounds per annum, I also let a flour & sawmill which I had built, for a similar sum & similar period...I have had pretty hard work to keep afloat since coming out here, now selling a spar, now a potatoe etc. All my personal property had likewise to be made available, & guns, furniture, books clothes etc. successively found their way up the spout and were converted into dollars & cents. I have done better for the men I brought out with me than for myself. I employed them at high wages, and have now established them on plots of land of their own...[8]

As Grant was leaving, the second independent settler arrived with his wife. He was Captain James Cooper, the former captain of the HBC ship *Columbia*. He established the 385-acre Bilston Farm in Metchosin.

In 1857 and 1859, Grant presented papers he had written on Vancouver Island to the Royal Geographical Society, of which he was elected a fellow. From all accounts, the papers were well received and very informative, giving detailed information about Vancouver Island.

The Crimean War had just broken out when Grant returned home. He signed up with his old regiment. Before the close of the war, he was promoted to lieutenant. The Scots Greys were ordered to India to take part in quelling the 1857 Indian mutiny. There was no transportation for their horses, so they sailed without them and had to find mounts in India. Grant was asked to find horses for his regiment. He did, and was promoted to lieutenant colonel. He was present at the siege of Lucknow. A few days before he was to return home, he had an attack of dysentery and died within 48 hours in Saugor, Central India, on August 27, 1861.

Joseph W. McKay left his recollection of Grant. In part, it reads:

> Grant was a man of fine Physique. He stood over six foot two and was well proportioned. He was a good scholar, had many accomplishments, was a good linguist and had traveled extensively. His general affable manners have left sunny memories in the minds of all whom he came in contact. He was a good conversationalist, his flashes of wit and intelligent discourse would enliven the social chat round the evening fire whether in camp or in cabin. Through all the changes and vicissitudes of his career he never lost the calm dignity and cool manner incident to his race and early training. He never forgot that he was a Highland chieftain firm as the rocks of Craigellachie. His motto was ever "Stand sure" befitting attributes of British Columbia's first settler.[9]

Walter C. Grant has been portrayed as a pioneer settler in a rugged country. Despite his failures as a surveyor and farmer, he was an educated gentleman, and a personable individual.

The Scottish Farmer: Kenneth McKenzie

There were several farms developed in the Fort Victoria area by the Company. Beckley Farm, North Dairy Farm and Uplands Farm were initially established to provide food for the fort. The PSAC, a subsidiary of the HBC, had four larger farms managed by a bailiff, or a gentleman farmer, and were worked by Company servants brought out from Great Britain on five-year contracts, at the end of which they would be granted 20 acres of land. These farms were Craigflower, Constance Cove, Viewfield and Colwood.

Viewfield was established in 1850 and was the first and only PSAC farm managed by an HBC long-term employee rather than a bailiff brought out from Great Britain. Donald MacAulay, from Diris-Gill on the Isle of Harris in the Hebrides Islands, joined the Company in June 1832 and served as a labourer in various forts within the Columbia District before his PSAC appointment in 1850 to farm Viewfield in return for a half share of the profits.[10]

When his contract expired in 1857 and was not renewed, Viewfield and Constance Cove farms merged under Thomas J. Skinner. MacAulay's final employment was as keeper of the Royal Navy's powder magazine at Esquimalt. He accidentally drowned in Esquimalt Harbour. Macaulay Point, between Esquimalt Harbour and Victoria Harbour, is named for him.

Captain Edward E. Langford managed the Colwood Farm, now the Royal Colwood Golf Club, and Thomas Skinner, the last bailiff to arrive in 1853, managed the Constance Cove Farm. Skinner, who was from the south of England, arrived on the *Norman Morison* on the same voyage as McKenzie. His farm was also known as Oaklands.

The best-known farm was Craigflower. It was managed by Kenneth McKenzie, who named it for Governor Andrew Colville's home in Fifeshire, Scotland. Seventy-three labourers and tradesmen were recruited, mostly in Scotland, for the McKenzie farm; some of them brought wives and children. Many of them settled later in Metchosin or Sooke.

By 1854, Victoria had changed. The townsite was laid out, 79 houses had been built close to the fort, and the population of the town, including the officers and men of the fort, had reached 232.[11]

McKenzie was born in Edinburgh in October 1811, the son of a surgeon and grandson of a chemist in the city. When his mother died in 1820, he went to live with his paternal grandparents while attending school and Edinburgh University. But the professions did not interest him, and after leaving school in the late 1820s, he became the manager of his father's estate, known as Rentonhall, in the Parish of Morham, Haddingtonshire, in East Lothian.[12] The farm was about three miles from the market town of Haddington.

Scotland was in the midst of technological change in agriculture with the introduction of farm machinery, selective breeding of livestock—particularly sheep—and plowing to drain wet marshlands.[13] McKenzie gained valuable experience managing his father's farms and sheep runs, and while doing so also established a tile works, using local clay to bring more of his father's lands into production.

His father died in 1844, leaving McKenzie with mounting debt that forced him to put the land and estate of Rentonhall and its comfortable stone manor house up for auction in 1848. Unfortunately, between 1848 and 1851, Scotland experienced a deep depression and no buyer could be found. McKenzie responded to several employment advertisements for positions as factor, bailiff or land steward on estates in Scotland, Cornwall, northern England and northern Ireland, all unsuccessfully. In 1851 he was finally able to sell the property for 4,925 pounds sterling.

Through a friend's influence, the governor and committee of the HBC granted him an interview in London. The Company was looking to fill the position of bailiff, or overseer, for one of four farms proposed under the PSAC near Fort Victoria. The position of bailiff was not new to the Company in farming areas such as Red River. Although the name presently has a legal context, then it was merely a management position of master to servant. The interview was successful, and McKenzie signed a contract on August 16, 1852. His salary would be 60 pounds a year, and he would share one-third of the profit or loss of the farm beginning at the expiration of three years. His five-year term was to commence when he landed on Vancouver Island.

McKenzie spent the next few months of 1852 recruiting

labourers, blacksmiths, carpenters and a schoolteacher for his new Scottish settlement on Vancouver Island. The plowmen and labourers were to be paid 17 pounds a year, including room and board, with a five-year contract. After that period, they could claim 20 or 25 acres of land, valued at one pound an acre in their own name, and could pay for them in instalments of 15 pounds a year as a premium for their work for the Company. The blacksmith and carpenters would receive 25 to 30 pounds a year and could claim 40 or 50 acres at the end of their contract period.

The teacher hired was Robert Barr, and under the terms of his agreement he would be paid 50 pounds a year, with 50 or 60 acres of land attached to the school, a free house and free passage to Vancouver Island. Barr was not given much time to think about the position, as McKenzie informed him in June he would have to leave on the Company ship at the end of July. Barr and his wife joined McKenzie's contingent bound for Fort Victoria.

Kenneth and his wife Agnes, whom he married in 1841, would have eight children. Six were born in Scotland: Agnes, Jesse, Kenneth, Dorothea, William and Wilhelmina Blair, nicknamed Goodie, who was only three months old when they embarked on the journey to the Colony of Vancouver Island. Two more sons, Andrew and Robert, were born in Victoria. The McKenzie family, along with 22 men and 3 servant girls, plus wives and children—in all, a contingent of 73 persons—left on the *Norman Morison* when it sailed from Gravesend, England, on August 18, 1852. The passenger list also included Thomas Skinner, who was appointed bailiff for Constance Cove Farm, another PSAC farm, and his workers.

Agnes McKenzie's brother, Thomas Russell, and Robert Melrose, who kept a diary of his years with the Company, were part of the McKenzie party. The list of men, women and children hired by McKenzie included two blacksmiths, Peter Bartleman and John Russell; four carpenters, Andrew Hume, Duncan Lidgate, Robert Anderson and George Deans; two grieves, James Stewart and Robert Weir; plus labourers John Bell, Robert

Melrose, Joseph Montgomery, James Downie, James Liddle, Joseph Thornton, Thomas Russell, James Wilson, James Whyte, James Deans and David Wilson.[14] Most of the men had wives and children; only three were single, and one was a widower with four children.

Those who signed on with the PSAC had faced uncertainty in Scotland; the country was in an economic decline, and the future looked grim. In the colony, they perhaps hoped for some job security, as well as a place to live. Being unemployed in Scotland at this time often meant being homeless. Cottages that were deemed surplus to the needs of the farm were pulled down, and any new building was rigorously controlled.

The *Norman Morison* anchored at Fort Victoria on January 16, 1853, after a stormy passage during which little Wilhelmina Blair's behaviour earned her the lifelong nickname Goodie. The weary passengers were given temporary accommodation in makeshift quarters at Fort Victoria. James Deans wrote about their accommodation:

> After landing at Fort Victoria, Vancouver Island, we young and old were huddled into an empty storehouse, where we had to make our beds on a dirty floor, until we made beds for ourselves with boards lying around. Our destination being a new settlement upon Victoria farm, which afterward got the name of Craigflower. No houses being ready for us, we had to live at the Fort.[15]

So shabby was the accommodation offered McKenzie on arrival that he threatened to return home. Douglas persuaded him to stay by taking him to see the site of his farm. It worked: McKenzie decided to stay. A week later he moved his carpenters and blacksmiths to the farmland allotted to him at Maple Point, between Esquimalt Harbour and the tidal inlet known as the Gorge. However, Deans continued to lament about their housing; he was feeling homesick for Scotland:

In order to help along the work all us single chaps, had to go to Craigflower, where we lived in a half finished frame house. The change from the cottage homes and fertile fields of East Lothian to the dense and dreary primeval forests of Vancouver Island, was so great that we felt it terribly bad, more especially on the Saturday afternoon when we had a half holiday. So much did I feel the change, and so home sick, I used to wander out in the bush and sit down, give vent to my grief in a flood of tears. In order to lighten my troubles I used to put my thoughts in rhyme.

McKenzie's family had to wait until April before they could join Kenneth at the farm. They lived in temporary housing until the main house was ready for occupancy on May 1, 1856.

During the spring and summer of 1853, McKenzie and his men built more houses, planted crops and gardens, and set up a seven-horsepower engine brought from Britain to run a sawmill and grind grain. Work also began on the brickworks and a lime kiln to produce plaster and whitewash.

While the farm was being established and the workers housed, schoolteacher Robert Barr's future took off in a different direction. No sooner had he landed than he was seconded by Douglas to teach at Victoria School. There was little opposition from McKenzie, who was preoccupied with the farm. The move, however, did not go unnoticed by HBC governor Andrew Colville, who more or less reprimanded Douglas but concluded another Scottish teacher would be found to replace Barr at Craigflower.

A year later, Colville still had not found a suitable Scottish schoolmaster. He wrote to McKenzie admitting his failure and said he had to resort to hiring an Englishman, Charles Clark, who decided to marry before leaving England. He and his bride, Eliza, joined the maiden voyage of the *Princess Royal,* a horrific voyage, well documented in history. This voyage brought 24 coal-mining families from Staffordshire, England, to work the mines in Nanaimo. Clark began teaching at Craigflower in November 1854. Sadly, Eliza did not live long, and a year after her death, Clark remarried Matilda Botwood in 1856.

To say that life on the farm ran smoothly would have been an overstatement. Many problems plagued Craigflower, which had grown to be more than just a farm. There were now a tile-making operation, brickworks, a kiln, a sawmill, a blacksmith shop, a bakery and a schoolhouse for the workers' children. McKenzie had recognized the poor quality of the soil at the farm and so had diversified to give more opportunities in the area.

The lack of an available labour force was a problem in the early days of the colony. To boost his workforce, McKenzie sometimes used sailors from the HMS *Trincomales*, when it was anchored at Esquimalt, and he also hired several Natives, but they did not prove to be steady workers.

Douglas appointed the four bailiffs of the PSAC farms as magistrates and justices of the peace in an attempt to provide some measure of authority and lawfulness on the farms.

In September 1856, McKenzie reported that he had supplied the navy with nearly 1,000 pounds of meat and 400 pounds of vegetables per day. He also provided flour to the navy bakers who often used McKenzie's ovens. In 1860 he entered into a regular contract with the Pacific Squadron to supply 10,000 pounds of biscuits within 24 hours of demand, and an unlimited quantity within 14 days of demand.[16] Produce was also sent down the Gorge to Fort Victoria.

McKenzie and his wife, Agnes, had their large farmhouse modelled after their Scottish home, Rentonhall. It became a social centre for navy and colonial officials. The McKenzie girls, particularly the beautiful, tight-laced Goodie, were courted by visiting officers. Sometimes Douglas or visiting British naval officers discussed world affairs before a blazing fireplace at Craigflower Manor. Built to last, the farmhouse survives today, with its hand-hewn beams and nails made in the blacksmith's forge.

Top left: Craigflower School, a rare survivor of Victoria's pioneer past. Top right: interior of the school, which is open to the public. Above: Craigflower Farm was established in 1852 as one of four Vancouver Island farms of the Puget Sound Agricultural Company, a subsidiary of the Hudson's Bay Company. Seen here is Craigflower Manor, which is now being restored.
IMAGES COURTESY OF JAN PETERSON

The farm showed small and intermittent profits after 1857, but the Company was concerned by the "confused and incorrect" accounts submitted by McKenzie. In 1861, his second five-year

Mrs. Agnes McKenzie (née Russell) seated next to eldest daughter Agnes. Standing, left to right, are daughters Dorothea, Jessie and Wilhelmina Blair, known as Goodie. IMAGE A-01447 COURTESY OF ROYAL BC MUSEUM, BC ARCHIVES

contract as bailiff was cancelled and he was given a two-year lease renewable on a year-to-year basis for a total of five years, as long as he held the contract with the navy.

In 1854 the colony's farms all performed poorly, and in an attempt to fix the situation, McKenzie, who was judged the most experienced of the four bailiffs, was appointed agent and superintendent of all the PSAC farms in an attempt to consolidate efforts to improve. Unfortunately, this did little to reverse fortunes, since the farms had inexperienced farm managers working on substandard agricultural lands.

McKenzie could not reduce the debt against the farms satisfactorily, and in 1864, he was told his lease of Craigflower Farm would be terminated on October 31, 1865. On that date he mortgaged his Lakehill and Dallas Bank properties to the Company to secure his indebtedness to them, which totalled 3,376 pounds. In 1866 he moved his family to their new home at Lakehill, but the debt

Kenneth McKenzie, who arrived on the *Norman Morison*, managed Craigflower Farm. In this photo he is seated on the left and his son Kenneth is the right. Standing from left to right are sons Andrew Colville, Robert Gregory and William Blair McKenzie.

IMAGE A-01445 COURTESY OF ROYAL BC MUSEUM, BC ARCHIVES

continued to plague him for the rest of his life. The Lakehill sheep farm included Christmas Hill and extended south of present-day McKenzie Avenue. This was the same farm where shepherd Peter Brown had so tragically been killed years before.

Although the agricultural venture of Craigflower was a failure, McKenzie did succeed in settling more than 22 families in the Colony of Vancouver Island. Kenneth McKenzie died of heart disease at his Lakehill Farm on April 10, 1874, and is buried in Ross Bay Cemetery, Victoria. Agnes also died at Lakehill Farm, in 1897.

The Farm Workers at Craigflower

Many of the Craigflower farm workers came from Haddington, situated on the River Tyne in East Lothian, east of Edinburgh.

It was once one of the largest cities in Scotland, and was notably the birthplace of preacher John Knox. Some of the men hired had worked for McKenzie in Scotland before they signed a five-year contract to work for the PSAC on Vancouver Island.

The worker best remembered was Robert Melrose, who was known mainly for the diary he kept of the day-to-day happenings on the farm, and for providing historians with an insight into life at Craigflower. He was obviously an educated man, unlike some of the other workers hired by Archibald Barclay, secretary to the governor and committee of the HBC. In the spring of 1854, Melrose was one of the educated Scots who contributed to a lecture series given for the Craigflower community on subjects ranging from geographic descriptions of Scotland and England to discoveries of optical science.

Melrose's diary notations were often preoccupied with the farm workers and their heavy drinking: "James Wilson, ½ drunk. The Author ¾ drunk." He also complained about the labouring class being left off the guest list for festivities held by the governing class: "Great Ball held at Victoria, riff-raff excluded." [17]

Melrose and his wife, Ellen, had only one child, a daughter named Ellen, or Nellie, born on May 19, 1854. She is listed as a pupil at Craigflower School. She married Frederick Douglas in 1883. The young couple had six children. Robert Melrose died in 1898 at age 70; his wife died in 1883.

Robert Melrose wrote in his diary an account of how Christmas Day and New Year's Day were celebrated at Craigflower. Christmas Day was marked with "Fiddling, dancing, singing, eating, and drinking," and New Year's Day was "celebrated in a glorious Bacchanalian manner." [18] In 1854, Fort Victoria seemed to have a shortage of liquor. His entry for January 1 is short: "Drouthy New Year."

New Year's Day, a day above all days, for rioting in drunkenness, then what are we to expect of this young, but desperate Colony of ours; where dissipation is carried on to such

extremities my readers will be expecting to find nothing in my
Almanack, from Christmas, till past the New Year, but such
a one drunk, and another drunk, and so on; how different is
the scene, then what must I attribute the cause of all this, too,
must I prescribe it to the good morals of the people; no! no! my
friends, no such thing could be expected here; the grog-shops
were drained of every sort of liquor, not a drop to be got for
either love or money, had it been otherwise the case, there is no
saying whither my small Almanack would have contained them
or not; it would almost take a line of packet ships, running
regular between here, and San Francisco to supply this Island
with grog, so great a thirst prevails amongst its inhabitants.[19]

Craigflower blacksmith Peter Bartleman was born in 1823
in Haddington, where he lived with his mother, an agricultural
worker. In 1852 he worked as a blacksmith at Gifford Gate,
Haddington. It is unclear why he decided to join the McKenzie
exodus to Vancouver Island, but no doubt the depressed economic
situation in Scotland played a role, and he was recently married.
Also, the free land he would receive at the end of his contract
would have been a good incentive.

On March 4, 1853, a temporary blacksmith shop was erected
at Craigflower. In June, Bartleman and the other blacksmith,
John Russell, and three other workers refused orders and left the
farm. Three days later, Victoria police constable Thomas Hall was
summoned, and McKenzie paid to have five warrants issued to
apprehend five escaped workers.

It was not uncommon for some of McKenzie's workers to be
found drunk. Some even deserted to the US, where they were
apprehended and jailed for 30 days, but Bartleman was particularly
troublesome. He refused orders, left work without permission and
on several occasions was found drunk. Robert Melrose recorded
in his diary for March 21, 1854: "John Russel & Peter Bartleman
fought a battle. J. Russel ½ drunk."[20]

Bartleman tried to set up his own blacksmith shop on the Craigflower property, using McKenzie's coal to fuel it. This resulted in McKenzie "attacking and destroying" the shop and taking him to court. Due to some technicalities in the case, McKenzie's attempt to control his blacksmith was thwarted, with the end result that Bartleman "set up on his own account with Captain Cooper."[21]

The situation with Bartleman did not improve and reached new heights on April 12, 1855, when he was sentenced to be sent home. This didn't happen, for a year later, Bartleman addressed a letter to Mr. Margery of Esquimalt, stating:

> At the time (he) left Mr. McKenzie, there was a balance in my favour of 2 pounds, 9 shillings, 10 pence, which you say is forfeited. I beg to say that I never received any money from Mrs. McKenzie and from what transpired, I do not see that I am liable for passage money.

In the 1891 census, Bartleman was listed, at age 65, as living in Saanich with his children. He died at the age of 82 in the Kamloops Old Men's Home on May 10, 1907.

One of the four carpenters hired for Craigflower Farm was Robert Anderson, from Edinburgh. He was 29 and his wife, Jessie, was 27 when they arrived with their two sons, John, 7, and Robert, 5. A baby daughter, Eliza, was born at sea shortly after the *Norman Morison* had left the River Thames. She was therefore christened Eliza Norman Morison Wishart; Wishart was the name of the ship's captain.[22]

Anderson helped with the early construction of the buildings at the farm, but by August 1853 he had left McKenzie after a disagreement about the terms of his employment. McKenzie had him arrested and imprisoned in the bastion at the fort for one month for breaking his contract. Ultimately, he was allowed to serve out his contract as a carpenter for the HBC; he helped construct the original Christ Church and parsonage. By 1857 he had completed his contract and purchased land from the HBC under the terms of the agreement, and established a farm, Loch End, at the head of Portage Inlet.

The Andersons had six more children: Sarah Livingstone (1855), Helen Crampton (1857), Jessie Murray (1860), Grace Henderson (1862), Isabel Bruce (1865) and Peter Murray (1866). Robert Anderson died in 1883 and Jessie in 1897; both are buried at Ross Bay Cemetery.

The Deans brothers, James and George, are well known as the "Deans of Craigflower" due to the literary efforts and poetry written by James, and the letters written by George's wife, Annie, to relatives in Scotland, now in the BC Archives.

James Deans had originally planned to go to New South Wales, Australia, but withdrew his application and then signed on with his brother in 1852 to work at Craigflower. He had already written several poems in Scotland as a schoolboy, and now the thought of leaving his homeland inspired another poem. These are a few select verses:

> The hour draws nigh that must us sever,
> Friends I love and fatherland,
> Exiled from thee, perhaps I'll never,
> Scotia, see thy rugged strand.
>
> Can I cross the briny ocean?
> Must I part with friends so kind?
> Yes, I must but with emotion,
> I shall leave them all behind.
>
> Lost to view, Dear Caledonia,
> Shall I never see thee more?
> Still I'll love thee best of any,
> Thou art the land which I adore.

Farewell, farewell, dear Caledonia,
Heath clad hills and birkinshaw,
Farewell, East Lothian's braes sae bonnie,
Thy bards farewell, when far awa.

Another poem, entitled "Summer," composed in May 1853, shows that James was now resigned to remaining on Vancouver Island. The fourth and fifth verses are as follows:

Cheer up, sad heart and while I stray,
Sadly o'er Craigflower woody brae
Come fancy paint each glad and glen,
With waving corn and homes of men.

Then lay aside, your hopes and fears,
A change shall come with passing years,
A time will come when you will say,
This is my home, here I will stay.

This change in heart was the result of the sad news he received of losing his sweetheart. James wrote:

Jean Robertson was an old sweetheart of mine. I wrote for her to come to Vancouver Island. Her father said she could come if I could come home for her when my time was up. Before the five years was up she took sick and died.

George Deans was hired as a carpenter. Shortly after he and his wife, Annie, arrived in Fort Victoria on January 16, 1853, their daughter Mary Jane was born, on May 8. The couple had three more daughters: Ellen Gillies (1855), Anne (1861) and Katie Stewart (1869), and two sons, Alec (1857) and George (1859). By this time the George Deans family lived on a farm at Shelbourne and Hillside that they named Oakvalle. Mary Jane was only 15 years old when she died of diphtheria in 1868.

George died on February 4, 1879, after an accidental kick from a horse. He had tried to catch the horse in the corral when it turned and kicked him in the stomach. The doctor was unable to save him.[23] Annie died of Bright's disease in 1890.

The Hudson's Bay Company probably had no great interest in promoting colonization, even by British subjects, and even though it was part of the contract entered into with the Crown. The importing of workers and bailiffs for the PSAC farms was designed to keep the resources of the colony exclusively in Company hands. There was no program developed to introduce independent settlers to the Island unless under the auspices of the Company. In that, it succeeded, for in the early days, only those with interests in the Company held a monopoly of available land near the fort. This kept at bay outside influences and stopped them from settling. Those workers who came under contract for the farms helped colonize Vancouver Island.

The Spirit Merchant: James Yates

James Yates was born on January 21, 1819, in Linlithgow, West Lothian, about 20 miles west of Edinburgh, Scotland. His father died when he was only six, and his mother remarried and moved with James and his sisters, Isabella and Helen, to Dysart, on the north shore of the Firth of Forth, near Kirkcaldy in Fifeshire.[24] He signed on with the Company as a carpenter, and from May to October 1848 was assigned to the Company ship *Prince Rupert* on voyages to York Factory on Hudson Bay.[25] He married Mary Powell of Montgomeryshire on November 13, 1848, and two weeks later the newlyweds sailed on the *Harpooner*, along with the first contingent of mining families destined for Fort Victoria.

From 1849 to 1851, Yates worked as a shipwright aboard Company ships such as the historic *Beaver,* and the US ship *Cayuga*, which anchored in Esquimalt Harbour to be loaded with lumber from the Company sawmill. With the imminent arrival of the first governor, Richard Blanshard, in 1850, Yates was seconded from the ships to put his carpenter skills to work building a house for the governor. Blanshard arrived on March 9, but while his house was still under construction, he remained aboard the HMS *Driver*, the paddlewheel sloop that had brought him from Panama.

Yates moved from the barracks to a completed house just in time for the birth of the couple's first daughter, Emma Frances, in 1850. Reverend Robert John Staines baptized the baby, naming her after Staines's wife, Emma Frances, who was the child's godmother. Their second daughter, Harriet Elizabeth Sinclair, was baptized on April 27, 1852.

Yates didn't like the Company's rigid discipline and bought out his contract 18 months after his arrival. He was granted independent status on January 29, 1851, and chose to remain in Victoria.[26]

In June 1851, Yates purchased two waterfront lots, 201 and 202, north of Wharf Street. Yates Street was the first main street in Victoria. The next year he built Victoria's first saloon, the Ship Inn, at the corner of present-day Yates and Wharf streets, and applied for a liquor licence. The licence fee for this first retail liquor licence issued in the colony was 120 pounds sterling a year. (Douglas imposed licences for liquor sales in 1853; before this time, liquor sales were unregulated.) There was not much competition for Yates until the Fraser River gold-rush miners arrived in 1858. Before long, others applied for and received licences when they saw the thirsty miners lined up at Yates's saloon. Profits from his business were converted into land purchases. He purchased 400 acres along the Gorge waterway and built another house between the water and Burnside Road. More children were born: Mary, James, Stuart and Harry, plus another daughter Agnes, who died in infancy. Amelia Douglas acted as midwife in the birth of the children.

Yates was an outspoken man, especially regarding politics. He grumbled a lot about the rule of the colony and advocated that elections be held for a parliament. Dr. John Sebastian Helmcken described him as a "radical, growler, cantankerous yet earnest, who hated the Governor and the Hudson's Bay Company."[27] Yates joined forces with an anti-Company group that circulated a petition advocating a British style of parliament. The group included Staines, Edward E. Langford and James Cooper. Governor Richard Blanshard encouraged the group in this, and its members continued to agitate for elections.

When the London office of the Company informed Douglas that he must introduce an elected assembly, he was a little disturbed by the orders, for he knew nothing of electoral law or parliamentary procedures, but he set about complying. Only those with 20 acres of land were qualified to vote; this disenfranchised nearly everyone living in Victoria. Yates was elected to the first legislative assembly in 1856, joining Dr. John Sebastian Helmcken, Joseph Pemberton, Thomas Skinner, Joseph William McKay, John Muir and John Kennedy. Chief Justice Cameron swore in the legislators.

The first meeting of the new legislature was held in the Bachelors' Hall, a building constructed of squared logs within the walls of the fort. Generally, the new assembly was regarded with some amusement because of the size of the voting public. Chief Factor John Work wrote to an old acquaintance with a caustic remark about "7 members chosen by about 40 voters."[28] However, it was a beginning, and it was almost democracy in action.

A decade later, James Yates was one of the richest men in Victoria. The Yates family was well liked by those less fortunate, and, according to the outspoken Annie Deans, never let their riches go to their heads. Income from investments was enough to keep the family comfortable for the rest of their lives.

Yates's sister Isabella came from Scotland to stay with the boys while James, Mary and the girls visited Scotland in October 1861. Isabella married engineer Edward Stephens in 1874. The family visit to Scotland may have been an exploratory one for Mary, and her daughters never returned to Victoria. James came back only to sort out a legal problem over land ownership, which was then in

This photo of James and Mary Yates and their son Harry was taken in Edinburgh around 1864. James and Mary arrived in Fort Victoria on the *Harpooner* in 1848. Harry was born in Victoria in 1859.

IMAGE COURTESY OF MAUREEN DUFFUS

some disarray after the colony reverted to the Crown. The HBC authority to act as land agents ended when its contract expired without renewal in 1859. James returned to Scotland with the boys to permanently live in Edinburgh. James, 7, remembered watching from their New York hotel as civil war soldiers straggled along the street. The boys were educated at Edinburgh Collegiate and Edinburgh University.

In Edinburgh, James Yates was listed in census records as landowner, fund holder or "merchant retired," and generally known as a person of independent means. Both sons returned to Victoria. They married two sisters, Annie and Nellie Austin. James practised law in the city from 1881 to the 1940s, and died in 1950 at age 92. Harry died in 1907. Both lived in houses they built on the Gorge estate. James Yates Sr. had a troubled relationship with his sons, eventually cutting both out of his will.

The daughters married well. Harriet became Lady Woodhead after her husband, a Cambridge pathologist, was knighted for perfecting a method of purifying water for troops during the First World War. Emma married Alec MacGregor and moved to Copenhagen. Mary Isabella married J. Harper, head of a tea plantation in Ceylon.

Mary Yates died in 1898, and James Yates Sr. died in 1900 in Edinburgh.[29]

The Cooper from Orkney: John Flett

Like James Yates, John Flett came to Fort Victoria on the *Harpooner*, arriving in 1849 with the first group of Scottish miners. Flett was born on April 16, 1827, and signed on with the HBC at Stromness in the Orkney Islands.[30] He was the second of three sons born to David Flett and Isabella Sinclair, who farmed West Leafea as tenants of the Watt family of Breckness. The 12-acre farm offered no future for John and his younger brother, James. The Reverend George Barry, writing about such young men in his classic *History of the Orkney Islands*, lamented:

> [Because of] the low state of agriculture, the smallness of the farms, and the little respect in which those connected with

the cultivation of the soil are held, it has become the custom for too great a proportion of our young men to enter into the profession of tradesman—when their apprenticeships are over, they frequently leave the place, in the hopes of a better life in another country.[31]

John Flett was one of these young men. He had completed a seven-year apprenticeship as a cooper on a herring boat. When Fort Victoria requested the Company agent in Orkney recruit a blacksmith, a biscuit baker and a cooper, John signed on as the cooper.

His skill as a barrel maker was valuable in the new colony, but it was not a guarantee of steady work. His salary as a cooper was 25 pounds sterling a year. For the first five years, he worked making barrels for the export of salted salmon. It was during this period that he was stationed on San Juan Island, where the Company established a salmon fishery in 1851, using Natives as fishermen. The first year, only 60 barrels of salmon were cured, less than expected. However, over the next few years, the annual output was between 2,000 and 3,000 barrels. The fish taken here were from the Fraser River. The fishery was terminated for British North Americans by the San Juan Water Boundary decision of 1872.[32]

The Company had been exporting salmon since 1821, when it got the exclusive right to trade with Natives. At first, it obtained salmon mainly to augment the food supplies for its various trading posts. However, when the fur catches failed to equal the rich harvest reaped in the northern departments of the Company, cured salmon became a welcome addition to the articles of trade.

Besides sending money home, many Orcadians left advance notes on their pay, cashable with Edward Clouston, the HBC agent in Stromness. Clouston wrote to Dr. Archibald Barclay, secretary of the London Committee in October 1848, noting that someone holding an advance note for John Flett had been "enquiring frequently whether the note is yet due."[33]

This plaque (top) on a wall at the edge of Victoria's harbour commemorates the HBC ship *Harpooner*, which transported John Flett and other indentured workers from Scotland to Fort Victoria in 1849. The plaque was presented by Flett's grandchildren in 1968. Plaques commemorating the other two ships that brought over Scottish workers, the *Norman Morison* and the *Tory*, are located nearby. IMAGES COURTESY OF JAN PETERSON

After Flett's contract with the Company expired in 1854, he returned to the Orkney Islands, where he married his first cousin Janet Flett, daughter of Peter Flett and Helen (Nelly) Sutherland. The couple married on August 28, 1854, at St. Dunstan's Anglican Church, Stepney, London. He was then 27 and she was 33.

Janet had also been born in the Orkney Islands, but she had lived in London for a few years, keeping house for her widowed brother, Captain Peter Flett, a sea captain, and his two children. It is said that her mother-in-law did not approve of the marriage, holding that Janet was "too stylish," a consequence perhaps of too much exposure to the ways of London and the English.[34] Her life in London must have been comfortable, for among the possessions she brought to Fort Victoria were six lovely silk dresses.[35]

Three weeks after their wedding, John and Janet Flett boarded the *Marquis of Bute*, a supply vessel of the HBC. They sailed on September 19, 1854, and, after a three-week stopover in Hawaii, arrived at Fort Victoria on April 1, 1855. Janet was one of five brides aboard, but for her the voyage of over six months was probably especially uncomfortable. Four months after their arrival at Victoria, their first son, John William (1855), was born.

John signed another contract with the Company, remaining in its service until 1870, but he switched to fur grading, a trade in which he is said to have made a reputation for fine judgment. During this time, Janet gave birth to three more sons: James (1857), Alfred (1859) and Peter (1861). All the boys were baptized in Christ Church, Victoria.[36]

The Flett family lived in three houses in Victoria: the first at the corner of Wharf and Johnston streets, the second on Broughton Street and the third and last, a house they built in James Bay. They sold the first of these for $600 only to see it change hands again a few months later for $6,000. This was during the period of the gold discoveries on the mainland that converted Victoria into a boom town.

John Flett left the Company service in 1870 and exchanged his Victoria property with the Randall family for their 150-acre Herd Road farm in Maple Bay. His choice of this location was probably influenced by visits made by the family in 1868 and 1869 to his younger brother, James, who had a farm between Maple Bay and Quamichan Lake. John's farm adjoined his brother's property.

The Fletts came to Maple Bay by steamer from Victoria on March 5, 1870. Their belongings were brought to the farm by ox cart. Along the way one of the wheels broke, but the solution was simple: the men just sawed a thin round off a log, pierced it with a hole to fit the axle and carried on their way.[37]

John Flett was a skilled barrel maker from the Orkney Islands who came with the first contingent of workers to Fort Victoria in 1849. He and his wife, Janet, were among the first settlers in Maple Bay. IMAGE 1991.06.2.1 COURTESY OF COWICHAN VALLEY MUSEUM & ARCHIVES

The Fletts transformed the undeveloped land into a productive dairy farm. With their sons' help, timber and brush were cut by hand and burned. Oxen were used for plowing, as there were no horses in the district at this time, but there were lots of cougars and wolves, always a threat to farm animals and children. John became involved in community affairs, serving as a trustee of the Methodist Church that had been built the previous year, and in 1873 was elected a member of the District of Comiaken.

John Flett died an untimely death in 1886. A wound on his leg turned septic, then gangrene set in and his leg had to be amputated. The operation was performed on the kitchen table of his son Jim's James Bay home. The shock proved too severe, and he died on February 5. He was buried in Ross Bay Cemetery in Victoria. Janet and other family members are buried in the Pioneer Methodist Cemetery at Maple Bay.

John was known to be a stickler for the truth. The story is told of a dispute over ownership of a heifer when he lived in Victoria. The dispute was referred to Douglas for arbitration. When told that John Flett was one of the claimants, Douglas without hesitation came down in his favour.

Flett was a man of quiet disposition, and it was said he never praised his sons. His obituary noted he was "a fine specimen of a true man in every relation of life, a worthy and exemplary Christian."[38]

Janet was well liked in the Maple Bay community. She survived John by 23 years, living alternately between the homes of her sons John and Peter. In later life she weighed about 250 pounds and walked with the aid of two sticks. When travelling by democrat (horse-drawn buggy), she would enter by means of a plank along which she was guided from the veranda of the house. She died on June 7, 1909.

William, the eldest son, married Mary Elizabeth Evans in 1893. She was the daughter of MLA John Evans, a pioneer in the Cowichan area since 1877. Evans farmed what is now known as the Tansor area, and became reeve of the municipality of North Cowichan before being elected MLA. William and Mary had three children: Alf, Mabel and Arnold.

Alf was born in 1912 at the Herd Road farm. He farmed, logged and worked at different times as a tax collector, but foremost he was a photographer. For a short time he operated a studio in Duncan. He met his wife, Agnes Jones, in 1938, and the couple married soon after. They had three children: Rosalie (Fraser), David and Ruth (Bankhead). Alf and Agnes (Aggie) contributed photographs to the CBC; their enthusiasm resulted in many news scoops, not only for the Vancouver TV station but also the CBC national network.

The Alf Fletts moved in 1960 to Nanaimo, where Alf immersed himself in community life and served two terms as alderman. He was a staunch Social Credit supporter. Agnes was a columnist with the *Nanaimo Daily Free Press* and Victoria's *Daily Colonist*.

When Alf Flett was chief factor of Post No. 3, Native Sons of B.C., he spearheaded a funding campaign to restore Nanaimo's historic bastion, turning it into a local tourist attraction. He was also well known as an ornithologist. When he died on March 15, 1991, former mayor Frank Ney paid tribute to his dedication and contributions to the civic affairs of the city.

CHAPTER 4

The First Mining Families Arrive

Douglas Makes Preparations

Douglas would have been one of the first people the Scottish miners met when they arrived in Fort Victoria; he was known to greet every ship when it arrived in Fort Victoria. Whether his father's Scottish background and his own early education in that country made any difference to how he viewed the newcomers is unknown. For the next few years of their lives on Vancouver Island, this man would dominate every decision.

The miners came to Vancouver Island on the HBC ship the *Harpooner*. When coal was first found at Fort Rupert, on northern Vancouver Island, the Company immediately began recruiting miners for a workforce. In anticipation of coal production being successful, the Company signed a contract with the American Pacific Mail Steamship Company to provide 1,000 tons of coal between May 1849 and May 1850, at 50 shillings per ton. Before long, Scots began signing indenture agreements to work for the Company for a period of three or five years.

Financial inducements must have figured prominently in their decisions to leave Scotland, or perhaps they saw an opportunity to make a new life in a new country. Miners were promised a yearly salary of 50 pounds sterling and a monthly quota of 30 tons of coal, plus a bonus of two shillings and sixpence per ton over quota. This wage was similar to that paid in Scotland, but the additional bonus made it seem like a better wage. The problem was that there was no workable coal seam underground on Vancouver Island, and it was impossible to earn a bonus. Men were offered free passage for their families and rations onboard ship for up to two children. Any other children had to have food purchased for them by their parents. They were also offered a grant of land upon completion of their contracts as an incentive to stay. This was more than would have been possible, or imaginable, in Scotland, and at a price they could afford.

The first Company workers arrived at Fort Victoria on June 1, 1849, on the *Harpooner*. The passengers included the eight workers hired by Captain Grant, and the Ayrshire miners destined for Fort Rupert coalfields, plus a carpenter, a cooper, a baker and a surgeon. This was a small group when compared to the passenger lists of the ships that followed. The official return dated 1852 states that the number of persons sent out by the HBC and the PSAC at their own expense between 1848 and 1852 was 435[1]:

	Men	Women	Children	Total
1848	21	5	6	32
1849	67	5	0	72
1850	99	25	27	151
1851	28	2	0	30
1852	56	43	51	150
Total	271	80	84	435

This shipload of workers may appear to be a small number of people to found a British colony, but to Douglas it appeared to be an alarming influx of population that taxed his resources sorely. There is a sense of this concern reflected in a letter to Douglas from Archibald Barclay. In August 1850, Barclay wrote:

The Governor and Committee are anxious on all occasions to select for the country the best men that they can obtain and they endeavour to adapt the number engaged to the exigencies of the service—it is better to have too many than too few. You seem to think that the number sent out this year should be limited to 10, but in this opinion they do not concur. You will have seen by my letter of the 5th, that they have resolved to forward by ship to sail in September eighty persons, of whom perhaps sixty may be fit for any kind of labour—and as you will require additional hands for improvement of the new road from Fort Langley to the Interior, for the cultivation of the land at Fort Victoria, and probably to supply the place of deserters from the service, that number will, it is conceived, not be more than will be wanted.[2]

Another letter from Barclay over a week later extolled the virtues of building houses from wood:

With respect to the difficulty of preparing House accommodation for the emigrants on their arrival, I refer you to the following Extract of a letter, dated California, May 30, 1850. "Wooden houses here are all the go. You would be astonished to see the immense quantities of wooden houses, and what splendid edifices are turned out in wood. You can have a large wooden house put up in a single day; they can build a city of them in a week, and comfortable strong houses too."[3]

Douglas may have been overwhelmed by the newcomers, but more arrived over the next few years, and somehow he managed to accommodate all.

Those aboard the *Harpooner* included the first families recruited to work the coal mine at Fort Rupert. They included the Muirs, McGregors, Turners and Smiths, all from Ayrshire, Scotland; only the Smiths were not related.

John Muir, with years of mining experience in the Kilmarnock area, had four sons and two nephews in the industry. Muir had seen an advertisement in a newspaper in Manchester, England, for coal miners to work on Vancouver Island, and good land was available at one pound an acre, with the minimum allowed being 100 acres. This seemed like a good opportunity for his family. Company agent David Landale hired the mining family after the terms of their employment contract were worked out.

John Muir was hired as oversman, or manager, and seven others as colliers and labourers. Free passage home would be provided at the end of the contract unless the miner was dismissed for cause, and there would be a money allowance for the miner but not for his family. They also had to build their own home with wood supplied by the company. They knew nothing about Vancouver Island except what the Company agent told them, and that was probably a coloured description.

A Difficult Voyage

In November 1848, the families gathered at the seaside village of Irvine, Ayrshire, waiting for orders, but the ship was not ready and they were told to remain there until called to London. Irvine is a seaside town located on the Firth of Clyde and was once a busy shipping port. Its history dates back centuries.

John Muir's son, 23-year-old Andrew, documented their journey in his diary. On November 9, 1848, he wrote that they had agreed to serve for three years on Vancouver's Island. "We were to sail from London on the 10th, but owing to the vessel not being ready we got orders to remain at Irvine until called for, so here we are knocking about at Rossholm no knowing what to do." Rossholm Farm stood near the banks of the Annick Water, about a mile east of Irvine.

Waiting for the call were his father and his mother, Ann, both in their late 40s, and his brothers John, Jr., 21, Robert, 19, and Michael, 16; also the Muir's widowed daughter, Marion Turner from Kilmarnock, and her two children, John, 8, and William, 9. The McGregor family, cousins from Kilmarnock, was also in the group. They included John Sr., 41, his wife, Mary, 30, and their three children, Archibald, 5, Mary, 3, and John Jr., 1. Also waiting, but not related, were John and Marion Smith, in their mid-20s, and their infant child, from Kilmaurs, Ayrshire.

When the call to London finally came, they travelled by train farther down the west coast to Troon, where the steamer *Royal Consort* transported them to Fleetwood, in Lancashire. The 16-hour sailing was very rough, and most were seasick. From there they boarded the Preston and Ware Railway for the 50-mile trip to Manchester, where they stayed overnight. The next day they changed their pound notes for gold. However, in doing so, they were obliged to pay a five percent exchange rate, and this annoyed the thrifty Scots. They left the next day on the North Western Railway for London, where two taxis took them to the West India docks. Much to their dismay, the offices were closed for the day, but they found accommodation in Mr. Montague's "Jamaica Tavern." Fortunately, the Company was paying all expenses. The next day Andrew and his father went to the HBC office on Fenchurch Street, where they met the person responsible for hiring them, Dr. Archibald Barclay, secretary for the London committee. Andrew does not say why they went to see Barclay, only that they were warmly received. No doubt this contingent of Scottish miners was as important to the Company as it was to them.

They boarded the *Harpooner* on November 29; Andrew described the ship as "a very fine vessel." Those on board included surgeon Dr. Alfred Robson Benson. (The Passenger Act required that all ships carrying passengers must have a doctor on board.) Others included Captain Grant's eight workers, James Yates and his wife, Mary, baker James Cathie and blacksmith William Walker. The ship was towed from the West India Docks on Friday, December 1, 1848, to Gravesend, where they anchored for the night. For the next two days, all fires aboard ship were put out as a precaution as they loaded volatile black powder on board. The voyage got under way on December 5. Everyone took turns doing chores on the ship. Andrew wrote:

> John Smith and I are Stewards today. It is not at all a bad job. Lifted anchor about 3 p.m. We walked away, very pretty indeed with very little sail.

They got as far as Margate, where the weather forced them to anchor two miles offshore, and there they remained until the 9th, when they sailed to Deal in Kent, to anchor for the night. A new steward boarded that afternoon, and finally their epic journey to the New World got under way the next day. By this time, the open Atlantic showed its teeth; most of the passengers were sick. It was about a week later before Ann Muir and Mary McGregor appeared on deck.

The ship sailed passed the scenic Portuguese Island of Madeira and the Spanish Island of La Palma, one of the Canary Islands. On January 21, they learned from a passing ship that Louis-Napoleon had been elected president of France on December 10, 1848. They crossed the Tropic of Cancer on February 23, and on February 24 rounded Cape Horn, or "Cape Stiff" as it was nicknamed, which lived up to its reputation on this occasion. The Cape Horn route around South America is one of the most dangerous nautical passages in the world. Waves can reach a height of over 65 feet. Freezing gales and mountainous waves tossed the *Harpooner* around like a toy in the water. Eventually they encountered dangerous swells as the little ship set a course northward. There were still three months to go before they would reach their destination.

A voyage that began with so much optimism was soon clouded by despair. The Muirs were more fortunate than most, as they had a cabin. Andrew shared a bunk with his cousin, Archibald Muir, and they joked when the ship's movement made them roll over on top of each other. However, there were no jokes for those who signed on as labourers; they were herded together in steerage below deck by the cargo hold. For them, there were no bunk beds—only damp boards where personal items could be spread out—and there were no windows. The only light came from oil lamps that gave off an offensive smell that filled the musty air. Most were resigned to their plight.

While conditions below deck were grim, overcrowding and rudimentary sanitary facilities were facts of life aboard many ships travelling to the New World. Travelling by sea was full of perils and discomforts.

On March 27 the ship arrived at one of the islands of Juan Fernández, off the coast of Chile, where they went ashore to get fresh water. Andrew noted that only a few people lived on the island. Some of the passengers went ashore to stretch their legs. They found peaches in abundance, quinces, vegetables, poultry, eggs, goat meat and lots of fish.

Each passenger took turns cooking on the voyage, with Andrew doing more than his share. He was young, and viewed everything as a new experience. He was even willing to try new foods such as prickly pears, turtle soup, American beans and wild fowl caught on Clarion Island, also known as Santa Rosa.

An issue over food arose only three weeks into the voyage when Andrew learned they were being denied fresh meat. He was angry, and voiced his displeasure:

> I gave them to understand I was not a tool in their hands to be used as they thought proper... One day I shall be able to see justice done to their full extent and that the transgressor may be punished.

Most of the trouble on this voyage, and other similar voyages to come, was over the distribution of food.

On May 28, Vancouver's Island was sighted, and Andrew's "long confinement," as he described it, was nearing the end. When the *Harpooner* entered Juan de Fuca Strait at Cape Flattery, "the ship became becalmed for one day," and to their surprise and alarm a number of Natives came aboard and refused to leave until pushed away. This was the newcomers' first encounter with the Island's First Nations, and it was a bit unsettling, as the two cultures eyed one another with suspicion:

> On reaching their canoes, they made an oration in their own tongue which we could not understand. We thought it was nothing good; with about forty canoes round the vessel and making such an unearthly noise and being forced off the deck, we flew to our Arms ready for action. The Indians had all bows and arrows; fortunately a breeze struck up which took us away out of their reach.

As the ship sailed toward its destination, the Natives were more peaceful. Andrew wrote:

> On our way up the Straits we traded with the Indians alongside the ship—salmon for articles of trifling value and tobacco—all very peaceable going off again as soon as they traded their salmon.

The ship docked at Fort Victoria on Friday, June 1, 1849. Andrew and his brothers were excited about what lay ahead in their new life; the adults were not so optimistic. Despite the importance of the new arrivals to the future of the Company's coal industry on Vancouver Island, there was no welcoming envoy. Dressed in all their finery, they awaited the presence of James Douglas. There was no cannon blast to welcome them, and no one to help escort them ashore. All on board were required to personally carry their possessions into the stockade of the fort. The Scottish miners had expected to continue their journey to Fort Rupert but were informed the fort there was still under construction and they would have to remain in Fort Victoria for several months. During that time the men were employed blasting rock for a ship slipway, and digging a well.

The miners finally set out on August 27 aboard the brig *Mary Dare* and, after what Andrew called "a very tedious passage," arrived at their destination, Beaver Harbour, on September 24. The long journey took them up the outer west coast of Vancouver Island and around the northern tip into Queen Charlotte Strait, then south to Beaver Harbour. Senior naval officers had recommended using the outside route because of the difficult Seymour and Dodd narrows that stood in the way of the inland route; it was easier to go around the outside of the Island.

The Fort Rupert Experience

The winter of 1849-50 in Fort Rupert was characterized not only by stormy weather so typical of the north Island, but also the stormy relations between the proud Scots and Company management. The workers had left secure mining positions in Scotland to fulfill a dream of a better life in the New World, and that dream turned sour when the Muirs and McGregors discovered there was no coal mine as such at Fort Rupert, only the anticipation of one.

Fort Rupert was built to last. Like most other HBC forts, it was a formidable structure, with its 18-foot-high stockade of logs shipped from Alaska and a network of bastions armed with cannons. Captain William McNeill, the officer in charge of constructing the fortress, wanted to build the best fort the Company ever had. Every effort was made to design it so that it could be defended by a handful of employees. The fort's main gate was an impressive piece of architecture, with tall and sturdy palisades on either side, and bastions positioned at each corner of the walls, creating a tunnel through which all visitors passed to gain entry.

Prior to construction of the fort, no Natives had settled there, but they knew the site as a safe harbour and a rich clamming ground. As the post was being built, Natives rushed to the area to take advantage of the new trading post. Almost overnight, cedar-planked houses appeared on the beach.

McNeill was a former sea captain from Boston who joined the Company when his ship the *Llama* was purchased by the HBC in 1832. In 1837 he was master of the *Beaver*, before being appointed chief trader. Five years later he travelled to England and became a British citizen. McNeill was tough as nails: a difficult man with a bad temper, but a well-respected disciplinarian. The young people in Victoria especially loved him because he brought firecrackers from the Hawaiian Islands for the first time.

His assistant was his son-in-law, George Blenkinsop, a good-natured Cornishman who joined the Company in August 1840 and had served in various positions such as steward in the Columbia Shipping Department, as well as postmaster and clerk at Stikine, where he married the adopted daughter of McNeill in July 1846. Blenkinsop was appointed clerk-in-charge at Fort Rupert for the term 1849 to 1850.[4]

Blenkinsop's apprentice clerk was Englishman Charles Beardmore, who served at Fort Rupert from 1849 until 1851, when he was permitted to retire from service. Dr. Helmcken described him as "a tall, active, red, curly-haired, fearless, energetic, wiry and a little harum-scarum, good natured fellow, who always carried a sort of shillelah."[5]

These three men managed Fort Rupert, setting the tone for the community's day-to-day life and ruling the lives of the Scottish miners.

Sir George Simpson, who recommended the establishment of a fort in northern Vancouver Island, viewed it as a regular HBC post, whose purpose was mainly in trading furs and fish from the area, and, as an aside, a very limited trial of coal development.[6] However, the new era of steam navigation required an adequate supply of coal to fuel Company vessels plying the coastal waters. Like other parts of Vancouver Island, the area was rich in forest resources. Ironically, it would be spars and shingles that would fuel the economy of Fort Rupert for many years, not coal or furs.

The first recorded shipment of coal was loaded in 1846 on the HMS *Cormorant* at Suquash, about six miles from the site of Fort Rupert. Natives had simply dug the coal from the surface with trade axes. Two years later, the Company signed a contract with the American Pacific Mail Steamship Company to sell coal at 50 shillings a ton; the ship carried mail between Panama and the Oregon Coast. Coal was in great demand—the Americans wanted it, the HBC needed it and the British Navy required it for their ships in Pacific waters.[7]

When the *Mary Dare* arrived on September 24, the population of Fort Rupert was 35. This included French Canadians, some Kanakas (Natives of Hawaii) and management staff. The addition of the Scots gave this small community an almost international flavour. The Native population had also increased, lured by the opportunity for jobs and trade.

The day after the Scottish miners arrived, the local Kwakiutl returned from a successful raid on a neighbouring tribe. There were 16 canoes drawn up on the beach, and 16 poles erected, each with a head impaled on it. Ann Muir, being the oldest female in the group and the first white women ever seen in the area, was offered her choice of any 2 of the 16 heads, as these were highly prized presents. Ann diplomatically declined the offer and told them she felt unworthy of such recognition. To everyone's relief, her decision was accepted and they gathered up their belongings and left.

The coal situation at Fort Rupert was not what the miners had expected when they signed their contract with the Company. There had been no exploration of the coalfield whatsoever, and it was now left to the miners to find a site for the mine plus build their own housing. It is doubtful that the Scottish miners had ever built a house before, although they had agreed to do this in their contract. Most of the building had to be done by other Company servants who were already hard-pressed building the new fort. "The miners more or less looked on, to the accompaniment of complaints from the fort management in the Fort Journal, kept by the clerks."[8]

On September 26, 1849, Andrew Muir wrote:

> Mr. Wark [Work] of Fort Simpson, Mr. Muir, Manager for Coal Work, McGregor and I along with some Indians started in a canoe after dinner in the direction of McNeil's Harbour to examine the coast for the most eligible place to commence operations at the coal... On October 1st, I was superintending Kanakas building chimneys—other men was digging a well in Fort—and until the 24th I was employed along with the others getting our houses [ready] in order to stay in.

On October 25, the five Muirs started to sink a shaft to look for that elusive coal, while McGregor and Smith continued to work on building their homes. John Muir had explored and tested many places, but the coal outcrops were not promising. The miners had anticipated an average wage of 50 pounds sterling for 310 days' work. The rest of their wages would be paid to the Company store for extra provisions for their families. There would be no bonuses awarded for digging this coalfield!

While the labour problems at Fort Rupert have been historically well documented, it is interesting to view them in the context of the Scottish miners: what they left behind, their expectations and the grim reality they now faced. The miners were asked to do all manner of jobs, work they had not agreed to, and they now believed the Company had broken its agreement with them. When they worked outside the fort, there was no protection of any kind. On one occasion, Natives came down to the pit, threatening to shoot them unless compensated for their land rights. The miners returned to the fort, demanding more protection, but their request was denied. They were told that if they didn't work, there would be no rations; they reluctantly returned to work. A shaft was dug deeper and deeper into the earth, but still there was no sign of coal. The disgruntled Scots wished for transportation home.

The Scottish miners got some unexpected support from an unlikely source. Not particularly wanted in Fort Victoria, the new governor of Vancouver Island, Richard Blanshard, took a trip to the north Island to see Fort Rupert in March 1850. He recognized the Scottish miners' plight after spending several hours talking with the Muirs, listening to their complaints and lending a sympathetic ear. The miners' grievances were added to his report to the Colonial Office. This gave ample credence to those in the colony who viewed him as an unnecessary intrusion into their affairs, and no doubt brought about his quick departure from Vancouver Island.

All work at Fort Rupert stopped on April 16, 1850, when the miners went on strike. Andrew Muir explained:

> Our watchman with our supply of arms and ammunition was forced to run leaving us without any protection at all. How could we be expected to stay and defend ourselves without them? We had to stop work and returned to the post.

Andrew Muir's diary detailed the charges and countercharges exchanged between workers and management. The final straw seemed to be when he and John McGregor were ordered to cut a drain in the fort below the Kanakas' house. "The place had such a bad smell hardly fit for a pig to live in," he wrote. They asked for a handwritten note stating they were to be used as labourers for the remainder of the contract. Only with that note in hand would they do it. George Blenkinsop flexed his muscle by threatening to shoot them "like so many crows." He said he was not afraid to die along with them. Andrew said he wanted no quarrel with him, and went back to work on the drain.

On April 26, Blenkinsop charged Andrew Muir and John McGregor with neglect of duty and imposed a penalty of 50 pounds. He claimed they were "working slowly and sitting about idly." Andrew said that was false and that he was only doing his duty. He was a miner, not a labourer. "Since we could not please him at what we do, we might as well stop work until the matter is settled." Vancouver Island's first labour strike had begun. When they refused to return to work, and demanded a fair trial under English law, the two men were put in irons.

> I was placed in the upper bastion and McGregor in the lower
> ˏ with nothing else than bread and water. I did not dare speak to
> my mother over such disgraceful proceedings that was being
> carried out in a British Colony that was governed by British
> Law. It is a disgrace, for it is said that slavery was abolished,
> here it reigns in full force. They have slaves that crawl at the feet
> of the officers of the Hudson's Bay Company.

They remained imprisoned for six days. On the first night, Andrew caught a cold that left him partly deaf. "With irons at night and no bed I could not keep myself warm." His request for a doctor was refused. "I will never forget the treatment I received, for they laughed at me in my torment." On the third night their request to have the irons removed for the night was granted. They were allowed to huddle together for warmth. During the day they were sometimes allowed to go for a walk on the gallery for exercise. They had soup for dinner twice, otherwise only bread and water.

The irons were removed on the seventh day, and the men were taken into the hall to appear before McNeill, Blenkinsop, Beardmore and Dr. Helmcken. The two men were ordered to state their mind freely, which they did. This was a great change from the day before, when they were told not to utter a word. They were implored to return to work until summer, when they could be tried as requested. Andrew and John said "no." They had been falsely imprisoned and would not work until the Pacific Mail Steamship returned, when their case could be tried and settled. The Company had hoped, by that time, to have found coal and it needed the miners' support to fulfill the steamship contract. The men were returned to the bastion, but not in irons, and rations were issued to their families to cook for them. Andrew received treatment for his ear condition. On May 11, they were freed but warned not to speak to any of the men or attempt to go outside the fort, and they were not to have any rum, powder or shot for three weeks.

The barque *England* arrived at Fort Rupert on May 24, under Captain Brown, to take on coal before returning to Britain. The ship planned a stop at San Francisco. Aboard were the four deserter crew members from the *Norman Morison*. The striking miners saw their opportunity to head down to California, where they could mine gold and not coal. They asked to be released from their contract, and when this was refused, they slipped aboard the vessel.

The *Beaver* arrived in Fort Rupert from Fort Victoria on June 27. The crew deserters panicked and thought the steamer had come for them. At the first opportunity they slipped over the side and escaped into the bush. Rumours circulated at the fort about the plight of the sailors—one had drowned, and the Natives had murdered two. Sometime later, their naked bodies were found shot through the heart.

Blanshard visited the fort once again, and, learning of the labour troubles and the consequences that had brought about the failure of the coal-mining venture, gave the HBC permission to abandon the coal operation as being unfit for commercial purposes. News of the trouble at Fort Rupert reached London. Douglas received a letter that severely reprimanded the actions of McNeill, Blenkinsop and Beardmore. They had no right to imprison the men, let alone put them in irons. Dr. Helmcken, who had been appointed as justice of the peace and advised to sort out the trouble at the fort, submitted his resignation to Douglas. He had had enough of the coal experiment at Fort Rupert.

On July 2, 1850, six miners and six labourers left by canoe "determined to make for some Christian place." (John and Ann Muir and their children, Michael Muir, and Mary McGregor and her children all remained behind in Fort Rupert.) Only the brave, uninformed or desperate would venture out in a canoe not knowing where they were going. These men were desperate. They thought they could hide among the islands until picked up by a passing ship. A week later they were picked up "very badly off" by the *England*. The goldfields of California looked very inviting. On July 20, they arrived in San Francisco.

In Fort Rupert, a pregnant Mary McGregor decided to join her husband, John, who had made his way to Astoria (Fort George) at the mouth of the Columbia River. When the *Cadboro* arrived, she gathered her children and possessions and went aboard. Muir's daughter, Marion Turner, joined Mary on the ship that took them as far as Port Townsend, and from there they journeyed on the backs of mules for almost 200 miles before reaching their destination. Mary was fortunate to have Marion along as a companion, as she was able to assist in the delivery of Isabella, Mary's fourth child, in March 1851.

McNeill was allowed a furlough in 1850, and Blenkinsop was appointed clerk-in-charge. No doubt McNeill's experience at Fort Rupert had taken its toll and he needed respite after all the trials and tribulations with the miners. A year later, he was appointed chief factor at Fort Simpson. McNeill retired on June 1, 1863, to a farm at Gonzales Point in Oak Bay, where he died in 1875.[9]

The discouraged Scottish miners from Fort Rupert, and the Muirs and McGregors, returned to Fort Victoria from San Francisco and Astoria in 1851. The McGregors left their eight-year-old son Archibald behind in Astoria with Muir's sister Marion Turner, who had married Dr. Curtis Trenchard and settled there. When his contract expired late in 1851, John Muir Sr., his wife Ann, and son Michael returned to Fort Victoria and moved west to Sooke, where the family purchased 100 acres from the Company, next to Captain Grant's farm.

Gold Find at Gold Harbour

Company officials at Fort Simpson had learned of gold-bearing quartz on the Queen Charlotte Islands and were sufficiently convinced of the find to investigate further. In October 1851, John McGregor was placed in charge of the miners who were to work there for shares. They left on the brig *Una* with Captain Willie Mitchell in command. McNeill was also on board, hoping to establish another post.

The voyage was long, difficult and plagued by rough weather. They found safe anchor and used the ship as a base for operations until a camp could be established ashore. The site is now called Gold Harbour, or Mitchell's Harbour.

The miners were divided into two work groups and were guided to possible sites by local Natives. McGregor kept a record of all the samples. For a time it looked like their efforts would be in vain, but then a seven-inch quartz vein was found. All the miners were gathered to an area that revealed up to 25 percent gold in some places. A fault cut off the main seam completely, so holes were drilled for blasting powder, and a charge was inserted and fuses lit. The blast split the ground open into gold-dust-bearing particles, instead of a clean vein. Miners and Natives fought over the gold particles.

After all had been picked, the Natives became troublesome, refusing to carry supplies or guide any farther. McNeill took all the gold and put it into small sacks, then into a large chest with a padlock. Then he and the miners proceeded to Fort Simpson for fresh water and supplies. McNeill promised the men they would share equally in the profits when they reached Fort Victoria. However, McGregor and the miners remembered their previous dealings with McNeill, and refused, preferring instead to have Douglas make the division. The *Una* then sailed for Fort Victoria, its crew hoping to reach there by Christmas.

The day before Christmas, they encountered a storm that forced them to take shelter in Neah Bay in the US. The ship struck a rock and was in danger of sinking. Canoes came out from a nearby village, intent on plundering the stricken vessel. The miners fought the raiders and tried to save the ship, but it was too late. Captain Mitchell ordered all to abandon ship, but not before he retrieved one 16-ounce gold nugget. The men boarded small boats and were picked up by the American schooner *Susan Sturgis*. A few shots were fired over the heads of the raiders, but by this time the *Una* was ablaze: the Natives had attempted to burn out the brass fittings. The ship sank, taking the precious ore to the bottom.

The men were taken to Fort Victoria, where McGregor and Mitchell reported to Douglas. A party of men and Mitchell were sent on the *Recovery*, under the command of Captain Charles Dodd, to capture those responsible for the loss of the *Una*. They met the chief of the village and found he had already dealt with the offenders. The leader of the raid had been buried alive and nine others shot for bringing disgrace to their village. Dodd and Mitchell returned to Fort Victoria. Mitchell called together those from the *Una*. He and McGregor had agreed to lessen the men's disappointment by having them share in the proceeds from the sale of the nugget he had saved. When news of the gold leaked out, prospectors were soon on their way from California and Oregon. This resulted in Douglas proclaiming the Queen Charlotte Islands a Crown Colony.

The Muir Family of Sooke

Andrew Muir may have had a chip on his shoulder from his experience at Fort Rupert, but Governor Douglas recognized the tenacious nature of the man and offered him a position as the colony's first sheriff in Fort Victoria. It was a job Andrew embraced, and he took great pride in enforcing the laws that empowered him "to take charge of the gaol, pursue and arrest felons, and administer lashes in a public forum."[10] His life seemed to have turned a corner when he married Isabella Weir in January 1854. Isabella was the daughter of Robert Weir, one of Kenneth McKenzie's labourers at Craigflower Farm.

As sheriff, Andrew was kept busy maintaining law and order and was often headlined in the newspaper apprehending drunks or stopping skirmishes in the frontier town. He also enjoyed a drink or two, but after Isabella's death in childbirth in 1857, Andrew plunged into despair. Their baby daughter, Isabella Ellen Muir, went to live with her grandparents. Andrew busied himself in his work as sheriff and was unanimously named sergeant-at-arms. Isabella Ellen Muir was baptized in Christ Church Cathedral, Victoria, on January 13, 1859, the same day her father's death was reported. Andrew died on January 11, 1859; he was only 32 years old.[11] He had been ill for a few days and was found dead on the floor of his room. This was devastating news for the Muir family. An autopsy was held, and the coroner found an enlarged liver, a sign of chronic alcoholism; the kidneys and stomach were also diseased. It was a sad end for a young man who had come to Vancouver Island with such high hopes for a new life.

John and Ann Muir, and their other sons John Jr., Michael and Robert, were now established landowners, farmers and entrepreneurs. John built a home on their farm they called Woodside, today a Sooke landmark. Eventually his holdings included 582 acres of land facing Sooke Bay and harbour. Michael's 71 acres adjoined Andrew's 92 acres, and Robert took up 100 acres and built Burnside at the corner of Muir and Maple avenues. John Jr. took over Captain Grant's home, renaming it Springside. Their homes were constructed of rough lumber from the forests nearby; even the downspouts were fashioned from wood.[12]

In the meantime, John Muir Sr. and his sons Robert and John Jr., and cousin Archibald signed another two-year contract with the Company to work the new coalfield discovered in Nanaimo. They mined coal from September 1852 to 1854, when the contract expired and John Sr. and Robert returned to Sooke, leaving John Jr. and Archibald behind.

The Muirs looked for ways to increase their income. From the forests of Sooke, the production of ships' spars seemed a possible

The John Muir family and friends sit on the steps of their home, Woodside, in Sooke around 1905. The Muirs helped establish the mines in Nanaimo, built a successful sawmill business, launched a fleet of ships and were pioneers in the Sooke district. IMAGE A-09168 COURTESY OF ROYAL BC MUSEUM, BC ARCHIVES

business venture. They came to an agreement with Thomas Munro, Grant's former employee who had taken over the mill, to work as partners; the mill had sat idle since Grant had left. The Muirs purchased the mill and all the land from Grant for $4,000.

In 1855 they acquired the engines, boilers and machinery from a wrecked steamship, giving them the means to build the Island's first steam sawmill. By 1859 they were exporting 40,000 board feet from its wharf, and in 1860 they opened a lumberyard at Victoria. The mill became the main employer in the area for years. Robert Muir negotiated the first contract to supply piles for the harbour in San Francisco.

The biggest obstacle to living and working in Sooke was the lack of a road to Victoria. In 1854 the Muirs petitioned Douglas to have such a road built, as the cost of transportation by canoe was so great. Douglas approved their application, and that winter had the line surveyed and cleared of timber. The road was built using Native labour paid $8 a month, as white workers could not be hired for less than $2 a day. Douglas maintained he could not afford to employ them. The road led from Woodside Farm to the Sooke River, which then had to be crossed by any means available, and then from the river to a point where it met the Metchosin Road to Victoria.

The Muirs went into the shipbuilding business with their *Ann Taylor*, 115 tons, launched in 1861, the largest sailing ship built in the colony at that time. It carried lumber to San Francisco and Hawaii. They also built the steamer *Woodside* in 1878; it was wrecked 10 years later.

John and Ann Muir and their descendants continued the Scottish tradition of Hogmanay, a New Year celebration, but there were no "first footers" to their remote wilderness home in Sooke. However, the family threw open their doors to friends and strangers alike from Fort Victoria to share in their warm hospitality and welcome in the New Year. Old Scottish songs were sung, and dancing continued until the celebration ended with the singing of Auld Lang Syne.[13]

In 1856, London informed Douglas he must introduce an elected assembly in the new colony. Knowing little about the niceties of electoral law or of parliamentary procedures, Douglas set about meeting the wishes of Whitehall. Since London's proposed electoral qualification—ownership of 20 acres of land—would have disenfranchised nearly everybody living in the colony, he liberalized the property requirement and gave the vote to every freeholder owning property worth 300 pounds sterling. Four electoral districts were established: Sooke, Esquimalt, Victoria and Nanaimo.

John Muir was elected to the first House of Assembly for the Colony of Vancouver's Island on July 22, 1856, and served until 1861. This was the first parliament west of the Great Lakes. He joined James Yates, Edward Langford, Thomas Skinner, Joseph William McKay, Joseph Pemberton, Dr. John F. Kennedy and Dr. John S. Helmcken as Speaker. Douglas, however, held a veto over all legislation. Dr. Helmcken gave a thumbnail sketch of some of the new legislators:

> Mr. James Yates, radical, growler, cantankerous yet earnest, who hated the Governor and the Hudson's Bay Co., although he had come out in their service. Thos. Skinner, a genial gentleman, a sort of liberal conservative, Bailiff of the Puget Sound Company's farm at Esquimalt. He liked the smell of the fox and to follow the hounds; but preferred this to being the fox. Jos. Pemberton, Surveyor General, who always endeavoured to induce both sides to agree, in medio tutissima, his motto. Jos. McKay, lively and active, who knew everything and everybody. The patriarchal Muir, one of the led, who had been in the Hudson's Bay Service at the coal mines at Fort Rupert—who said Aye or Nay when present. Dr. Kennedy, who voted; and last, J.S. Helmcken…innocent and ignorant of politics, a London sparrow, too fond of nonsense and cigars.[14]

The young Colony of Vancouver Island now had a seven-member elected government in a colony with only 774 European inhabitants, according to the 1855 census. The 1855 census listed 4 dwelling houses in Sooke, 7 stores, 18 outhouses, a sawmill, a flour and threshing mill—all the property of the Muirs.

John Muir's nephew Archibald remained in Nanaimo and became a respected miner in the community. In 1871 he married 17-year-old Julia Bevilockway, whose parents had arrived on the *Princess Royal* in 1854. The couple had six children, but only three survived their father: Annie Frost, Joseph Edward Lewis and Janet Maud Julia. Sadly, Archibald died in the May 3, 1887, explosion of the Number One mine. Julia also lost her brother Herbert in the same disaster.[15] Julia later married Edward Brown and had several more children.

Archibald and Julia's son, Joseph (Joe) Muir, born in 1875, earned the respect of Nanaimo residents for his contribution in recording its history, and for being "Keeper of the Bastion" for over 25 years. He married Agnes Paterson from the Cranberry District in 1901. He was a charter member of Post No. 3, Native Sons of B.C., and its chief factor in 1900 and 1962. He was also a member of the Ancient Order of Foresters, and a Mason. On his death in 1963, the Bastion flag flew at half-mast.

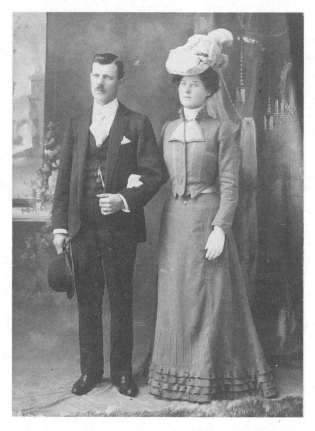

Mr. and Mrs. Joseph Muir on their wedding day, November 19, 1901. Joseph Muir helped record Nanaimo's history and was "Keeper of the Bastion" for over 25 years. PHOTOGRAPHER A. SAVARD, VANCOUVER. IMAGE 12-54 COURTESY OF NANAIMO MUSEUM

In this photo taken around 1952, Joseph Muir, right, "Keeper of the Bastion" and a descendant of one of the first miners, John Muir, poses with Mr. Melville and Bob Wilson.

IMAGE 1992 025 A-P70 COURTESY OF NANAIMO COMMUNITY ARCHIVES

CHAPTER 5

The Nanaimo Coalfield

Colvilletown (Nanaimo)

The situation changed for the miners at Fort Rupert when news came of a coal discovery at Wentuhuysen Inlet (Nanaimo). The story of the coal discovery is legendary. Snuneymuxw chief Che-wich-i-kan was having his gun repaired at Fort Victoria, and while watching the blacksmith at his forge, noticed the coal and told the smithy there were plenty of black rocks near his village. He was offered a bottle of rum and told there would be no charge for gun repairs if he would bring some of the black rocks to Fort Victoria. The following spring, the chief returned with a canoe loaded with coal. Company clerk Joseph William McKay was sent immediately to investigate, and he confirmed the chief's claim.

Douglas wanted to see for himself this new find, and he made a canoe trip to Nanaimo with John Muir Sr., surveyor Joseph Pemberton and Richard Colledge, Douglas's secretary. He was anxious to prove that the Company coal-mining venture on Vancouver Island could be a reality, and he wanted to put the failure at Fort Rupert behind him. They found several coal beds in various parts of the harbour. Douglas concluded that the mineral wealth of Vancouver Island had not been overrated. In 1852, McKay was ordered back to Nanaimo to take charge of the coal beds. Douglas also sent his most experienced miners, John Muir Sr., his son Robert and his nephew Archibald Muir, and John McGregor Sr.

The discovery of coal in the Central Island area, at Wentuhuysen Inlet in the traditional land of the Snuneymuxw, was a bonus for the Company. The area, sheltered by two islands on the east side and a mountain in the west, was first named Colvilletown in honour of HBC governor Andrew Colville. The name "Nanaimo" became official in 1860.

Scattered along the shoreline and the Nanaimo River were a number of Native villages and longhouses, large barnlike structures that accommodated several families. Each band retained its own tribal customs, spoke the same dialect and united against a common enemy. Early contact with Fort Langley on the mainland resulted in the Snuneymuxw having no fear of the Company men. They had traded fish and furs for blankets—familiar items of trade for years. The post in Nanaimo would be no different.

The Company's Nanaimo operation was established solely to extract coal; it would never be a "fort" as such, since there were no expectations of any fur trade, although some trading did occur. The Company thought that this venture could operate under the same management system as the fur trade and saw no need to create a separate organization. However, it later discovered this was what was required, but by that time its holdings had been sold. In 1862, Alexander Grant Dallas separated the coal operation from all other Company activities.

When Company surveyor Joseph Despard Pemberton and his assistant Benjamin William Pearse made an initial survey of what was known earlier as Wenthuysen Inlet, they found an excellent deep-sea harbour that would play a large role in the development of the city.

The face of the town was established during this period, when the Company imported miners to work the coal in Nanaimo. Unknowingly, it created a community dominated by labourers,

This early photo of Nanaimo, with the Bastion at centre left and coal being loaded on a sailing ship in the harbour, shows the frontier ruggedness of the coal-mining village. IMAGE HI-47 COURTESY OF NANAIMO MUSEUM

unlike Fort Victoria, which attracted the middle class, retired Company traders, and professional and business-oriented men. Nanaimo became a Company town, and its residents looked to the Company rather than the government for any local improvements. In the early stage of development, it was the coal company that built the roads and bridges, built the houses and improved the town economically. Some miners served out their contract and then sought other opportunities in town, in agriculture or in the service industry.

Joseph William McKay, 23, was appointed officer-in-charge of Nanaimo. He was a very junior man in the Company hierarchy, having worked in the sales shop at Fort Victoria. Douglas kept a close eye on every aspect of the Nanaimo operation, for he wanted it to succeed. John Muir and his sons, John and Robert, and nephew Archibald had signed another two-year contract with the

Company and were assigned to Nanaimo, arriving on September 6, 1852.[1] John McGregor was ill and would follow shortly. They were housed in the first log cabin, which was covered with cedar bark.

The next morning four labourers arrived from Fort Rupert with instructions to assist Muir wherever needed. James Stove, James Linklater, William Ritch and John Malcolm brought drilling equipment, hand tools and black powder. A few French Canadians and Kanakas were also sent along to assist and provide security—a lesson learned from the Fort Rupert experience. Initially, the coal was extracted by the same method used at Fort Rupert, by Natives digging surface seams. Soon Muir began sinking shafts in areas too deep to be worked from the surface.

Within days, this small complement of men managed with the help of the Snuneymuxw to fill an order of 480 barrels of coal and load it aboard the *Cadboro,* destined for Fort Victoria. Five days later more coal was loaded on the *Honolulu Packet,* and a few months later the first shipment was made to San Francisco. To save McKay the trouble of providing food for the miners, Douglas advised him that the miners would be allowed one shilling per day instead of rations and would have to provide their own food.[2]

Boyd Gilmour arrived on December 9, 1852, from Fort Rupert, and joined Muir as manager. There were now two managers whose duty it was to oversee five miners and half a dozen labourers. It wasn't long before Gilmour quarrelled with the miners under his control, which resulted in a strike. A month later, when Douglas arrived on another inspection trip, he was met by striking miners who presented him with a long string of grievances. Douglas managed to placate the angry miners.

Mary McGregor joined her husband, John, in Nanaimo in October 1852, bringing the newest addition to the family, Isabella, who was born in March 1851. She and John Jr. had stayed on at Sooke with Mrs. Ann Muir. John McGregor began building a house in Nanaimo, but without the means to finish it, offered it to the Company for four cows and a young bull.[3] The Company gladly accepted the offer, as it was short of housing. On January 4, 1854, the Daybook noted, "Commenced dividing the new house purchased from McGregor into four rooms."

In 1855, Mary McGregor travelled in a Native canoe to Victoria, where she gave birth to son William.

When James Douglas visited Nanaimo in 1853, the settlement consisted of 12 houses, a forge and a lumber store, and the white population was 125. They were totally outnumbered by the Snuneymuxw, who were also enumerated that year: there were 159 "men with beards," 160 women, 300 boys and 324 girls, giving a total population of 943.

January 1854 was very cold. Ice covered the Nanaimo harbour to the head of Commercial Inlet. When the *Otter* arrived, it anchored inside of Tide Staff Point (now Gallows Point) because it could not get closer; the ice was estimated to be four inches thick. Then the brig *Rose* arrived from Victoria, chartered by the Company to take a cargo of coal to San Francisco. Men were put to work clearing a passage through the ice from the coal wharf to the ship before they could begin loading. The ice at Long Lake was measured at 15 inches. McKay could not believe this, so sent two men to find out if it was true. They returned from the journey quite late, only to report they had found a herd of elk, so had shot two. No report about the ice!

From this modest beginning, the new community of Nanaimo was born, and a new industry put on firm foundations. During this visit, Douglas listened to the miners' concerns. They asked that a school be established; he then transferred teacher Charles Bayley from Victoria, and also promised residents he would provide for the community's religious life. He recommended to his superiors in the Company that

> the party selected for that office should be a member of the Free Kirk of Scotland, the miners being generally of that persuasion, and not disposed to receive instructions from the clergy of any other denomination.[4]

This last request might have been a more difficult promise to fulfill, for it wasn't until 1855 that the first missionary appeared, and he was Catholic bishop Modeste Demers, the consecrated bishop of Vancouver Island, who was also responsible for the British territories on the mainland.

Work in the mines progressed slowly, with occasional punctuality issues on the part of some of the miners; in the fall of 1853, only two tons of coal a day was being mined. During the Company's operations in Nanaimo between 1852 and 1859, 25,000 tons of coal were shipped, mostly to California.

Schoolteacher Charles Alfred Bayley gave a good account of how Native women were used in this fledgling coal industry:

> Loading ships was done in a very primitive manner in early days. Hundreds of Natives, mostly women, being employed who conveyed the coal alongside the ships in canoes—it was a curious sight to see the string of Natives of both sexes working like ants in one continuous line over the trail to where they deposited their loads.[5]

The women received tickets for every tub of coal they carried. These tickets were then exchanged at the Company store for a variety of trade goods. Men were employed in constructing shafts and transporting the coal to the pithead. The Snuneymuxw were very accommodating, so much so that the Company store occasionally ran out of trade goods to pay them.

Conflicting Personalities

After completing his contract, John Muir Sr. and his son Robert returned home to Sooke, leaving son John Jr. and nephew Archibald in Nanaimo. John McGregor joined Boyd Gilmour as a second oversman (mining manager). If there was any Scottish bond between them, both having come from Kilmarnock, Ayrshire, it wasn't evident in their workplace, for they did not get along. McGregor had a quick temper, and Gilmour was a lonely and unhappy man. His wife, Jean, refused to live anywhere but Victoria, and she kept their children, Jean, Joseph, Mary, Marion and Boyd, with her. Gilmour shared a cabin with his nephew Robert Dunsmuir and his family.

Perhaps it was inevitable that the two men would clash. The HBC Nanaimo Daybook recorded a disagreement between McGregor and Gilmour at Omitted Creek on May 1, 1854. McGregor refused to work under Gilmour's orders.[6]

McGregor may not have been the easiest man to get along with, but he was an experienced miner. In 1856 he had an altercation with the next oversman, George Robinson, when he was accused of negligence and of being absent from work one day and leaving work early on two occasions. The two men began arguing at the top of the hill, by the Bastion. Robinson said McGregor was impertinent. The argument continued down the hill to the black-smith shop, where McGregor continued to shout at Robinson. The argument gathered a few onlookers as it progressed. Robinson left to report the incident to Charles Edward Stuart, who had succeeded McKay as officer-in-charge. An angry McGregor yelled after him, calling him a liar and a hypocrite. Robinson had had enough! In a rage, he grabbed a heavy hammer left by the smithy and "dealt McGregor a blow on the head which knocked him down."[7] McGregor walked up to the surgery, where Dr. Thomas bandaged his head wound. Fortunately, the wound was not dangerous; McGregor had suffered no serious injury.

Meanwhile Robinson, alarmed at his own lack of control, reported the incident, which he believed was understandable, considering McGregor's angry words. He felt sure he would be reprimanded or sent away; instead, it was McGregor who was sent to Victoria to cool off. By this time, McGregor probably had had enough of the HBC's attempt at coal mining both in Fort Rupert and now Nanaimo, for he did not return to Nanaimo until there was new management, the Company having sold its holdings to the Vancouver Coal Mining and Land Company. Robinson continued on in Nanaimo until his contract expired in 1859.

Three Generations of Miners: The McGregor Family

The John McGregor family returned to Sooke, but it wasn't long before they acquired 180 acres of land in the Metchosin District. The land was registered on October 6, 1857. There, John built a family home they named Oakwood. The following year, another 100 acres from the adjoining property were added to their estate. Three more children were born here: James, Agnes and Jean Katherine (Kate).[8] Their eldest daughter, Mary, was married at Oakwood in 1861 to John Van Houten of Hawaii. The couple had six children, three sons and three daughters: Ernest, Charlie, Walter, Eva, Myrtle and Rose. After her husband's death in 1877, Mary Van Houten moved back to Nanaimo.

The McGregors sold their property in January 1863 to return to Nanaimo, where John went back to work in the mines now owned by the Vancouver Coal Mining and Land Company (often referred to simply as the Vancouver Coal Company). John died suddenly on January 12, 1866, aged 55, at his home on Front Street and was laid to rest in the Pioneer Cemetery at the corner of Wallace and Comox Road in Nanaimo. Mary stayed on in Nanaimo and raised her children there.

After John's death, the burden of providing for the family fell on his young sons John, 19, and William, 11, who worked in the mines; they were joined by James when he reached 10. There were few luxuries in Mary McGregor's household as they struggled to make ends meet. The brothers worked at various jobs as door trappers and mule drivers, but they also found time to educate themselves, and they were ambitious.

John, being the eldest, was the breadwinner in the family, but he died after a long illness in 1873 at age 26. It was not the

Four generations of McGregors. Seated is Mrs. John McGregor (Mary), flanked by daughter Mary Van Houten of Nanaimo (left) and granddaughter Eva Coldwell (right). Eva married Alderman C.A. Coldwell, of Vancouver's first city council. The child is Charles Coldwell, born at Hastings Mill in 1880. In later years, Charles was an official of the Union Steamship Company. PHOTOGRAPHED BY BOYDEN STUDIO, NANAIMO, BC, IN 1885. IMAGE COURTESY OF THE MURPHY FAMILY

first time illness had afflicted John—he had contracted smallpox in 1862, when the disease had spread through Victoria and the surrounding area.[9] It was believed it had reached Victoria from San Francisco, where several cases had been detected. Within two years the epidemic had spread up the coast, killing 20,000 of the 60,000 Natives in the colony.

The onus was now on William to take care of the family. He worked hard, studied and, at age 29, was appointed general manager of the Vancouver Coal Company mines. He married Amanda Teresa Meakin in 1875. Amanda was born in Nanaimo in 1857. Her parents were from Staffordshire, England, and came to Nanaimo in November 1854 on the *Princess Royal*. The couple had six children: Jack, Alice, Agnes, William, Kate and Ernest.

The biggest disaster in Nanaimo's mining history happened on May 3, 1887, and greatly affected William and Amanda. At the Number One Esplanade mine, an explosion killed 148 miners and 1 rescuer. The couple grieved along with the community: Amanda lost her father, John Meakin, and her brother Arthur, and William lost his cousin, Archibald Muir. Almost everyone in the community lost someone in the tragedy. William joined Sam Hudson, a Northfield miner, in an attempt to rescue some of the men, but they were overcome by afterdamp. Both were unconscious when finally found. William proved to be as tough as his father and recovered, but Sam couldn't be revived. William was carried home to Amanda. A few hours later, when she checked on his condition, William was gone; he had returned to the mine site.[10]

William believed in education and served several terms on the Nanaimo School Board, and he loved sports. As a track athlete, he won awards in high jump and long jump, and encouraged others to participate in sports. He was the first president of the Nanaimo Athletic Association Football Club, which was formed in September 1889.[11]

At the end of an afternoon shift at the Number One mine on November 12, 1897, William was seriously burned in a mine explosion along with seven other men. Gas had ignited an open-flame lamp on one of the miner's caps as he and his partner left for the day. Another explosion followed seconds later, causing a fire that could not be extinguished. Seven men died from their injuries, including William, who was only 43. This must have been a very difficult time for Amanda. She had lost her father and brother in the 1887 explosion, and now her husband was dead, leaving her with six children to raise on her own.

William's funeral was one of the largest in the city's history, with an estimated 3,000 people attending services held in several churches, including enough people from Wellington to fill four railroad coaches. At St. Andrew's Presbyterian Church, on November 22, 1898, the minister eulogized this distinguished son of pioneer miner John McGregor. James Dunsmuir and his brother-in-law, John Bryden, were among the mourners.

William's son Jack was in the Klondike with his cousin Arthur "Duffy" McGregor and other men from Nanaimo when he got the tragic news about his father. He made an urgent call home, then started on the long journey back to Nanaimo in mid-winter by dogsled over the ice toward Skagway, where he boarded a steamer for Seattle. He arrived home 27 days later.

Jack taught in Cedar Public School for two years, travelling by bicycle back and forth from Nanaimo each day; he was well known as a professional cyclist. Like his father, he was active in sports and seldom missed a sporting event. He played in the Nanaimo lacrosse team, and was also on the hose-reel team. He married Catherine McArthur Thompson, who came from Glasgow as a child. They had two children, Pat and William. For over 20 years, Jack worked with Pacific Coast Coal Company of South Wellington, where he was master mechanic. Later he became chief engineer of Canadian Collieries (Dunsmuir) Ltd. at the Number Five mine until it closed in 1935. During the Second World War, he worked in the Nanaimo Shipyard. After retirement, he served on the City of Nanaimo parks and recreation board from 1952 to 1954. He was also one of the founders of the Nanaimo Yacht Club and was its first commodore, from 1931 to 1935.[12]

Jack's uncle James, once manager of Number Five Southfield Chase River mine, had left the mining industry and in 1891 had gone into the retail clothing business. Three years later, he was elected a member of the provincial legislature for Nanaimo City.

His election was viewed as a popular one. The *Colonist* reported:

> He has the confidence of the business men and the miners know that in him they have a man who will look after their interests as well as a man actually engaged in digging coal.[13]

James did not stand for re-election in 1898, for that year he was appointed Inspector of Metalliferous Mines. He later became inspector of mines for the West Kootenay and Boundary District, with headquarters at Nelson. On June 3, 1900, he and Alice Emily Gooding (who had previously lived in Nanaimo) were married in Rossland.

The couple moved in January 1920, when James was appointed chief inspector of mines for British Columbia, with headquarters in Victoria. James had been ill for over a year when he retired in

1923; he died in Victoria on May 28, 1924.

James's sister, Isabella McGregor, who was born in 1851, married Isaac Johns, the Deputy Collector of Inland Revenue for the Port of Vancouver. She and Isaac had five children, two sons and three daughters. Isabella died in 1888 after a short illness, and Isaac died in Vancouver in 1890.

Margaret McGregor, born in March 1854, was the first white girl born in Nanaimo. Her recollections of her early life in Nanaimo were documented in Elizabeth Forbes's *Pioneer Women of Vancouver Island.* Margaret recalled attending school in a log cabin that doubled as a post office as well as the teacher's living quarters. She remembered that children were given a holiday to join in the excitement when an animal was slaughtered for food in front of the Bastion, and that noon and summertime were announced from the Bastion by the beating of a suspended crosscut saw against a triangular piece of steel. Later, a man beating a brass tambourine marched along the winding paths to give the time at regular intervals. When the Company imported a bell from England, the settlers turned out en masse to see it installed on a 30-foot scaffolding in front of the Company store. Thereafter the bell gave the time of day.

Jack McGregor, grandson of miner John McGregor and son of William McGregor, was one of the founders of the Nanaimo Yacht Club. Jack was known as a Klondiker; he first taught school, then later became a master mechanic, and was a sports enthusiast for many years. PHOTOGRAPHER SCHWARZE OF NANAIMO. IMAGE COURTESY OF THE NANAIMO YACHT CLUB

> Mail day was a big event. As soon as the little boat showed around Jack's Point, men, women and children hurried to the rock below the Bastion to wait until it eased in and tied up, and the mail was brought ashore. Even if no letters arrived it was

contact with the outside world just to stand and watch the boat discharge its cargo and perhaps talk to the captain who gave verbal news of persons in other ports of call.[14]

Margaret married Thomas Watson Glaholm in March 1870. Thomas was from England, and at age 13 travelled with his brother John William to the California gold rush. The two young men arrived in Nanaimo in 1864. Margaret's sister Kate married John William in 1887.[15]

Thomas worked in the mines before becoming a teamster. Then, in 1879, he became a partner in A.R. Johnston & Co., wholesale and retail grocers on Bastion Street. The store offered everything from groceries and grain to general farm produce, and was also the agent for the steamers operating to San Francisco and Portland, as well as for the east coast steamers. He and Margaret and their five children lived on Chapel Street, just a few blocks from where Margaret was born. The children were Flora, John William, Mary, Winnie and Agnes. Margaret's mother, Mary, lived with her until her death in 1905 at age 85. Margaret also had a long life; she died at the grand old age of 88 in 1942.

Margaret's oldest daughter, Flora, married William Sloan, a partner in the company Sloan and Scott. The couple had one son, Gordon McGregor Sloan, who became chief justice of British Columbia. William Sloan was another Klondiker, but one of the few who actually made money in the gold rush. He served as minister of mines and always looked for ways to improve the safety of the mines. As provincial secretary, he advocated for old-age pensions, improved health care and hospital facilities. He was one of Nanaimo's most popular politicians and had a long career, both federally and provincially. After Flora died, he married Catherine McDougall and they had two children, William and Barbara Jean.

Jack McGregor's son William was the first McGregor not to be involved in the mining industry. Most of the mines closed in the early fifties. William was an employee of Nanaimo Electric Light

Teacher Miss Agnes Waugh stands with her class in this South Wellington School photo taken in 1914. Jack McGregor's daughter Marion (Pat) is in the front row, fourth from left. (For the names of other children in the photo see Appendix IV.) IMAGE COURTESY OF THE MURPHY FAMILY

& Power Co., served an alderman for the City of Nanaimo for 10 years and was chairman of the parks and recreation commission for 14 years. He married Angie Clovis and they had one son, Malcolm. Like all the McGregor men before him, William was also active in sports.

John and Mary McGregor's family were part of Nanaimo's history from the earliest days of coal mining. Descendants still live in the area, although all do not carry the McGregor name. Only Malcolm McGregor, son of William, remains as a direct descendant in name, and he now lives in the Interior.

McGregor Park on the Nanaimo waterfront was named for the McGregor family, and as a memorial to all the other Scottish families who came to mine coal and settle in Nanaimo.

CHAPTER 6

The Coal Baron:
Robert Dunsmuir

Destiny Intervenes

The story of Robert Dunsmuir is not a-rags-to-riches story of a poor immigrant lad who came to the Colony of Vancouver Island and ended up building a castle for his bride. Rather, it is the fulfilled destiny of an educated coal miner and an astute business-man who took advantage of the opportunities presented to him. His father and grandfather before him were successful coal miners in Scotland.

The family lived in Hurlford, a small village a few miles east of Kilmarnock, Ayrshire, in an area dotted with coal mines and made famous by Scottish poet Robert Burns. The villages of Burleith, Riccarton and Hurlford were all closely tied to the main town of Kilmarnock, and all had mines. Tragedy struck the family in 1832, when Robert Dunsmuir was seven years old: his parents, grandmother and two of his sisters died during a cholera outbreak, leaving him and his four-year-old sister Jean in the care of his grandfather.

Cholera was a devastating disease that struck Scotland in the spring of 1832. It spread from town to town so rapidly that in some localities, a fifth of the population was swept away; in one village in the Highlands, half the population died. In July it broke out in Kilmarnock. Many of the deaths were so sudden that individuals who were hale and hearty in the morning were dead in the evening. A temporary hospital was mobilized. People retreated to their homes, and others moved to another town. However, compared to other places in the west of Scotland, Kilmarnock suffered slightly. When the disease disappeared in October, 250 had died, unlike Glasgow, where the epidemic killed 3,000. In Kilmarnock, the victims were interred in a piece of ground obtained for that purpose at the south corner of Wards Park. Cholera again broke out in January 1849, but fortunately it was less virulent than in 1832; only 130 people died in this outbreak.[1] Today there is a monument commemorating the dead from the cholera epidemic in Howard Park, Kilmarnock.

Three years later, Robert's grandfather, 57, also died. Jean stayed in Hurlford with her maternal aunt, Jean Hamilton, while Robert was sent off to school at Kilmarnock Academy. This school, which opened in 1808, provided a high standard of education, teaching the Latin classes necessary for university entrance. However, without government funding, it was largely dependent on the fees paid by the students' parents, and with the working-class industrial nature of the town, few people could afford to attend or stay on at school.[2] One of the school's former pupils was Sir Alexander Fleming, who discovered penicillin.

After Kilmarnock, Robert was sent to Paisley, where he studied at the Mercantile and Mathematical School, located at No. 4 Meeting House Lane in Paisley. His teacher was Alexander Macome, a well-known figure in the educational history of the town.[3] Paisley is known for its weaving industry and the famous paisley pattern.

When his education was completed, Robert joined his uncle, Boyd Gilmour, in the mines, learning about their day-to-day operation. Boyd Gilmour was married to Robert's Aunt Jean (Dunsmuir).

Robert Dunsmuir married a Kilmarnock woman, Joanna (Joan) Olive White when she was 19 and he was 22; they wed on September 11, 1847. Joan, pregnant with Robert's child, gave birth eight days later to daughter Elizabeth. The Scottish kirk did not look kindly on unwed mothers, and the young Dunsmuirs were banned from attending services or having Elizabeth baptized until they confessed their sin and paid penance. They pled guilty to "antenuptial fornication together."[4] After they were rebuked for their sin, they were absolved of the scandal and readmitted into the kirk.

Another daughter, Agnes, was born before Boyd Gilmour presented the young couple with an opportunity to start a new life in the new colony.

An Uncle's Choice

Boyd Gilmour signed a three-year contract with the HBC in December 1850. He was the son of a day labourer in Kilmarnock and worked as a "spirit dealer" in Kilmarnock in 1838, but by 1850 he was working as a mining oversman in Kilmarnock.[5] His brother Allan was a coalmaster at nearby Hurlford. Gilmour and Jean Dunsmuir were married on June 26, 1835. Their first child, Jean, was born a year later. Three more children were born before the Gilmours left for Vancouver Island.

No sooner had Gilmour signed on with the HBC when word came of the unhappy circumstance of the Muir family at Fort Rupert, who had signed on two years earlier. Gilmour expressed his concern to the Company agent David Landale, who reassured him of the integrity of the HBC and guaranteed he would be treated well. He and his family were due to sail on the *Pekin* on December 7, and he felt committed to go. The three other young men who had signed with him were not as committed. One decided to go; Archibald French joined his brother Adam. The two others were replaced, one by Arthur Queegly, the other by Robert

Dunsmuir, who was given only a day to decide. Considering the turmoil in Dunsmuir's life caused by the church's reaction to his marriage, this might have been an easy decision.

The *Pekin* sailed on December 19, 1850, with the Gilmours, Dunsmuirs, French brothers and Arthur Queegly. It would have been a difficult voyage for Joan Dunsmuir and Jean Gilmour, as both were pregnant. As the ship edged up the Columbia River toward Fort Vancouver, Jean gave birth to a son they named Allan Columbia Gilmour on June 20, 1851. Allan's birth register noted he was born on the Columbia River, America, Oregon Territory. The ship finally arrived at Fort Vancouver on June 29, 1851. Joan gave birth on July 8 to a son they named James.

The stay in Fort Vancouver did not impress the weary passengers and crew. After 191 days at sea, short of food, sick with scurvy, and tired of low wages, the crew deserted for the goldfields of California. Miner Arthur Queegly and blacksmith William Preston joined them. The ship's cargo had to be unloaded then reloaded aboard the *Mary Dare* by local Natives for the trip up the coast to Fort Rupert. On July 18, they left for Fort Rupert, a trip that lasted three weeks.

Gilmour's job was to prospect for coal, but it soon became evident he had difficulty with this chore. Robert Dunsmuir worked steadily, and wisely said little to upset management. Perhaps both men were saved by the discovery of coal at Nanaimo in 1852. Douglas began moving his workers to the new coalfields, and Gilmour and Dunsmuir were ordered to Nanaimo.

Gilmour had as much trouble finding coal seams in the Nanaimo area as he had in Fort Rupert. There were coal outcroppings on Newcastle Island, but he soon discovered a layer of conglomerate rock; the coal on the surface, he decided, was an isolated pocket. He abandoned Newcastle Island in favour of a Chase River site. Again, this proved unsatisfactory. On his third attempt, he finally uncovered black diamonds—Douglas's coal—and a workable seam in a good location on the west side of Commercial Inlet.[6] The job of drilling through the coal seam went to his nephew, Robert Dunsmuir.

Starting in August, Robert Dunsmuir drilled for four months through layers of conglomerate, sandstone and shale before striking a second seam, and that was good news for everyone concerned, including Douglas in Victoria, who wanted mining in Nanaimo to succeed. Within three years, two small mines were developed, and a decade later, at this same location, the Douglas Pit would be the first major producer of coal on Vancouver Island.

Only a former spirit dealer would request wine to be supplied in the wilderness of Vancouver Island, where the population had trouble getting food, let alone alcohol. On September 24, 1853, Gilmour made inquiries about a requisition he had sent to the Company store for some wines he hadn't received. This prompted a reply from Douglas to McKay: "Mr. Gilmour's requisition was not attended to, because there was not wine for sale, but I will endeavor to procure a small supply for him."[7] This was in the same dispatch informing Nanaimo that the *Colinda* had sailed with more Ayrshire miners and their families.

The contracts signed by Gilmour and Dunsmuir were due to expire on August 8, 1854. They had an option to return to Scotland, or they could stay on and sign new contracts. Douglas made a trip to Nanaimo to meet with the men. They had decided to stay, but only if the Company made it worthwhile and increased their wages. Douglas was not so inclined. He wrote:

> I was prepared to hear many absurd proposals but was certainly not prepared for the extravagant demands they actually made. From the idea that their services were indispensably necessary, they supposed they might command their own terms. I positively refused all their demands for an advance or anything beyond their former rate of wages.[8]

Douglas informed them that the *Princess Royal* had sailed from London carrying 24 English miners and their families to Nanaimo.

Gilmour countered saying he would not consider working beyond his contract without a raise in pay. Douglas had had enough of Boyd Gilmour and did not encourage him to remain in the Company. He concluded that Gilmour might be "a good honest man," but he was also "indolent and deficient in energy," a man who knew "just enough of Physical Geography to confuse himself and everyone about him. He has now made up his mind to leave the country and I have not pressed him to remain in the service."[9]

Gilmour returned to Scotland with his family in January 1855 on the *Princess Royal*'s return trip, just a few days after Jean gave birth to their seventh child, John Gilmour, born on December 24, 1854, at Fort Victoria.

They were home only a year when Jean died of enteritis. Boyd remarried. He died on March 26, 1869.[10] His obituary appeared in the *Kilmarnock Standard*, on April 3, 1869:

> Boyd Gilmour at Riverside Cottage, Galston. He was coalmaster of the firm Boyd Gilmour & Co., Burnbank, Ladyston, and Goatfoot Colleries. He served as magistrate of the Burgh in Galston. It is our painful duty to record the decease of one of our most respected and enterprising townsmen, Mr. Boyd Gilmour, coalmaster, who died on Friday night last, in the 54th year of his age... On the adoption of the New Police Act in Galston, he was elected one of the Magistrates of the burgh, and until his decease was one of the most active Commissioners, devising and, by his practical experience, carrying out schemes for the improvement of the place. He possessed a store of general information, had traveled much and read largely, was a gentleman of benevolent disposition, and universally respected. He leaves behind him a widow and a large family to mourn his death.

A Licensed Free Miner

Dunsmuir began working for himself when his contract expired. The Nanaimo Daybook recorded, "Dunsmuir commenced working on his own account."[11] In October 1855, he and Edward Walker were granted the first free miners' licences issued by the Company. Dunsmuir reopened the mine on Commercial Inlet that Gilmour had abandoned, hired his own workers and then sold the coal to the Company. When the English miners went on strike over low wages and poor working conditions, some even deserted to the American rival mines of the Puget's Sound Coal Mining Association at Bellingham Bay, where coal was discovered in 1852. Dunsmuir's mine was the only one operating in Nanaimo producing seven tons of coal a day.

The Vancouver Coal Mining and Land Company manager, George Robinson, did not like Dunsmuir and let Douglas know of his discontent with the young Scot. He claimed the Company paid too much money for Dunsmuir's coal. Douglas walked a fine line between the two men, not wishing to upset either, and not wanting to lose the services of Dunsmuir.

With a promised share in the profits, Dunsmuir then went on to manage the Harewood Coal Company for Dr. Alfred Robson Benson and his partner, the Honourable Horace Douglas Lascelles, seventh son of the third Earl of Harewood. Dunsmuir's employment there was short-lived. After a year of trying to make the mine profitable, he left the troubled company, which had no easy way of getting the coal to the harbour for shipment. The Harewood Mine lay outside the city limits, and out of HBC control. Later the Company built a tramway to carry the coal from the mine to the harbour. This partially solved the delivery problem, but it was only a one-year wonder, and, plagued with mechanical problems and lack of parts, the mine closed. Eventually the Vancouver Coal Company purchased it.

In 1858, Dunsmuir built a grand family home at the corner of Wallace and Albert streets in Nanaimo and named it Ardoon. The attractive rustic log home drew public attention with its beautiful gardens, trees and shrubs, and view of the harbour. This was an improvement over the simple log cabin the family first called

This charming early sketch is of a peaceful and even pastoral-looking Nanaimo Harbour. IMAGE 1998 032 M PRT 1 COURTESY OF NANAIMO COMMUNITY ARCHIVES

home on Front Street. Joan now had paid help from a Swedish gardener, a Chinese cook and an English parlour maid, all befitting this woman of substance.

Finding Black Gold

A coal-prospecting trip with friends in October 1869 changed forever Robert Dunsmuir's fortune and the coal industry in the Nanaimo area. The seam of coal he discovered resulted in the development of the Wellington mines and the town of Wellington, a few miles north of Nanaimo. He raised capital for the mining venture from Lieutenant Waldham N. Diggle of HMS *Grappler*, who signed on for $12,000, enough to get his name on the ownership papers of Dunsmuir, Diggle & Company. There were seven other partners, who, with Diggle, accounted for half the shares. Dunsmuir's two sons, Alex and James, were also named as partners, though perhaps in name only, for all the decision-making was done by their father, now a 20-year veteran miner.

Another partnership was developed with San Francisco businessman Henry Berryman to distribute Wellington coal to his office in San Francisco. Over the next decade and beyond, coal ships made regular trips between Departure Bay and the Golden Gate. Dunsmuir also signed a five-year contract with the Pacific Mail Steamship Company to supply coal for its company ships.

In the days before banks were the norm, Dunsmuir had his own banking system. He received shipments of gold from the ships that came from San Francisco to Departure Bay for coal. He kept a stock of 5-, 10- and 20-dollar gold pieces at his home for the convenience of any merchant who wanted gold. Old-timer William Lewis recalled, "I often went to his home for rolls of gold coins, wrapped just the same as you wrap silver today."[12] Dunsmuir used the pursers on the coal boats to take gold down to Victoria and deposit it for him in the bank there.

The town of Wellington grew to be greater in population than Nanaimo. What began with a few cottages for Dunsmuir miners, blacksmiths and joiners' shops emerged into a small city with a theatre where the great names of vaudeville and stage entertained, a hotel, boarding houses, a school, shops and a bicycle racing track reported to be the finest in the Pacific Northwest.

Nanaimo now had a growing population of Chinese residents. Dunsmuir recognized the potential workforce and had no qualms about hiring them, unlike his competitor, the Vancouver Coal Company, which excluded the Chinese workers. When the Royal Commission on Chinese Immigration held hearings, Dunsmuir spoke favourably for his Asian workers:

> If it were not for Chinese labor the business I am engaged in, especially coal mining, would be seriously retarded and curtailed, and it would be impossible to sell this product and compete favorably in the market of San Francisco.[13]

In August 1876, Dunsmuir named his son James, now 25, superintendent of the Wellington mine operation. James was not like his outgoing, friendly father, but was cautious and wary, often regarded as cold and haughty, a bit impatient and quite demanding. He did not warm to the miners, and in his first two years, he experienced labour trouble.

The Dunsmuirs paid workers $2 to $4 per day for white men and half as much for Chinese. They used a considerable number of Chinese workers in their mines, which caused ill will among whites looking for work. There was no effective union, and attempts by the men to bring pressure on management by withdrawing their services were met by importing strikebreakers. Ugly situations developed several times, notably in 1877, when troops were brought in to maintain order.

In 1878, 88,000 tons of coal was mined, and the output that year had doubled from the previous year. The next year it increased again, to 113,000 tons, making the Wellington Colliery the largest producer of coal on Vancouver Island.

Family Connections

Robert and Joan Dunsmuir had arrived on Vancouver Island with two daughters, Elizabeth and Agnes. The family increased in size when James was born at Fort Vancouver and Alexander in Nanaimo. Six more daughters rounded out the family: Marion, Mary Jean, Emily Ellen, Jessie, Annie and Henriette Maude. Giving birth every two years and raising eight children could not have been easy for Joan, especially in those early years when they could not afford to hire a housekeeper or nanny.

The two boys garnered the most attention from their father, as they were considered heirs to the coal empire now being developed. Dunsmuir considered Alex the most business savvy of his sons. Alex attended college in Ontario, and in 1874, when he returned to Nanaimo, went to work for his father and became his right-hand man. Alex is credited with successfully circulating a petition that resulted in the incorporation of the City of Nanaimo. Four years later, Alex was sent to San Francisco to manage the office there, his father having decided he no longer needed the expertise of Harry Berryman.

James apprenticed with the Willamette Ironworks in Portland, Oregon, and then attended the Virginia Agricultural and Mechanical College in Blacksburg, studying mining engineering before joining the family's Wellington mine operation.

Over the years, Robert Dunsmuir had grudgingly gained the respect of the miners, who referred to him as "the old man." He was a hard-working, hard-drinking Scot who was a homegrown success story. He was everywhere and on every committee that functioned in the small community of Nanaimo, a member of the school board and the court of revisions, and was justice of the peace. There was little that happened in Nanaimo that didn't get his attention. Complaints were handled directly, and he kept a keen eye for business opportunities. The *Nanaimo Free Press*, which began publishing in 1874, praised him for his efforts on behalf of the community:

> When you see a spirited man have the grit to go into an enter-
> prise, run chances and when he succeeds that man deserves
> credit. The people of Nanaimo can look Mr. Dunsmuir in the
> face and say they feel proud of him. He started on a small capi-
> tal and through his industry and sagacity; he is today a credit
> to himself and an honour to Nanaimo.[14]

When the Nanaimo Literary Institute was founded in 1863, it was not so surprising to see Robert Dunsmuir's name listed as one of the founders, alongside Mark Bate, who became the first mayor of Nanaimo. In 1869, these two men, along with John Bryden and a group of citizens, petitioned Governor Anthony Musgrave for financial aid for public works and the Literary Institute, plus construction of a proper schoolhouse, and urged reciprocity with the United States. Their petition was printed in the *Colonist*, October 25, 1869.

The Colony of Vancouver Island was unsure about Confederation, and there were some who favoured joining their neighbour to the south. President Ulysses Grant received a petition signed by 43 Victorians in favour of joining the United States. The Nanaimo petition added fuel for the movement against Confederation. The *British Colonist* dismissed the petition as the work of "foreigners," men of European ancestry who had come to the Island by way of San Francisco, which could be said for most of the people on Vancouver Island at that time.

Dunsmuir was kept busy with all his business interests, but he took time off in January 1875 to preside at the Burns Supper in Nanaimo, on the 116th anniversary of the birth of the Scottish poet. He spoke of how the poet's memory was revered. He told his audience that he had seen the thatched cottage where the poet had lived, and how glad he was to see so many present to honour Burns.[15]

Historical references to Dunsmuir seldom refer to his speech pattern, probably because few can write the Scottish dialect. Without a language of their own, the Scots have found a unique way of communicating with each other. A manuscript in the British Columbia Archives written by Michael Manson is the exception. Manson, from the Shetland Islands, Scotland, came to Nanaimo to look for work and went to Wellington to ask Robert Dunsmuir for a job. Dunsmuir's Scottish accent comes out loud and clear in Manson's recollection of his meeting:

> and when I saw him he asked me where I came from
> and when I told him I came from the Shetland Islands,
> he said, "Ay man ye will ken gay weal how to handle they
> mules."[16]

Dunsmuir told him to come back on Monday and he would give him a job. Manson didn't go to work in the Wellington mines, but instead began working for the Vancouver Coal Company in Nanaimo.

There was another Scot in Dunsmuir's life, John Bryden. He was born in Riccarton, Ayrshire, in 1831, and like Dunsmuir, had served his apprenticeship in the Ayrshire mines before being signed on by the HBC. There is little information about him before this time. He was hired in 1863 to take over as "coal viewer" for 300 pounds sterling per year, and in 1866 he was assistant manager of the Vancouver Coal Company mines.

Bryden, a tall, handsome man, cemented his role in the community by marrying Dunsmuir's eldest daughter, Elizabeth, in 1867. The young couple was married in St. Andrew's Presbyterian Church in Nanaimo on September 27, 1866. The new son-in-law was admired and respected by Dunsmuir, who considered him a valued friend and confidant. When Bryden resigned his position with the Vancouver Coal Company, Dunsmuir offered him a job as manager of the Wellington mine. Meanwhile, James, who had struggled as manager, was given the less demanding job of loading the coal carriers on the Departure Bay wharves.

In 1883, Dunsmuir bought out his partner, Diggle, thus taking total control of the company, which now realized profits of $500,000 a year. The company was renamed R. Dunsmuir & Sons. With the company firmly in family control, Robert Dunsmuir began to seek new challenges.

Building a Railway

When British Columbia entered Confederation in 1871, one of the conditions under the Terms of Union was the construction of a railway connecting the eastern provinces to the Pacific coast. Construction was to begin in 1873. The railway would meet the sea at Bute Inlet, cross Quadra Island and bridge Seymour Narrows to reach Vancouver Island, 85 miles north of Nanaimo and 160 miles from the proposed terminus at Esquimalt, east of Victoria. However, surveys of the route showed the impracticability of building a railway connection to Vancouver Island. The route on the island itself also had problems, especially finding a way around the mountainous Malahat Ridge north of Victoria.

In 1874, in anticipation of a railway, the BC government established a railway land reserve 20 miles in width along the east coast of the Island between Seymour Narrows and Esquimalt. The legislation became known as the Esquimalt and Nanaimo Railway Act. Vancouver Island residents considered the construction of a railway from Nanaimo to Esquimalt a necessity, and when no progress was made on its construction, they threatened secession.

John Bryden, an Ayrshire miner, was hired as a mine manager for the Vancouver Coal Mines in Nanaimo. He married Robert Dunsmuir's daughter Elizabeth.
IMAGE 11-250 COURTESY OF NANAIMO MUSEUM

So serious was the situation that an arbitrator was sent to calm the troubled waters. Lord Carnarvon, the British Colonial Secretary, ruled that the section of line between Nanaimo and Esquimalt must be an integral part of the railway system, and it was a Dominion Government responsibility to arrange construction of such a railway.

Dunsmuir formed the Esquimalt and Nanaimo Railway Company and petitioned the British Columbia Legislative Assembly to give it authority to construct the railway. Dunsmuir knew about railways, having built several to service his coal mine in Wellington. In 1875, Prime Minister Alexander Mackenzie introduced a bill in Parliament to give cash and land to Dunsmuir's company to build the railway. The bill passed the House but was defeated in the Senate by a vote of 23 to 22. Residents of British Columbia were incensed because they believed that Mackenzie had rigged the vote. So angered were they that Governor General Lord Dufferin was sent to the western province to heal wounds. He was met in Victoria by a banner proclaiming "Carnarvon Terms or Separation."

The railway problem on Vancouver Island had yet to be resolved in 1882 when another Governor General came to Victoria hoping to bring about a resolution and promote better feelings between the two levels of government. The Marquis of Lorne, and Princess Louise, Queen Victoria's daughter, visited the province and met with Dunsmuir, who was reluctant to put his own money into the construction and operation of the railway. When the Marquis persisted, Dunsmuir consented, but under his terms. He wanted land, coal, a money subsidy and freedom from taxation for the railway lands, and both levels of government had to agree to his terms.

This same year, Dunsmuir was elected to the provincial legislature to represent Nanaimo. He never campaigned, knocked on doors or held public meetings to garner support. Instead he relied on the recognition factor; his name was a household word in Nanaimo. The most important issue of the day was the railway. He was so sure of his election that he went off on a trip to Scotland.

Dunsmuir's first attempt to get the railway contract had failed, but now he felt certain he would get approval. Unknown to him, a competing bid had been submitted from a San Francisco syndicate headed by Lewis Clements, who proposed a line all the way to Seymour Narrows. Prime Minister John A. Macdonald decided the province should decide between the two bidders. The House dissolved in April, with only the Clements bid receiving government approval. Dunsmuir was in Glasgow when he learned the news. His concern was only short-lived when he heard that Clements did not have secure financial backing and had not asked for a cash subsidy. Dunsmuir was back in business when Clements's contract collapsed.

Dunsmuir was the right man at the right time in the right place: he could have remained in the coal industry, acquiring a fortune even before the railway was an issue, but he chose to accept a new challenge. His demands, or terms, have made many shake their head in disbelief that he could have been so bold. Residents of the Island were outraged when they learned of the terms. Prime Minister Macdonald shrugged off all criticism. He said:

> We want more Dunsmuirs, more men of action, less men of straw and cheek, and more men of brains and energy to complete our provincial destiny.[17]

In addition to the 1,900,000 acres, Dunsmuir received $750,000. Only the land pre-empted by settlers was excluded from the vast tract of land along the east side of Vancouver Island. Where Native reserves, Crown grants, military reservations and leases existed, he and his partners were given an equal area of land in the Peace River Block. In addition, all coal, coal oil, ores, stones, clay, marble and minerals were granted, all free from taxation, just to construct 73 miles of railway. If there was a downside, it was that Dunsmuir had to raise over $2 million—but the sale of forest lands alone, from only a small portion, netted him $25 million.

The contract to build the railway was signed by Robert Dunsmuir, James Dunsmuir, John Bryden and four American railroad tycoons of the Central Pacific Railroad: Leyland Stanford, Charles Crocker, Collis Huntingdon and Mark Hopkins. Construction of the railway began on May 6, 1884. The formidable Malahat section lay in the way of the route to Esquimalt. Dunsmuir knew a young engineer, Joseph Hunter, who had searched for railway passes for the CPR on the mainland, and on a single sheet of paper he instructed him to "build the railway." The young man was able to overcome the mountainous obstacles that confronted him.

Meanwhile, the Canadian Pacific Railway (CPR) neared completion of its transcontinental rail line into Port Moody. The Last Spike ceremony was held on November 7, 1885, at Craigellachie, a place few in British Columbia could spell or even pronounce, and named for a mountain in Morayshire, Scotland.

The E & N rails were laid into Nanaimo on February 26, 1886. The Island railway also had a spike ceremony when Sir John A. Macdonald hammered in a silver spike on a rail near Shawnigan Lake on August 13, 1886, declaring it an extension of the CPR. He congratulated Dunsmuir on the completion of the railway. Dunsmuir and Macdonald were both Scots and friends, and shared the same political views and love of whisky. The story has been told many times of how after a meal at the Royal Hotel in Nanaimo, the two men went to inspect Dunsmuir's mine, and there they privately toasted the completion of the railway in traditional Scottish fashion with a wee dram o' whisky. Daily rail service began in September, leaving from Russell's Station in Victoria West at 8:00 a.m. and returning at 5:40 p.m. During the first year of operation, the company's four Schenectady-built 4-4-0 locomotives, four passenger cars and 70 freight cars handled 13,000 passengers and over 8,000 tons of freight. However, it was not until March that trains entered Victoria, after a swing bridge across the harbour was completed at Dunsmuir's expense.

A Castle for Joan

I will make a palace fit for you and me.
Of green days in forests and blue days at sea.
—*Robert Louis Stevenson*

Dunsmuir moved from Nanaimo to Victoria to live, leaving James, Alex and John Bryden in charge of the mining operation.

The Royal Hotel on Wharf Street was where Sir John A. Macdonald and Robert Dunsmuir began celebrating the completion of the Esquimalt and Nanaimo Railway on August 13, 1886. They finished the toast below ground with a little whisky, away from the prying eyes of their wives.

IMAGE 2000 032 A-P16 COURTESY OF NANAIMO COMMUNITY ARCHIVES

Dunsmuir had promised his wife, Joan, a castle, and in 1882 he purchased land with a view over Victoria. More land was acquired until he had 28 acres, enough to build a spectacular castle. Until it was built, the couple lived in Fairview, across the street from the legislative buildings. The castle, with a tower, was named Craigdarroch after the Scottish home of Annie Laurie, the woman made famous by Scottish poet Robert Burns. Portland architect Warren H. Williams designed it, and the castle was said to be the most expensive residence ever built in western Canada. Construction began in 1887. Craigdarroch Castle contained a billiard room, a ballroom, a library, 35 fireplaces and a living room 63 feet long. The exterior was of sandstone quarried in the Duncan area, but items such as the leaded glass windows came from Italy.

Robert Dunsmuir had Craigdarroch Castle built in Victoria for his wife, Joan. It took three years to complete, from 1887 to 1890. Craigdarroch means "rocky oak place" in Gaelic.

Dunsmuir was re-elected MLA for Nanaimo in 1886, even though he now lived in Victoria; this fact did not seem to trouble his hometown voters. They knew this man and knew he would represent them well. A year later, he became president of the executive council, a post he held until his death.

The death of Dunsmuir came as a shock to the province, his friends and his family. He had been ill for a few days but was not considered in danger. Then, late in the evening of April 12, 1889, he died at his residence with Joan by his bedside. The couple had been together 42 years. He never saw his castle completed, nor did he have the anticipated knighthood bestowed by the Queen, but he did see the E & N Railway arrive in Victoria, probably the most satisfying achievement for the veteran miner. Son-in-law John Bryden completed Dunsmuir's term as MLA.

Robert Dunsmuir's funeral on April 16, 1889, was the largest ever held in Victoria, with an estimated 12,000 people lining the route to St. Andrew's Church and on to Ross Bay Cemetery. The mines at Wellington and Nanaimo closed; hundreds took advantage of free passes on the E & N Railway to attend his funeral. All schools and shops in his hometown and Victoria closed, and flags flew at half-mast.

Six days later, this special remembrance sketch, entitled "The Old Man of the Mountain," appeared in the *Nanaimo Free Press*:

> That the Old Man learns with deep regret of the death of Robert Dunsmuir, for his energy, perseverance and enterprise have made the valley skirting Mount Benson blossom as a rose, while the smoke issuing from the tall chimneys showed that he was extracting the "black diamonds" from the Millstream Valley to warm many a fireside and make home cheerful.
>
> The Old Man feels that in the death of the "coal king," as he familiarly called, the needy and the distressed have lost a kind and generous friend. The Old Man feels confident that the young Dunsmuirs will follow closely the pathway trodden by their departed parent.
>
> That more people were to be seen on Commercial Street this afternoon, than for some weeks past, Nanaimo is beginning to resume its former air of rush and business which is very interesting to the Old Man who has taken a paternal interest in the City for many, many years.

Dunsmuir was survived by his wife, Joan, their two sons, James and Alex, and eight daughters: Elizabeth, Agnes, Marion, Mary, Emily Ellen, Jessie, Effie and Maude.[18] Robert Dunsmuir left control of the estate to Joan. James became president of the Wellington Colliery, and Alex became president of the Esquimalt and Nanaimo Railway Company. Alex continued living in San Francisco, while James moved from Departure Bay to Victoria

Robert Dunsmuir, the canny Scot who built a mining empire, a railway and a castle, and became the richest man in the Colony of Vancouver Island.
IMAGE COURTESY OF CRAIGDARROCH MUSEUM SOCIETY

to take over the company office.

Joan took a trip to Scotland. Craigdarroch Castle was not yet completed, and she left Fairview to James and his family. She signed over power of attorney to her sons, and then left them to finish the castle construction and manage the mines. Robert Dunsmuir probably thought he had done the best for his family by leaving Joan in charge of everything, but in fact this action left the family divided. Joan moved into Craigdarroch Castle in 1890 with her daughters and shocked everyone, including her sons, by announcing she was selling Wellington Colliery. Alex and James had worked all their lives in the mining industry; neither had received salaries, but were advanced money when needed. They helped the family prosper, only to see all the profits now go directly to their mother, who had no interest in keeping the mine.

Joan was convinced to relinquish control over the San Francisco operation managed by Alex, and after months of arguments she gave her sons a share in both the E & N Railway and the mines, but she kept control of other family holdings such as the Canadian Pacific Navigation Company, the Albion Iron Works

Hatley Castle was James and Laura Dunsmuir's rather grand home in Victoria.

and real-estate properties in Nanaimo and Victoria. She eventually sold the Wellington Colliery to James for $410,000. He moved the town and the mining operation south of Nanaimo, to Extension. By this time, the Wellington mine was almost played out.

After years of excessive alcohol consumption, Alex died on January 31, 1900, leaving James in total control of the mines. He was now one of the richest coal-mining operators in Canada and the province's largest employer. The Dunsmuir name was recognized throughout the province and across Canada, a legacy left by his father, and like his father, James knew where the power lay and so in 1898, he entered politics and was elected MLA in Nanaimo South. In 1900 he became premier of British Columbia, and in 1906 was appointed BC's Lieutenant-Governor.

Joan was firmly established in Craigdarroch Castle when James built his own mansion, which he named Hatley Castle, completed in 1908. It was situated on 650 acres overlooking Esquimalt

Lieutenant-Governor James Dunsmuir followed in his father Robert's footsteps in the mining industry. He then entered politics, becoming premier in 1900 and lieutenant-governor in 1906. He remained in that post until 1909.

IMAGE COURTESY OF CRAIGDARROCH MUSEUM SOCIETY

Lagoon outside Victoria. Samuel Maclure, the leading architect of the time, designed the castle, which was surrounded by beautiful gardens. These two castles remain landmarks today in Victoria.

When Joan died in 1908, the contents of her home were sold at auction and the estate subdivided. In 1910, James sold the family mining operation to Donald Mann and William Mackenzie for $10 million, adding to his already substantial fortune. The E & N Railway had already been sold in 1905 to the Canadian Pacific Railway.

James and his wife, Laura, enjoyed a good life; their home was the setting for many parties and balls enjoyed by their 10 children. Unfortunately, the carefree days ended when their third son, known as Boy, went down with the *Lusitania* when it was torpedoed in 1915 en route to engage in battle in the First World War. The lights went out at Hatley Castle! The death of his son was a devastating blow for James; it is said he secluded himself in his study, where he played a record with the tune *Where Is My Wandering Boy Tonight?*

In spite of all of James's accomplishments and his large healthy family, he was not a happy man. He may have been a millionaire, but money did not bring him contentment. His last few years

Resembling a row of little angels, James and Laura Dunsmuir's daughters are all dressed in white for this photo. Left to right: Kathleen, Jessie Muriel, Joan Marion, Emily, Laura May and Elizabeth. PHOTOGRAPHER RICHARD MAYNARD 1893. IMAGE 12-107 COURTESY OF NANAIMO MUSEUM

were spent on his yacht *Dolaura*. When he died at Cowichan in June 1920, he was the richest man in British Columbia; his estate was valued at over $3.5 million. Hatley Castle went to Laura, who also pined after her lost son. When she died in 1937, her surviving children had scattered and had no interest in business. The mining operation and the railway had already been sold. The Dunsmuir name, once so prominent in business and political circles, disappeared in the next generation.

CHAPTER 7

Colony Population Doubles

More Miners for Nanaimo

Another 80 new immigrants arrived in Fort Victoria on the barque *Tory* in the spring of 1851. As the ship entered the harbour, Charles Fish, who was in charge of the 16 cannons, fired the usual salute of welcome, using a blank charge from the fort's cannon. His brother had decided to join him and work for the Company, and as he stood at the railing of the ship waiting to disembark, somehow the cannon fired early and severed his right arm. As Fish searched for his brother, he lay fighting for his life. He died a few hours later. This was the only life taken by one of the fort's cannons.[1]

There were 125 labourers and their families aboard, including 18 recruits from Orkney, two with wives. These new arrivals almost doubled the number of people living in the colony. Unfortunately, there had been no attempt to provide accommodation for the newcomers, and they were herded like cattle into a number of Company sheds that held 25 to 30 people per building, married or single. The sheds provided no privacy, and pride was a luxury they had left behind in Scotland.

Some men were sent to farms, while eight others were sent to Fort Rupert. These included James Sabiston and John Malcolm, from

Stromness, Orkney. Sabiston's two other brothers, John and Peter, sailed on the *Norman Morison*. Others from Orkney included James Stove, a labourer and shipmaster; William Isbister, a stonemason; John and Margaret Work, and William Work, brother of John; and Peter Papley, a blacksmith. Papley's brother Alexander came on the *Norman Morison*. Also aboard the *Tory* were Mary and Andrew Hunter, a steam engineer from Kilmarnock, Ayrshire, and Adam Grant Horne, from Kirkwall, Orkney. All expected to find an active coal mine at Fort Rupert, but instead were put to work doing menial tasks, with no coal works in sight.

The First Engineer: Andrew Hunter

The *Tory* brought the first qualified engineer to Vancouver Island. Andrew Hunter, his wife, Mary, their daughter, Agnes, and sons John, Thomas and Andrew joined the ship in London on the long journey to Vancouver Island. The ship carried mining equipment valued at 1,000 pounds, including drilling rods and a steam engine for the mine at Fort Rupert. To ensure the engine was well taken care of, Hunter was hired in July 1850 at the request of John Muir, who knew him to be a "hard working industrious mechanick."[2]

The Hunters first viewed Fort Victoria on May 12, 1851. It would have been a glorious sight after such a long journey and a happy occasion for most passengers, but for the Hunters there would have been mixed emotions, for on the voyage their son Andrew suffered what was termed "an infection of the brain." He survived five more years and died in Nanaimo at the age of six.[3]

Andrew Hunter was born in 1812 in Beith, a small village with a population of over 3,000 located 18 miles southwest of Glasgow and 22 miles north of Ayr. In negotiating his contract, Hunter's main concern had been for his children and who would pay for their travel expenses. The Company reluctantly agreed to give him more travelling money and also to employ his oldest son, John, but his rate of pay would be left for the Fort Rupert management to decide.

The Hunters arrived in Fort Rupert only to discover there was no coal mine, only the hope that one could be developed. While waiting for the final decision on the location of the steam engine, Hunter worked at clearing John Muir's pit and helped with blacksmithing. Mary added to the family in 1852 with the birth of son William, claimed to be the first white male child born in the Colony of Vancouver Island.

When the Company workforce was slowly moved south to Nanaimo, Hunter remained behind until May 1853, awaiting the transfer of the steam engine. Life in Nanaimo for the engineer remained in limbo. He had looked after the engine as he was required to do, but it sat idle and had not been fired up; instead, he was employed building the coal wharf and the Bastion. When Hunter advised the office-in-charge, Joseph William McKay, that he had changed his mind about working coal, he was put to work building chimneys for John Muir's house.[4] At this stage of development in Nanaimo, it was just as important to house people as it was to find coal.

When the Hunter family first arrived in Nanaimo, they lived in one of the small log cabins built for the miners along what is now known as Front Street, and then later moved to a Company house located on the site of the present-day Palace Hotel on Skinner Street. Later Andrew built a large house for his growing family on Irwin Street. His son John lived on Haliburton Street, and son William lived on Nicol Street.[5]

Coal was slowly being mined, with some miners producing up to two tons a day. The HBC workbook made two entries—the amount of coal produced by the miners, and that produced by the Natives. The miners were paid by what they produced, while the Natives received trinkets or tickets for every tub of coal, which were then exchanged at the Company store for a variety of trade goods.

Douglas was pleased with the progress. After visiting the town, he declared that the settlement had every appearance of a little village. The surface buildings of the Number One Shaft sat in the

Eight miners take a break to pose for a photo outside the coal shaft. Standing, left to right: Andrew Hunter, Nels Nord, Robert Wenborn Sr., Fred Pafford. Seated, left to right: Timothy O'Sullivan, Robert Wenborn Jr., William Lewis, Horace Decker. IMAGE 03-2 COURTESY OF NANAIMO MUSEUM

middle of the village. The shaft had a square chimney of quarried stone built by Orcadian stonemason William Isbister, and a low log building housed the hoisting gear and the steam engine. A pithead frame built by a carpenter supported the steam engine.

Douglas expressed some anguish about getting Hunter's steam engine ready, but he was also concerned there would not be enough houses built to accommodate the additional 40 Scottish miners scheduled to arrive on the return of the *Norman Morison*:

> I fear the erection of the steam engine just at present will cause considerable delay, but I presume it cannot be deferred without retarding the operations in the shaft. Whatever is done in the premises keep two points constantly in view, that is to get out as much coal as you possibly can, and to get as many houses put up as possible for the reception of the miners on their arrival in this country.[6]

Providing housing for the incoming miners was difficult. The mining operation constantly needed a great deal of lumber, and there was not enough for both enterprises. McKay complained that the window sashes and doors took a long time to make, and suggested it would help if these and the lumber could be supplied from Victoria. He must have convinced Douglas, for he approved of the purchase. By September 1853, Francis Côte was contracted to build 20 detached houses, each containing four rooms and with a chimney in the centre, so each house could accommodate one or two families, with separate entrances for each family. The shingles were being shipped from Fort Rupert.

This must have been a difficult time for Hunter. He would have agonized over the state of his steam engine, for in preparing it for start-up, he found many of the parts were corroded, and it took time to clean and put all in working order. The engine had sat idle in Fort Rupert since it had arrived on Vancouver Island.

On November 7, 1853, the steam engine was started up. However, the feeding arrangements for the steam boiler were incomplete, and the engine was stopped until pipes were laid for feeding the boiler from the water discharged by the pit pump.[7] On December 2, a second boiler was connected to the engine.

Finally the big start-up day arrived, and it created a great deal of excitement in the village. Watching intently were special guests James Douglas and his wife, Amelia, who were joined by miners, labourers and Snuneymuxw, all anxious to see and hear the engine, now nicknamed the "Lady McKay," make its first splut-tering sound. Slowly the engine began pumping out water from the Number One Shaft. This must have seemed like a miraculous event for the Natives, who had never seen new technology at work. A year later a large circular saw blade was fitted to the steam engine flywheel, making it useful in sawing lumber, which was then cut into suitable lengths for building material.[8] Since the steam engine was only required for mining eight hours a day, it was used for sawing lumber for the remainder of each day.

In 1853 the Hunters took in a boarder who would become an important member of the family. He was Charles Alfred

Bayley, sent to Nanaimo by Douglas to teach the children of the Company's servants and "labouring class." The Bayley family had come from Essex, England; Charles's father was hired as bailiff for the Uplands Farm. Young Charles taught school in Fort Victoria until he was sent to Nanaimo.

The small school in Nanaimo was housed in a small log cabin on Skinner Street, behind the present-day Bygone Books, on Commercial Street. Later the school moved into the old Stone House on Front Street.

Bayley had signed a five-year contract as a labourer with the HBC in 1850 and had come to Fort Victoria on the *Tory*, the same ship that brought the Hunters. On board, he had run a library and conducted classes for the children and some adult passengers. Douglas did not find him useful as a labourer, so appointed him schoolmaster in 1852, at a salary of 40 pounds sterling a year. Parents added another pound for each child and supplied books and paper. Bayley has been described as "a small dapper man, a feisty Londoner, well educated, moral and fiery...full of sparkle and wit, he never took himself too seriously."[9]

Agnes, the Hunters' teenage daughter, and Bayley were married on Christmas Eve, 1854, by Douglas aboard ship in Nanaimo Harbour. Douglas was in town to sign a treaty with the Snuneymuxw, the last of the 14 treaties negotiated on Vancouver Island. The treaty was signed on December 23. Adam Grant Horne wrote in his diary this brief but succinct notice: "Mr. Bayley married at 7 p.m." This was the first recorded marriage in Nanaimo. Their first child, a boy, was born on October 1855. The couple would have five more children.

Unhappy with his appointment in Nanaimo due to the lack of supplies and salary, when Bayley completed his contract with the HBC in 1856, the couple returned to Victoria, where Charles opened a store selling supplies to gold miners. He later built the Bayley Hotel at the corner of Government and Yates streets.

Bayley served in the Third House of Assembly from September 3,

1863, to June 21, 1865, as Nanaimo's fourth representative. He was very familiar with the interests of the community. Yet, at a public meeting held in October 1864 to review his political career, Chairman Robert Dunsmuir quietly dismissed the dismal crowd of 13, whose number probably reflected the inertia of political opinion at the time.[10]

Thomas Cunningham, owner of the general store in Nanaimo, succeeded Bayley.

Bad health led Bayley to sell the Victoria store and move his family to Dallas, Oregon. Another move in 1870 took the family to San Francisco to seek further medical treatment. He died in 1899.

Andrew Hunter narrowly escaped death in a mine accident that occurred on May 3, 1876, taking the life of one man. It was an early spring day when Hunter and mine carpenter George William Gregor descended below ground at the Douglas Shaft. Reid, the hoisting engineer, was unaware of their presence until it was too late to stop them from stepping on board the cage, which then plummeted 300 feet to the bottom. Reid sounded the emergency whistle, and the mine rescue squad responded at the pithead. Harry Bolton volunteered to be lowered to the bottom of the shaft at the end of a 3.5-inch manila rope with his feet in a loop; he clung tightly, soon disappearing out of sight. When Bolton signalled to be brought up, the rope was attached to the steam engine and elevated him slowly. He emerged from the shaft holding the limp body of Hunter, more dead than alive. Bolton said he had found the cable coiled around on top of the cage and saw a figure emerge from the crushed cage. He'd taken a quick look inside and seen Gregor directly under the full weight of the cable, crushed to death. He was 35 years of age. Although in terrible agony, Hunter put his good leg into the loop and then halfway up, passed out with Bolton hanging onto him. Bolton was exhausted by the time he reached the top.

Hunter, his leg broken in two places, was rushed to the village hospital, where he remained to recuperate for several weeks.

Gregor's body was recovered and laid to rest in the cemetery on Wallace Street.

A board of inquiry heard the testimony of Reid, Harry Bolton and Andrew Hunter. Hunter said that he and Gregor had gone to the shaft to solve some problem underground but had not notified Reid they were boarding the cage. Although Reid was cleared of any responsibility, he resigned from his job: the shock of seeing a man killed was too much for him. The Vancouver Coal Company was found guilty of neglect for not having installed keepers on top of the shaft where the cage could rest. Only a lever controlled by the engineer could release the keepers before the cage could be lowered. Andrew Hunter said it was the sump at the bottom of the shaft that saved him from being crushed to death. He recuperated but was no longer able to go below ground, so was placed in charge of the machine shop and the Lady McKay. The steam engine was destroyed in 1880, when a fire engulfed the machine shop.

Andrew Hunter died at his home on January 4, 1884, at age 73. The *Nanaimo Free Press* obituary advised, "the funeral will take place from his late residence near the Vancouver Coal Company Machine Shops (Esplanade) on Sunday afternoon at 3 p.m. The deceased was a jovial companion and highly respected by his numerous friends." Mary died in 1904.

The young engineer, who had come to Vancouver Island with his wife and such high hopes for a better future, left many grandchildren to continue the Hunter lineage. Eldest son John married Mary Guillion, and they had 12 children; Thomas and his wife, Martha Smith Frew, had 5 children; William, who was born in Fort Rupert, married Mary Ann Wenborn, and they had 7 children.

Prospector Extraordinaire: John Dick

John Dick came from a large family of miners in Ayrshire. His parents, James and Sarah Dick, and siblings James, Robert, Archibald, Christine, Sarah and Isabella, all came to Nanaimo at different times. They were all educated in Scotland; when the boys reached 10 years of age, they became wage earners in the mining industry. John remembered working with his father and brothers in a coal mine in the small village of Dreghorn, about two miles from Dunsmuir's father's mines. The village, near Irvine in Ayrshire, is known as one of Britain's oldest inhabited villages, dating back 5,000 years, and was also the birthplace of John Boyd Dunlop, the inventor of the pneumatic tire.

John Dick, born in 1834, was the first one in his family to arrive on the coast when he joined other miners in California prospecting for gold. After returning to Nanaimo, he signed on with a group searching for coal in Burrard Inlet. John seemed to have the ability to find coal. He sunk a borehole 600 feet into a thick seam of coal at Deadman's Island, located in what is now known as Coal Harbour. The coal was of poor quality and was never mined, but the harbour became a centre for shipbuilding, sawmilling and other industries. Today these have been replaced by the Bayshore Inn and marinas.

For the next three years, John prospected for gold during the Cariboo gold rush, and when he returned to Nanaimo, he began working with Robert Dunsmuir and James (Jimmy) Hamilton, both independent miners, outside of the Vancouver Coal Company's jurisdiction.

In 1865 sisters Sarah and Isabella and their parents emigrated from Scotland to join John in Nanaimo. Sarah was already married to Alexander Galloway, and Isabella married William Reid in St. Andrew's Presbyterian Church, Nanaimo, in 1871. John, then 38, married 19-year-old Esther Ann Richardson a year later in the Wesleyan Methodist Church (St. Andrew's Presbyterian Church was without a minister at the time). Esther's parents, John and Seadonah Richardson, were *Princess Royal* pioneers.[11]

Over the years, John and Esther had 10 children, who remembered their father as being a kind man but a stern disciplinarian. Esther cooked oatmeal for breakfast every morning; the children could have nothing else until it was finished, and she was strict about church attendance. Every Saturday, all the shoes in the house had to be cleaned and left on a bench on their back porch ready for church on Sunday morning.[12]

When the City of Nanaimo incorporated in 1874, John was elected to the first city council under Mayor Mark Bate, joining John Bryden, Richard Nightingale, Richard Brinn, John Pawson, William Raybould and John Hirst. He served only one term, but it was an important year for the city. The first official business was procuring a city seal, establishing an assessment roll and taking a census in the city. The population of the city was then 1,500.

A year later, John went into partnership with Adam Grant Horne and Peter Sabiston in what was known as the Sabiston-Horne Mine, today better known as the Jingle Pot Mine—an odd name for a mine, but according to folklore, when a lone miner wanted to come to the surface, he would jingle a pot full of stones that was suspended on a tripod to signal he wanted the man on the winch to pull him up.

Building contractor Jacob Blessing joined the partnership to open the mine. The Minister of Mines report for 1879 noted: "A first-class seam of coal was found under the estate of Messrs. Sabiston and Horne by Mr. John Dick. This very valuable property is within two miles of Nanaimo Harbour."[13] The mine produced excellent coal. Dunsmuir, Diggle and Company took over the mine from 1881 to 1896. John was among a group of miners who sat for their manager's ticket exam in 1878.

Robert Dunsmuir recognized John's ability to find coal and hired him to search throughout the province. As well as the Sabiston-Horne Mine, John also found coal for the Vancouver Coal Company at Chase River; at the East Wellington mine for Robert Chandler; and at the Cumberland and Comox mines and the Alexandra mine for Dunsmuir. He also supervised the building of the aerial tramway for the Harewood Mine, the tramway that carried coal from the mine to the coal wharves at Nanaimo.

In this photo of Nanaimo's first mayor and council, Councillor John Dick is directly to the right of Mayor Mark Bate, the central figure. At the top is Councillor John Bryden. IMAGE JI-2 COURTESY OF NANAIMO MUSEUM

In 1894, James Dunsmuir appointed John manager of the Alexandra Mine in South Wellington. The family's connection with the area is reflected in a street named Dick Avenue. John would have been right at home in the Alexandra Mine, as Scottish miners figured prominently in the workforce. This was not a large mine and only produced for a few years between 1882 and 1902. Locals called the area Mushtown because of the amount of oatmeal that was eaten there every morning. The Scots are known to enjoy a good plate of porridge to start their day!

The Scottish miners also kept the old country traditions alive by celebrating Hogmanay, the last night of the old year. Miners climbed a ridge above South Wellington and poured small amounts of blasting powder into the stumps of old-growth trees left over when the settlers pre-empted land. At the stroke of midnight they celebrated by lighting the powder; the blasts brought in the New Year in style. Adding to the noisy cacophony of sounds, the men fired their shotguns into the air. Then they went first-footing. Each home waited for a dark-haired man to come knocking on their door, carrying a lump of coal in one hand and a bottle of Scotch whisky in the other. The lump of coal was to signal good luck and a good year ahead. They were welcomed into the home, and the celebrations would continue into the wee sma' hours.[14]

A number of deaths in the family saddened the Dick family in the late 1890s. John's sister Isabella Reid died in 1895, and his other sister, Sarah Galloway, in 1898. Then a tragic accident in 1899 claimed the life of John's wife, Esther, and injured their daughter Christina. They were negotiating a hill near the settlement when the buggy they were riding in overturned and fell down an embankment, seriously injuring both women. Christina recovered from her injuries, but Esther died on November 7, 1899.[15]

John Dick died at age 68, on March 26, 1902, only a few months after he had retired. The *Nanaimo Free Press* obituary noted: "John Dick was one of British Columbia's greatest prospectors, and belonged to a class to which a province rich in mineral resources owes so much."

John's parents, James and Sarah Dick, lived on the southwest corner of Comox Road. Mark Bate remembered James Sr. as being good-natured, good-humoured and "a jocular man." He related a story that told a lot about the man:

> He kept inside his door an Aneroid Barometer, which was not apparently a very sensitive instrument. There had been a wet day, and night—the barometer indicated "Fair." Taking the Aneroid outside, Dick hung it up saying he "would let it see it was raining."[16]

Church records of St. Andrew's Presbyterian Church list Mr. and Mrs. James Dick, Archibald Dick and John Dick as among the 19 members who took the First Communion on December 30, 1866. The Dick family were lifelong members of the church. Also listed were Mr. and Mrs. Robert Dunsmuir, their daughter Elizabeth and her husband, John Bryden. The Reverend Robert Jamieson, a visiting missionary from New Westminster, conducted the Communion service.[17]

Sarah died in 1877 and was the first person buried in the new Comox Road cemetery.[18] James, who had spent all his life in the mines, both in Scotland and Nanaimo, died in 1885.

Inspector of Mines: Archibald Dick

Archibald Dick, born on Christmas Day 1840 in Kilmarnock, Ayrshire, was the youngest boy in the Dick family. Archibald made a name for himself in the mining industry in British Columbia by serving as a mine inspector for 30 years. When the family first arrived in Nanaimo, he worked for the Vancouver Coal Company. He was injured in an accidental explosion of powder in 1867. When gold was discovered in the Cariboo, he joined his brother John in 1869 to prospect for gold. Later he recalled "the dark days when night came on shortly after twelve o'clock noon, and continued until five in the morning."[19]

On his return to Nanaimo in 1872, he was hired as manager of the Baynes Sound Coal Company mine. Baynes Sound is a narrow stretch of water separating Denman Island from Vancouver Island. He remained there until the mine closed.

The government mine inspector for British Columbia was Edward Prior, who had been assistant manager of the Vancouver Coal Company in Nanaimo. Following the passage of the Coal Mines Regulation Act in 1877, he was appointed inspector of mines. When Prior resigned to go into business in May 1880, Archibald was appointed to the position and served in that capacity until 1910. Prior later became premier of British Columbia in 1902.

Archibald Dick was diligent in his job, as his mining reports will attest. He was a constant irritant to mining companies, who thought the Coal Mines Regulation Act was an infringement of their right to run their own business, as Dick demanded they comply with the new legislation. Dunsmuir was particularly stubborn, refusing to file coal returns or to post special rules informing the miners of safety problems associated with each mine. Somehow Dick worked his way through the quagmire, offering encouragement and sidestepping angry words. Safety in the mines was his mantra.

Archibald married Elizabeth Clara Westwood on January 1, 1879. She was the daughter of William and Fannie Westwood. The Westwood family operated a 650-acre farm three miles east of Wellington that was purchased in 1864 for a dollar an acre. When William died, he left his widow and their 10 children the Westwood Estate. The family sold 600 acres, with the coal rights, to San Franciscan Richard Chandler. This became the East Wellington Colliery. The Westwood name is well known in the Nanaimo area, and Westwood Lake Park is named for the family.

The young couple would have eight children: James, Fannie, William, Archie, Sarah, Clara Belle, Vallegjo and John.

Assistant Miners: The French Brothers

Adam French, 31, and Archibald French, 29, came from Muirkirk, Ayrshire, arriving on the *Pekin* in 1851 along with the Dunsmuirs and the Gilmours and signing on as assistant miners.

Their names appear many times in the 1852-54 HBC Nanaimo Daybook, but notations only give their work detail with no mention of the young men's personalities. Adam appears to have been a steady worker and diligent in his job, although on January 10, 1853, he and Robert Dunsmuir refused to empty the water out of the coal. No explanation was given about why they refused this order, or the outcome of their act of defiance. The early mines kept filling up with water, and it was not until the steam engine was used to pump out the water that the situation was resolved.

From January 1853 until August 1854, the brothers worked as assistants to Muir, Dunsmuir and McGregor. They were employed in some of the earliest Nanaimo mines. The first mine opened was in the area bounded approximately by Wharf Street, Bastion Street, Front Street and Commercial Street, including the HBC Number One mine, and extending south of Commercial and Wharf for about 200 feet. The second was the Douglas Mine, or Park Head Mine, south of Pioneer Square, under Nicol Street and Victoria Road. The third mine was centred on Front Street, at the location of the old Malaspina Hotel, and included the HBC Number Three mine. The fourth was the Newcastle Island Mine.[20]

Adzes and axes were soon replaced by picks and shovels made by the Company blacksmith, Raymond. This made the rugged hard work of digging for coal a little easier. Water was a constant problem in the early mines, and digging in the dark was another, and there were always shortages of everything needed to mine coal, including fish oil. Raymond made lamps for the miners, but they were not happy with them because the spout was only half the height of the lamp, and a greater quantity of oil was wasted than burned when the fish oil ran down the miners' foreheads.

McKay complained to Douglas and sent along a sample of the Kilmarnock lamp, which had a double spout made purposely to catch the waste oil. A hinged lid fitted snugly over the rim of the cover, which was bevelled and well soldered.[21] The sample lamp probably belonged to Dunsmuir or Gilmour. The Kilmarnock lamp was used by thousands of coal miners until electric lights replaced them in 1917.

On June 2, 1853, Adam was on the sick list. At this time, McKay wrote to Douglas, advising that only five of the assistant miners were in a healthy condition.

In August 1854, the French brothers neared the end of their contract, which expired along with Boyd Gilmour's and Robert Dunsmuir's. Around this time Douglas made a visit to Nanaimo, accompanied by his entourage of David Cameron, Dr. Benson and his secretary, Richard Colledge. He arrived on August 5, which was a Saturday, and on Sunday morning he conducted "Divine service on board the *Otter*. Prayers read by His Excellency the Governor."

On Monday he met with the miners whose terms of service had expired and came to an arrangement that the French brothers, Dunsmuir and Gilmour, would continue to work at extracting coal until a vessel was available to transport them back to England.[22] Dunsmuir decided to remain in Nanaimo, and in October 1855 he was granted a free miner's licence along with Edward Walker, whose contract had also expired. The two men were now free to work independently.

For the first time, on August 26, Douglas ordered "all" the miners to work on the coal. Gilmour was informed of the instructions. Until now, many had worked at building houses, taking care of animals, cutting logs and other chores that kept the village operating. The mining industry in Nanaimo had taken a major step forward.

Perhaps it was the thought of returning home that caused Archibald French to have a drunken encounter with a Native. On August 27, 1854, Captain Charles Edward Stuart, officer-in-charge, recorded the offence:

> Archibald French in a state of intoxication, and very riotous, running about with a loaded pistol and otherwise disturbing the peace at Nanaimo, and creating a disturbance with the Indians. Men were on the point of being taken to confine and secure him, when a stone thrown at him by an Indian whom he had beaten, which took effect behind the ear, that succeeded in silencing him. He afterwards went quietly to his home. Complaints were made about his riotous conduct by several parties.

Several negative comments were reported about his behaviour. Unfortunately, this was the last entry made about the French brothers before they returned with Gilmour to Scotland on the return voyage of the *Princess Royal*.

CHAPTER 8

The Orcadians

The Explorer: Adam Grant Horne

Adam Grant Horne was a simple but courageous young man and a valued employee of the HBC. His trek across Vancouver Island from Qualicum into the Alberni Valley (the Horne Lake Trail) opened up the Central Island and made him a celebrity of note among Vancouver Island pioneers. When he died on August 9, 1901, the *Nanaimo Free Press* reported, "Pioneer of the pioneers. Adam Grant Horne passed away yesterday evening. His personality a link between the first settlements and the living present."

Horne was born in Edinburgh on January 1, 1831, but spent his boyhood in the village of Kirkwall on his father's goose farm on the Orkney Islands. As a young man, he answered an HBC advertisement for workers for the Colony of Vancouver's Island and was signed on by Edward Clouston, the Company representative on the islands. On the long voyage to Vancouver Island aboard the barque *Tory*, he shared a steerage cabin with William Isbister, Thomas Smith, James Stove, John Malcolm and Robert Firth, all young men in their early twenties from the Orkney Islands who had also signed on with the Company.

For the next few months, the men worked as labourers in Fort

Victoria before being sent to Fort Rupert to join the other miners already recruited from Scotland. As the Nanaimo coalfield was being developed, the men were moved south in April 1853 to join miners John Muir and John McGregor, who were already there. Horne was put on the sick list, and it wasn't until July that the HBC Daybook reported he was assigned "light work that would do him no harm." There is no indication what his medical condition was at this time.

Horne never became a miner but found his niche working as a clerk in the Company store in Nanaimo. As clerk, Horne made the first formal application to Victoria to sell liquor in Nanaimo, an application that was renewed every year until 1862. The liquor was dispensed into any utensil the purchaser wished to use.

Within a few years he became fluent in Chinook, a mixture of French, English and various Native dialects that was used by traders and essential in trading for goods with the local Snuneymuxw and other area tribes. Some chiefs refused to trade with anyone but Horne, and judged him to be an honest and trustworthy friend.

A journal he started in 1854 is full of observations about fossils, coal, furs and compass readings; his entries are short and concise. He explored the east coast of the Island in Native canoes, making note of rivers, lakes and Native villages. The HBC showed its appreciation by promoting him from clerk to explorer and trader. Journal entries show meetings with chiefs of surrounding tribes and the establishment of fur-trading partnerships. Horne wanted to explore farther and indicated to Douglas a desire to make the difficult crossing of the Island between present-day Qualicum and Port Alberni, despite fears expressed by east-coast Natives about the Interior "lake Indians." Douglas called him to Victoria, where he met with Dallas and Finlayson. They agreed to provide the necessary equipment for the expedition. This was a journey that made Horne famous, and a story he told many times to his children.

The details of Horne's trek emerged in a conversation he had with Dr. William Wymond Walkem in May 1883; Walkem was the surgeon at East Wellington Colliery. His interview with Horne was published in 1914 in *Stories of Early British Columbia*. This source, plus an unpublished manuscript held by the family, detailed the dramatic expedition. The following account is from both these sources.

Nanaimo officer-in-charge Charles E. Stuart issued instructions to Horne "to proceed without delay by way of Qualicum Creek to the head waters of Barkley Sound for the purpose of opening a trade route for furs and to establish good relations with the tribes you encounter."[1] He was not to proceed farther than the highest mountain (Mount Arrowsmith), which was situated beyond the first lake (Horne Lake or Sproat Lake) in the Interior, but if the Interior tribes were peaceable, he could continue on to the sea.

Horne's travelling companion was Thomas (Toma) Quamtomy, later known as "one arm Tomo," an Iroquois employed by the HBC who had lost his arm in a fight with a young Cowichan. Others in the expedition included four Natives, three men and one woman. There was difficulty persuading any Snuneymuxw to come along on the expedition because of their previous trouble with the Interior tribes, but Horne found one whose wife had been kidnapped from the Interior when young. The other two recruits were Songhees from the Victoria area. A French Canadian named Francis Côte and an interpreter named Lafromboise also accompanied them. Côte was an experienced canoeman and knew the coast well. The expedition was supplied with strong Haida-type canoes that were excellent for rough weather. They carried with them HBC blankets for presentation to chiefs and various trinkets, mirrors and knives for trading.

The Horne expedition left Victoria at sunrise, and, after encountering strong winds and rough sea, camped overnight on Salt Spring Island and then continued the next day to Nanaimo. Horne left on May 10, 1856. He wrote in his journal:

Early the next morning Tomo awakened me saying big canoes were coming and whispered "Haidas." We all anticipated trouble. From the edge of the forest around us we could see the big canoes disappear behind the trees perhaps entering a small bay and we knew we would have to stay where we were and hoped they would be gone before the day ended. We stayed very quiet and did not light a fire. Then we heard sounds of battle and realized that a fairly large sleeping Indian rancherie or camp was being invaded. We saw a lot of smoke. Near noon the great canoes headed out to sea proceeding southwards, the men yelling and a few standing up holding human heads. We were horrified.

They lay quiet for some time, then proceeded northwest with some trepidation and saw the results of a horrific massacre. The camp was a smouldering heap. Some of the bodies were headless or mutilated.

At the edge of the camp, they found a badly wounded old woman. She was moaning, chanting and bleeding, and her face was pale. She looked at the strangers; they were the first white people she had ever seen. They gave her some rum and water, and with the aid of the interpreter, she told them what had taken place. The Haidas had carried off two young women, four little girls and two small boys. The massacre had been to avenge the killing of a Haida at Cape Mudge, where a warrior had attempted to carry off the daughter of the Euclataw chief. The Qualicums were a Euclataw sept (a division of the tribe), so the Haidas took their revenge on them. The old woman died and Horne and his party moved on.

We continued inland on our trek laden with the blankets and trinkets for peaceful tribes we hoped to see. It was very hard going carrying our heavy packs through bush, giant wide trees, slopes and creeks. We pushed on until late that day when we came across a placid large lake and there we made our camp.

We were up early the next morning, some to fish, and I took my musket and shot an elk calf which we needed for food. We hung part of the carcass high in a tree for use on the return journey. We proceeded west close to the lakeshore, preferring to be able to hide should we see Indians who could be unfriendly. A trail we found was difficult to follow and tortuous to climb with our heavy packs. Indians would never remove an object blocking a trail. They prefer to go distances around it. After fighting our way on the slight trail and up a large mountain we finally reached the top. We would see many lakes and another long arm of water which we later found to be salt water.

The expedition continued down the mountainside into the Alberni Valley, where contact was made with a tribe Horne recognized as belonging to the Nootkan group, known today as the Nuu-chah-nulth. The men wore hats made from cedar fibres with the design woven in of a man in a canoe hunting whales. Horne's height and white skin frightened them. Horne had been told that the majority of Barkley Sound Natives had never seen a white man, and they might be difficult to approach unless he succeeded in gaining their confidence and friendship.

Tomo made a fire, and they proceeded to have tea and biscuits. Horne beckoned the anxious Natives to join the party, but it was no use. Then he asked Tomo and the others to begin smoking—to make lots of smoke. Before long, one man approached and Tomo gave him his pipe, tea and biscuit. Horne had to take a bite before he would take it. Gradually, others joined them. They were given trinkets and mirrors. Later a boy approached the party

and told us he was a Songhee, captured by these Indians when he was a boy, and saying that I was the first white man they had seen, and that they were frightened. We told them we were friends and desired to meet their chief.

Tomo accompanied me while the others guarded our supplies. We were well armed. I refused to enter the chief's house when we met him. I had the Songhee tell the chief to make his men behave, to stay further away from us and not touch any of our equipment. The chief pointed to my gun. I showed him how my musket killed by downing two crows in succession, for there were many around. The men were frightened and dashed to the side of the rancherie and watched.

Horne presented the chief with a message from Finlayson inviting him and his band to bring furs and pelts to the Company posts. Then he presented them with several HBC blankets. The chief said he would trade with the great company. Many of the tribe had beaver and otter pelts, and wanted knives and blankets. After trading, they pitched camp several hundred yards away from the local tribe.

While cooking supper, the young Songhee approached and told them he wanted to return with them to Fort Victoria. The chief agreed to release him for the price of two blankets. The next morning the chief and two of his men arrived with the Songhee, and now demanded three blankets. Horne forcibly took him and ordered his men on alert and to load their guns ready for a speedy retreat. In a few moments, they heard war cries from a number of the tribe. They came armed with clubs and spears, prepared to do battle. Before they got too close, Horne fired a volley over their heads. The Natives ran into the bush.

On the return journey they approached Qualicum Creek cautiously, making sure the Haidas had not returned. The buildings were still smouldering, and wild animals had been at the scene of the massacre. They continued on toward Nanaimo to make a report to Stuart. As they approached the Nanaimo River, the Snuneymuxw gave them a friendly welcome. "On the second day after my visit to Nanaimo I arrived with my party at Victoria, and received the commendations of the chief factor."

It was learned sometime later that a young boy of the massacred tribe had escaped unharmed into the forest and apparently was found two days later by friends. As an adult, he lived in a little cabin by the mouth of the Qualicum River and was known as Qualicum Tom. He died shortly after the First World War.

Horne made other expeditions over this same route, although none as eventful as the first expedition:

> Sat. Sept. 20th, 1856. Mr. Horne returned after a successful expedition across the Island, bringing with him numerous skins, and accompanied by seaboard Indians of the tribe of See-Shaad (Tseshaht).[2]

While the Company's main interest in Nanaimo was developing the coalfield, it still continued trading in furs and pelts:

> Four consignments packed for Victoria were forwarded on December 27, 1854, and contained 49 black bear, four brown bears, two grisslies, 25 beaver, 29 otter, 22 racoon, 82 marten, 11 muskrat, 240 mink, 26 deer and one lynx.

Horne continued working in the Company store in Nanaimo, but his personal life changed in 1857 when the *Princess Royal* ship brought more immigrants to Nanaimo from England, including Mark Bate, who would become the first mayor of Nanaimo, and his sister Elizabeth. Their uncle was George Robinson, the new mine manager.

Two years later, Horne's entry in his journal gives a glimpse into the matter-of-fact nature of the man. On his wedding day, February 22, 1859, he wrote, showing little emotion: "At 12 a.m. I was married by the Rev. Dossen at Nanaimo in the schoolroom to E. Bate." His bride was Elizabeth Bate, born at Bromwich, near Birmingham, England; the minister was the Reverend Richard Dawson of the Church of England. Those witnessing the wedding vows were Captain Charles Edward Stuart, the HBC officer-in-charge in Nanaimo; Mark Bate and his wife, Sarah Ann (née

Cartwright); Elizabeth's cousin Cornelius Bryant, schoolteacher; and Caroline and George Robinson, Elizabeth's uncle and aunt. The Horne family bible has a notation from Stuart inscribed in it:

> To my friend Adam Grant Horne on the day of his marriage with best wishes for his health and prosperity, AD. 1859 Feby. 22nd Colvile Town, Nanaimo, Vancouver Island.[3]

Adam Grant Horne is wearing his HBC uniform in this photo of him and his wife, Elizabeth (née Bate), on their wedding day, February 22, 1859. IMAGE PN 454 COURTESY OF ALBERNI VALLEY MUSEUM

The newlyweds made a handsome couple: Horne was a tall (about 6 feet 3 inches), good-looking man with dark red hair, while Elizabeth was a pretty, petite woman with dark, almost black hair who reached in height to Adam's shoulders. Those who knew Horne said he spoke with a quiet, firm voice. Elizabeth was an ideal partner for this young Orcadian.

The first family home was at the southeast corner of Bastion and Commercial streets. The couple had 11 children. Three died before their seventh birthday: a boy, David, and two girls, both named Lucy. Their surviving children were Adam Henry, Ann Elizabeth, Sarah Maria, Herbert Lewis, Thomas Charles, Emily Maude, George Grant and Lindley Dallas.

Adam Grant Horne with his wife, Elizabeth, and five of their children; Annie is behind, Sarah is on the right, Tom is in front and Bert is in the middle. Baby Lucy died shortly after the photo was taken. IMAGE COURTESY OF TERRY SIMPSON

When the HBC sold all its holdings in Nanaimo in 1862 to the Vancouver Coal Mining and Land Company, Horne opened his own store, a wooden-frame building with access to the ramp leading to the old wharf. This same building was later used as a police station and as the first courthouse in Nanaimo.

In 1864, Horne rejoined the HBC service and was posted to Fort Simpson, at Chatham Sound, with Elizabeth and their two small children. There he joined Joseph William McKay, who was sent there when Britain went to war against Russia. The Company had part of the Russian coast under lease from the Russian American Fur Company and did not want the Tsimshian people to fall under the influence of the Russians. The Horne family stayed there for three years, during which time two more children were born. They were Lucy Amelia, who lived only a few years, and Sarah. They were the first white children born at Fort Simpson.[4]

The following year, Horne was sent to operate a small Company trading store in Comox, strategically located near the foot of Comox Hill. The area was still undeveloped: the first settlers, who had arrived only six years before, were scattered throughout the area. Horne remained there until the Company closed the store in December 1877.[5] More children were born here during this stay: Herbert Lewis, Thomas Charles, Emily Maude and David William.

Horne's colourful life continued in Comox. His granddaughter Carrie Brown Doney of Seattle wrote about an incident that took place in Comox:

> One night there was a lot of noise at the gate of the fort. Grandfather went out to see what was wrong and there stood a huge Indian with an oatmeal sack in his hand. He said the Indians had all been fighting and the chief had been scalped and grandfather was to go sew the scalp on him. They were all very upset about this. Grandfather refused to do it at first, and

Sarah Maria Horne, daughter of Adam Grant Horne, and Fred Seymour Brown on their wedding day, July 8, 1885. IMAGE COURTESY OF MILDRED SIMPSON

tried to get rid of him. He had a medicine chest that he used for small wounds but he had never done anything like that before. The Indians persisted and grandfather was afraid he would stick a spear in him, so he went.

The chief's hide was so tough that grandfather had to take his shoemaker's awl and make holes in his head and also through the scalp to sew it on. The old chief was so drunk that he could not feel a thing. Grandfather thought he would be dead by morning; he was very much alive and lived to be an old man.[6]

Sometime later, when Doney's mother was living in Union Bay, an old Indian came to the house with a bucket of clams. He began talking to her mother in the kitchen and then lifted his hair up, and there were the scars where Horne had sewn on his scalp many years before. "Every stitch had grown together perfectly."

The family returned to Nanaimo in 1878. Elizabeth wanted to be closer to her eldest son, Adam, her sister Lucy and her brother Mark. They built a house next door to Lucy and her husband, Peter Sabiston, at 149 Wallace Street. Their last two children were born here, George Grant and Lindley Dallas.

At this time, Horne leased a new building on Victoria Crescent, near the corner of Cavan Street, and opened his own business, A.G. Horne & Son. The store sold "fashionable hats," and the "finest and cheapest underclothing."[7] His older sons worked in the store, while the youngest delivered goods with a horse and buggy. The store gave credit to the miners and their families, allowing many to buy goods when the mines were idle and pay the bills when they worked. This business lasted until 1893. Horne's son Adam was postmaster in Nanaimo from 1890 to 1928.

During this time, Horne entered into partnership in a mining venture in the Mountain District west of Nanaimo with Peter Sabiston, Jacob Blessing and John Dick. Records show they operated the mine from 1879 to 1881. The mine was a success, and when it was sold, the partners divided the profits equally. Robert Dunsmuir eventually purchased it from the second owners for the grand sum of $30,000.

Horne was elected a city alderman in 1886, a pivotal year in Nanaimo's history, when the Esquimalt and Nanaimo Railway arrived in town. The aldermen signed a speech written by Mark Bate, welcoming the prime minister of Canada, Sir John A. Macdonald, to Nanaimo at the opening of the railway.

Adam Grant Horne's death on August 9, 1901, marked the passing of an era, a time of exploration and settlement on Vancouver Island. He helped open up the Central Island to trade and commerce; he settled disputes; he was a loyal servant to the HBC and a respected businessman. As the local newspaper so aptly described, "He was a pioneer of pioneers."

Horne Lake in Central Vancouver Island and a lane in downtown Nanaimo are named in his honour.

Harbourmaster and Hoteliers: The Sabiston Brothers

The three Sabiston brothers, John, Peter and James, all left their mark on Nanaimo. None were involved in the coal-mining industry, but they helped build the city. The brothers grew up on a farm at Castle Folly, Orkney Islands.

John Flett Sabiston got his sea legs from sailing around the world before he came to Vancouver Island. He then sailed on the historic HBC steamship, the *Beaver*, before settling down as Nanaimo's first harbourmaster. Sabiston was born in Kirkwall, Orkney Islands, on February 14, 1828, to George Sabiston and Margaret Brown. He was one of eight children. As a young lad of 13, he took to the sea, travelling in every kind of vessel afloat.

In 1849 he joined passengers on the *Norman Morison* leaving for Fort Victoria on Vancouver Island. He learned the *Beaver* was short an able seaman, so he signed on. The ship was then under the command of Captain Dodd and first officer Thomas Wade, who had been with the steamer for 10 years. Wade seemed well content with his position in life; however, sometime later, while the *Beaver* was docked at Stellacombe in Washington Territory, Wade was found dead in his cabin from an apparent suicide. There seemed to

DOMINION OF CANADA.

Pilotage District of Nanaimo, B. C.

Licensed Pilot No. 1

We, the undersigned Pilot Commissioners

being the pilotage authority having by law power to examine and license pilots for the pilotage district of Nanaimo, B. C., do hereby certify that John Sabiston of Nanaimo B. C. having been duly examined by us, has been found in all respects duly qualified, and is deemed by us to be a fit person to undertake the pilotage of vessels of every description, within the Harbour and throughout the said pilotage district of Nanaimo, B. C., and on this First day of April A. D. 1880, is by us licensed to act in that capacity. THIS LICENSE CANNOT BE LENT OR TRANSFERRED

Description of John Sabiston of Nanaimo B. C.

Age.	Height.	Complexion.	Color of Hair.	Color of Eyes.	Marks.	
52	5 ft. 8 in.	Florid	Gray	Blue	Cut on right cheek	Seniority 20th June 1879

John Sabiston was appointed Nanaimo's first harbourmaster in 1875. This certificate, dated 1880, is Sabiston's pilot's licence, verifying that he was a "Licensed Pilot No. 1" for the Dominion of Canada's Pilotage District of Nanaimo. NANAIMO COMMUNITY ARCHIVES JOHN SABISTON FONDS

be no reason for this rash act. US authorities looked into the death, but no report was ever issued on their investigation.

Built in England in 1835, the *Beaver* was the HBC flagship; it has been affectionately called "one of the bravest little ships which ever sailed."[8] The ship made the trip from Gravesend, leaving on August 29, 1935, and went around Cape Horn rigged as a brigantine, with her machinery dismantled, arriving at Fort Vancouver on April 10, 1836. She was the first steamship to ply the waters of the northern Pacific and was the first steamship to visit Fort Langley. In 1843 the *Beaver* transported James Douglas and his party to Vancouver Island when they founded Fort Victoria.

The gallant little vessel already had a history below her waterline when John Sabiston joined the crew. In the spring of 1851, the *Beaver* docked in Victoria to receive an overhaul. Sabiston and the crew were kept busy until the fall, when Captain Charles E. Stuart took command of the ship, giving Captain Dodd a much-needed rest. It then sailed for Nisqually in Washington Territory to pick up a cargo of cattle from the Puget Sound Agricultural Company. When American Customs detained the *Beaver* for unlawful entry into US waters, Sabiston protested the seizure. Captain Stuart left him in charge while he went to Olympia to sort out the problem. It was three weeks before Stuart returned with a paper from Washington, DC, allowing the release of the ship and the cattle that had been put ashore. No satisfactory answer was given over the seizure, but Stuart and others speculated that the US did not want to disturb the relationship between the US and Britain.

Captain Dodd returned and took command of the *Beaver* in 1853, just in time to be part of the first trial held under British law in British Columbia of two young Native men for the murder of shepherd Peter Brown in November at the sheep station near Victoria. Sabiston served on the jury in Nanaimo.

Sabiston began learning HBC trading procedures, a brisk and profitable business. He also learned from experience that a safe anchorage from the open sea was not always a safe place from hostile Natives, nor was it always safe to go exploring in Native territory. On one occasion, he and a shipmate were ransomed for HBC blankets after being captured on an excursion ashore. He swore he would never go exploring again in hostile country.

Driver Jerry McGill holds the reins atop the Particular Grocery cart outside an old Nanaimo building. Jerry married Margaret, a granddaughter of John Sabiston. IMAGE QI-5 COURTESY OF NANAIMO MUSEUM

There were several refuelling stations established by the Company along the coast where the *Beaver* took on firewood. When the ship had to travel further north, extra axemen were required. On one occasion, the ship arrived at the station to find no firewood. The boiler's fresh water supply was low, and firewood was needed. Sabiston, in charge of the axemen, went ashore to find out what had happened and then ordered his men into the forest to cut down some trees.

Suddenly, Natives surrounded the men. Sabiston spoke several Native languages, including Chinook, and was able to convince them to release his men and allow them to cut firewood while he was escorted to the nearby village. He was recognized as the white man who spoke many tongues and a fair man to trade with. Meanwhile, Captain Dodd received word that Sabiston would be returned in payment for some HBC blankets.

In the fall of 1854, while the *Beaver* was anchored at Fort Simpson for several weeks for repairs and to take on furs, Sabiston heard there was an opening at the fort. He decided it was time to try fur trading for a living. He settled at Fort Simpson and married Jane, a Native woman from Ketchikan, Alaska, then known as Russian America. He and Jane had two daughters and a son. Sabiston became a successful trader.

In 1858, Sabiston's contract at Fort Simpson expired, and with the *Beaver* not due to return until the spring of 1859, he disregarded the advice of his friends and headed south to Nanaimo in a dugout canoe with his wife and children. The journey took six weeks. His knowledge of the sea and the coastline served him well during this hazardous journey.

Back on solid ground in Nanaimo, he was placed in charge of Native labour working at the Company sawmill on Millstone River and at the pitheads. Sabiston never ventured into a mine if he could avoid it. He worked at various places around the community and sometimes at the loading chute where ships took on coal. One fateful morning in March 1860, he fell through a hole left by a broken plank on the dock above the coal chutes. Somehow he managed to hold onto a timber long enough until the coal had finished loading. Some deckhands saw him and rushed to extricate him. It was not until he was safely on the dock that he realized he had a nasty head wound. He was rushed to the doctor and received stitches.

After this foray on dry land, John Sabiston went back to sea again, signing on with the marine branch of the HBC, where he rose from able seaman to captain. In 1875, after British Columbia joined Confederation and the harbours came under the jurisdiction of the Dominion Government, Sabiston was appointed the first Nanaimo harbourmaster. The Governor General of Canada, the Earl of Dufferin, Sir Frederick Temple, signed the document appointing him to this position. Sabiston is described on the Pilotage District of Nanaimo licence as "Pilot No. 1, age 52, five-foot eight-inches in height, gray hair and blue eyes, with a cut on right cheek." Mayor Mark Bate and Alderman John Hirst signed the licence on June 20, 1879.

There is an amazing story told by explorer Sir John Franklin's wife, Lady Franklin, on her visit to Nanaimo and the Pacific Northwest in 1861. She wrote:

> May 6: We made an excursion yesterday between the islands, to a very small one beyond a mere rock, covered with lovely flowers, and more curious stone crop, which in colour and shape exactly resembles the flowers of Dresden china. Captain and Mrs. Spalding took us in their boat, with their two boys, quite filled. Strange to say, the man who pulled the stroke oar, who is a pilot here, was a boy in Orkney his native place when my uncle's expedition stopped there, and he drove my uncle from Stromness to Kirkwall and back again."[9]

Warner Reeve Spalding was the magistrate in Nanaimo, and the man with the oar was John Sabiston. One can imagine Lady Franklin's surprise at meeting an Orkney native halfway around the world.

John Sabiston served as City of Nanaimo alderman from 1876 to 1879 under Mayor Mark Bate. With the proliferation of hotels, boarding houses and pubs in the city, he suggested in 1876 that the pubs be closed on Sundays. Before this, there had been little regulation of the pubs beyond the requirement of a licence. From then on only medicines and medicinal alcohol could be sold on the Sabbath, and then only between one o'clock and five. This probably did not endear him to his brother Peter, who operated a hotel in town.

John was also warden of St. Paul's Anglican Church. He died at his home on Cavan Street, Nanaimo, on April 17, 1902, at the age of 77.[10]

John's wife, Jane, lived to the grand age of 93 years. She was born in 1828 at Ketchikan, Alaska, then a Company trading post.[11]

When she died at her home on Albert Street, she was considered Nanaimo's oldest resident and had lived in Nanaimo continuously at the same address.

John's brother, Peter Sabiston, worked at Fort Simpson, then returned to Nanaimo in 1858 and went into the hotel business. On January 8, 1864, he married Lucy Bate, sister of Mark Bate.

Nanaimo had had many hotels; at one time, there was estimated to be over 40 serving the community. Many were really boarding houses for the young single men working in the mines. The more established hotels became social centres where miners met after a long day underground.

Over the years Peter Sabiston invested in several hotels, including the Miners' Hotel on Commercial Street, which opened in 1869. The hotel was described as an old established house offering English and French wines, brandy, gin and ale, and was only a two-minute walk from the steamboat landing. It was later renamed the Central Hotel. Peter entered another partnership with J. Wilcox in the Commercial Hotel on Bastion Street, first licensed in 1875 at the same location as the present-day Commercial Hotel, which was rebuilt in 1913.

Peter also farmed to the west of Mountain District, where he grew produce for sale in town, and invested in the Jingle Pot Mine with Adam Grant Horne. He also built several buildings in town, including St. Andrew's Presbyterian Church and the Prideaux Street Bridge. Peter died on September 29, 1892, at 59 years of age. Lucy died on November 8, 1927.

The youngest brother, James, was a partner in one of the first Nanaimo saloons, the Identical, on Victoria Crescent. The Identical was designed and built by Bruno Mellado, a young man with a knowledge of architecture from Santiago, Chile, who settled in Nanaimo.

James and his wife, Catherine, had two children, Esther Jessie and Douglas Campbell. James died on October 20, 1875, at age 36.

Sabiston Street, in Nanaimo, is named for the Sabiston brothers, but it was John who developed the land the street led through.

Skilled Labourers: The Papley Brothers

Three more brothers left the Orkney Islands to make their way to Vancouver Island, and, like the Sabiston brothers, they brought their youthful enthusiasm and skills. The Papley brothers, Peter, 21, Alexander, 17, and Joseph, 15, signed on with the Company at the Firth of Stenness. The New World beckoned. Joseph signed on as a carpenter, Peter as a blacksmith and Alexander as a labourer. In fact, they were all farmers, and like most farmers, they were adaptable and able to put their hand to almost any task.

Unlike many of the immigrants from Orkney who were poor, working-class folk, their parents, John Papley and Betty Oman, were landholders, owning one quarter of the Farm of Garth, a piece of land valued at five pounds sterling. They signed on with the Company for a period of three to five years, so their father may have expected them to return to the Orkney Islands. The Company tried to attract Orkney agricultural labourers to Vancouver Island as settlers, promising them a free grant of land at the end of their contracts, but Orcadians did not view Vancouver Island as an agricultural settlement like Australia.[12] Later, in 1867, Alexander wrote home about the possibility of farming land around Nanaimo but noted that the land was covered with woods and thick brush. He wrote:

> You may think the Orknes [sic] is a poor place but I believe it this a better place for a man to Settle into (than) what this is yet...[13]

In the small mining village of Nanaimo, the young Papley men were needed. Peter was hired as a blacksmith, while Alexander worked as a labourer in the mines, and Joseph worked as a carpenter. After a stay in Fort Rupert, they were brought to Nanaimo. On

September 10, 1856, Alexander Papley, William Ritch and Thomas Mills accompanied Adam Grant Horne on another trip across the Island. The trip was judged a success when they returned 10 days later with "numerous skins." [14]

Alexander completed his contract with the Company and stayed on in Nanaimo, working for the Vancouver Coal Company. To friends, he was known as Sandy, "a large lusty man, unassuming and quiet, respected both by employer and employees for his rigid rectitude." [15] He worked as a labourer, at the sawmill, at the salt spring shed and around the mines, until the Douglas Mine became operational in 1862. Then he was appointed weighman at the pithead, a position he held until the mine closed.

Alexander wrote letters home to his mother telling of the work he and his brothers were doing and the great excitement of the copper ore discovery on Vancouver Island. This would have been the discovery at Mount Sicker. He also noted that the Harewood Coal Company mine was going "full blast" and that Robert Dunsmuir was sending 260 tons of coal a day to the bunkers for shipping. [16] (Dunsmuir was then working as manager for the Harewood Mine for a share of the profits.) In some of his letters home, Alexander discussed sending money to his sisters, who were still living on and farming their late father's one-quarter portion of Garth. [17]

Alexander married a Native woman, and they had a daughter named Mary Ann who was baptized on January 1, 1865, in Nanaimo. She attended a school taught by Cornelius Bryant. In 1884 she was living in San Francisco and using the name Marion. [18]

Alexander Papley built a small house on Nicol Street. Everyone had good memories about Sandy:

He will be remembered as a man who was strict in the performance of his duty, and one for whom all the miners had a good word. Those who at times, thought they had cause for complaint, who censured him for any of his work as a tallyman, invariably admitted, after hearing him, that he was just, and he feared not.[19]

Alexander died at age 51 on March 9, 1884, of pneumonia. Before he died, he dictated his will to two friends but died before it was signed. Meanwhile Joseph, who was named executor, had returned to the Orkney Islands to attend to urgent family matters. This may have been on the death of his father. Alexander's two friends, who had witnessed the will, took over its administration. Joseph reappeared in Nanaimo, but when friends saw him wearing a gold watch intended for his niece Marion, they laid a complaint with the magistrate. The bank account was frozen, and Joseph was restrained from disposing of any property. Alexander's house was worth $635, and he had over $3,000 in cash.

The HBC Daybook, now in the Nanaimo Community Archives, documents the day-to-day operations of the coal-mining village from 1852 to 1854. There are many references to the work done by Peter, who seemed to be moved around to wherever he was needed as a labourer. He quarried stones, built chimneys, loaded ships, cleared land for the sawmill and helped build the first log cabins.[20]

Joseph and Peter joined the gold rush in the Cariboo, and on their return in 1871 to Nanaimo, Joseph built roads and bridges and worked for Robert Dunsmuir, building wharves at Departure Bay for the Wellington mines. He didn't like outdoor work, especially during the winter months, but he earned $3 a day. When Peter returned, he also worked for Robert Dunsmuir, as a blacksmith.[21] Peter died accidentally on November 13, 1880, at age 52.[22] He was hit by a passing train when he was drunk, and died two days later.

In 1885, Joseph received a letter from his niece Marion in San Francisco. She was concerned that both her father and uncle were buried in unmarked graves, and she wanted him to install a monument with a railing around the grave. She was willing to help defray the cost but could not do it alone as "the Orkney relatives" had received most of her father's estate.[23] It is unknown if Joseph ever did as asked. There is no further record of him in BC. He may have returned to his family in Orkney.

Family Tragedies: John Work

John and Margaret Work, and baby daughter Margaret, lived at Wideford in the Orkney Islands. His daughter was only a year old when John, 23, signed on in 1850 with Company agent Edward Clouston in Stromness. John was a farmer and perhaps wanted a better life for his family. Work is an old Orcadian surname derived from the lands of Work in the Parish of St. Ola.

The young family sailed from Kirkwall on October 15, 1850, aboard the *Queen*, bound for London, where they boarded the *Tory* for the long journey to Vancouver Island. Aboard ship they shared a steerage cabin with John and Jessie Irvine and son Robert.[24] The ship arrived in Fort Victoria on May 14, 1851. According to HBC archival records, John first worked as a labourer at Fort Langley, and then in Victoria, and was discharged on September 20, 1852. He then signed another contract with the Company from 1853 to 1856.[25]

Friendships made on this journey stayed with the family as they made a new life for themselves in Nanaimo and Victoria. John Work and family arrived in Nanaimo on the *Beaver* in December 1852 along with four miners and their families from Fort Rupert to work the new coalfield.[26]

The family lived in one of the log cabins that had been built along Front Street to house the mining families. Two sons were born here: John Pearson on June 1, 1852, and James Leask on November 7, 1853.

The HBC Accounts book for Nanaimo has a list of items purchased by John Work at the store that shows their wants and needs in the frontier village. The list includes: "4 blankets, 2 pr.

Drawers [underclothing], 16 yds Druggets, thin felted woolen cloth, 2 lbs. comfits [sweetmeat confection], 2 lbs. almonds, 1 roll Irish tobacco, 1 bubb handle knife, ½ gal. Rum, 4 lbs. butter, ½ gal. rice, ½ deer carcass, ¼ lb. white thread, 2 gal. molasses, and 1 pr. Welty shoes [slip-on sole protectors].[27]

John would have smoked a pipe, since tobacco was charged to the account. Margaret may have used the yards of druggets for blankets, sheets, window coverings or clothing, and from the purchase of rum, it would seem that John was not averse to an occasional drink. Early Company records show the miners did their fair share of drinking. Liquor was a problem in the small mining village, and was also a problem for Natives until Douglas prohibited the sale of liquor to Natives on August 12, 1854.[28]

The young family was devastated by a tragic accident on April 18, 1856, possibly the first mining fatality recorded in Nanaimo. The incident is recorded in the HBC Daybook:

> An accident of a serious nature happened to one of the men working at Dunsmuir's level, named John Work, a piece of the roof falling upon him, causing fracture of several ribs, as well as severely injuring the spine causing complete paralization of lower extremities.[29]

Two days later, Margaret Work sent a canoe to Victoria for some necessaries for her husband, but John died of his injuries a short time later. His work contract with the Company would have expired by this time, leaving Margaret with no money for her passage home and three young children to raise on her own. If her husband had been under contract, she would have had free passage home for herself and her children.

After John's death, Margaret moved to Victoria. In letters to her former neighbour in Nanaimo, Christopher Finlay, she wrote of the difficulties she faced, and asked to be remembered to Mrs. Adam Grant Horne (Elizabeth) and Mrs. Dunsmuir (Joan). (Finlay and Horne had also been passengers on the *Tory*.[30]) In her

This railway locomotive, the Duke, was used in the early coal industry. In this photo, taken *circa* 1875, Robert Dunsmuir can be spotted wearing a top hat.
IMAGE 1993 028 A-P41 COURTESY OF NANAIMO COMMUNITY ARCHIVES

letter to Finlay, dated July 26, 1857, she expressed concern about her husband's grave and its marker:

> I hope you will finish my husband's grave as well as you can. I can tell you I have been sorry many a time for Nanaimo. I have got but very little since I have been down here. Irvin gave me a cow to milk for the children. The calf is to be my own. You see, that is all I have got, but spend the little I had. It was three weeks before I went to the Governor. When he saw me on the wharf, he spoke to me and asked if I was going to the Muirs. I said no. He wanted to know what was the reason. I would not tell him. So I went to him at last and he allows one ration and a half. John is going to school. Margaret is at Flett's. I am very uneasy at present but I hope I will have a home by and by. I would not advise you to come down. So comfort yourself for this (is) a poor place. You will find plenty of friends if you (have money).[31]

The "Irvin" she refers to is probably John and Jessie Irvine, who were fellow passengers on the *Tory*. In another letter to Finlay in September, she again advised him not to come to Victoria, that he was better off in Nanaimo, and asks him to look after John's grave. (In the early days of the colony's development, it was left to family members to care for the burial sites.) The Fletts referred to in her letter are John and Janet Flett, who were also from the Orkney Islands: John Flett was hired as a cooper, and made barrels for the salmon fisheries on Vancouver Island.

The *Victoria Gazette* of August 4, 1858, announced Margaret's marriage on August 1 to William Reid. She lived only a few years into her marriage, and died in 1862, possibly during the smallpox epidemic of that year. Reid remarried and did not want Margaret's children, so they were split up and sent to different families. Their eight-year-old daughter Margaret went to live with the Flett family, and son James Leask went to live with his guardian, William John Macdonald, in Victoria; Macdonald was another family friend from the *Tory*. Margaret's eldest son, John Pearson Work, left Vancouver Island aboard a sailing ship and settled in the New York area, working for the Long Island Railroad. He died in 1924. Daughter Margaret married and settled in the Seattle area and had two sons.

Trent River Bridge Accident

Margaret's son James Leask Work apprenticed with the carpenter firm of Hayward & Jenkinson in Victoria. After completing his apprenticeship in 1873, he returned to Nanaimo. He worked for Robert Dunsmuir in his Wellington mines, then later in the Cumberland mine. In 1894 he was sent to San Francisco to supervise the construction of the new coal yards and bunkers for Dunsmuir's coal from the Wellington mines.

James married a young English woman, Dorothy Akenhead, on August 23, 1876. Dorothy's father Walter established the What

Cheer House on Commercial Street, and later had a wholesale and retail meat business in town. The young couple would have seven children: Walter, Edith, James, John, William, Alex and Frank.

The year 1898 was a tragic one for the family. Dorothy gave birth to twins, one of whom died at birth. Then their son Walter, 20, who had worked as a carpenter for James Dunsmuir at Union Bay, was killed in the Trent River Bridge accident. Six people died in the accident, sending the Nanaimo-Wellington district into shock because so many families were affected by it.

The centre span of the Trent River trestle, a structure about 90 feet high and a quarter of a mile long, had collapsed when the first train of the day, a 70-ton locomotive pulling 20 coal cars containing 20 tons of coal each, was crossing it. The train fell into the

The centre span of the Trent River trestle in Cumberland collapsed on August 17, 1898. Five people were killed and three were injured in the accident.
IMAGE Q2-44 COURTESY OF NANAIMO MUSEUM

rocky ravine below, the locomotive and cars piled one on top of the other in a heterogeneous mass. The rear brakeman, Matthew Piercy, managed to jump to safety.[32]

Along with Walter, the dead included engineer Alfred Walker, who was killed instantly, leaving a wife and five children; the brakeman Alexander Melado, who left a wife and one child; Richard Nightingale, a long-time resident and pub owner in Nanaimo who had just returned from Wrangell, Alaska, and who also left a family behind in Nanaimo; and two Japanese men named Nanka and Oshana. There were also a number of injuries. Frances Horne, daughter of William Horne, the blacksmith at Union Wharf, died from hers.

The Trent River Bridge, only 10 years old, was a wooden bridge with a sharp curve. It had been well maintained and was regarded as safe. The rail line followed the Trent River until it reached a point one mile from the sea, where it crossed a gorge over a large bridge, truss and trestle before dropping to Union Bay and the wharves. There had been plans to have it replaced by a steel bridge in the future.

Walter's death was felt deeply in Wellington, where he lived; his easy-going nature had made him well liked.

When news of the accident reached Victoria, James Dunsmuir, John Bryden, C.E. Pooley, J. Hunter and Edward Gawlor Prior boarded a special train for Wellington. The coroner's report concluded that parts of the bridge known as the chords were rotted and may have caused the accident, as they were not strong enough to carry the weight. The Crown sued the Union Colliery Company for negligence, and the jury found that the company had neglected its duty to take care of the bridge and trestle.

One month later there was more bad news for the Work family, and again the *Wellington Enterprise* carried the report of another family tragedy: "On September 16, James Leask Work was killed by falling between two cars. Work, 45, had been the head carpenter at Union Bay." After the death of James and Walter, the two older sons, James and John, were taken on as apprentices at the Wellington shops of the E & N Railway to help the family financially.

John started a four-year apprenticeship in January 1899, just two months before his 14th birthday. He went to San Francisco after the 1906 earthquake that destroyed that city and worked as a carpenter during the restoration. By 1910 he was back in Wellington. He married Beatrice Doward of Northfield, the daughter of Enoch and Fanny Doward, from Wales. He and Beatrice had three sons, Albert, Walter and Jack. During the First World War, the young family lived in Victoria, where John worked in the shipyard building wooden ships for the war effort. By 1920 he had returned to work for the E & N Railway, where he spent his remaining years until his retirement in 1949.

What dreams and expectations John and Margaret Work may have had when they signed on with the Company in 1850! They had a short life together, much of it marked by tragedy. Despite this, the Work family thrived, and many decades later, their descendants are a living testimony to their presence during the settlement years on Vancouver Island.

The Stonemason: William Isbister

William Isbister was known as the man who built the Stone House and as a skilful stonemason. He was one of the *Tory* passengers arriving in Fort Victoria in 1850. He worked for a time at Fort Rupert, and then was "brought to Nanaimo to install boiler seats and chimneys at the No. 1 and No. 2 pitheads."[33] The chimney he built at Fort Rupert still stands today, the only remains of the old fort.

Isbister was born on January 4, 1829, and signed a three-year contract with the Company at Stromness, Orkney Islands, as a stonemason. The HBC Nanaimo Daybook noted that Isbister and several others arrived on the steamer *Beaver* from Fort Rupert on Sunday, April 18, 1853.

The historic Nanaimo bastion in its original location, *circa* 1885. It was built with squared timbers fitted together with wooden pegs. Note the miners' cabins remaining on the right. These were roughly constructed with logs from the forest nearby and roof shakes from Fort Rupert. IMAGE 2000 032 A-P3 COURTESY OF NANAIMO COMMUNITY ARCHIVES

Isbister's first job in Nanaimo was to lay the foundation for the Bastion, an octagonal fortress-like structure that was built to give security to the small mining village from marauding Natives who were enemies of the Snuneymuxw. It also served as a store, and later as a jail. Today it is one of the oldest buildings on Vancouver Island and a landmark in Nanaimo. At this time, Isbister was living on Comox Road with Henry Samson.

The Bastion took months to complete. Isbister's job was finished when the French-Canadian carpenters Leon Labine and Jean Baptiste Fortier began squaring the timbers for its construction. Two cannons were placed adjacent to the Bastion, perhaps to strike fear into unwelcome visitors, or perhaps in celebration of an official visit from Douglas.

In November 1853, when he refused to build a chimney on one of the new houses, Isbister was sent, for his insolence, "on board the *Archemedes* to work his passage in that vessel down to Victoria."[34] He returned to Nanaimo in May 1854, and with the help of Christopher Finlay, began building the Stone House on Front Street.

The Stone House was one of the first stone buildings erected in the Colony of Vancouver Island and was strongly built, like a fort, with walls two feet thick. It was constructed of stones gathered from the beach and lime made from crushed clamshells to form walls.[35] The Snuneymuxw called it the Tyee House. It was similar in structure to stone buildings in the Orkney Islands.

Over the years, the building served many functions: first as an administrative office for HBC officers-in-charge, and then as an office for the Vancouver Coal Company. The first schoolmaster, Charles Bayley, used part of the house as a classroom, as did his successor, Cornelius Bryant. The building served as the second city hall in 1874. Isbister was hired to give a rough cast to the outside walls in 1879. City council moved to another location in 1887, and the Stone House became a branch office for the Bank of British Columbia for a year, until it too moved to another building. Meanwhile, the building continued to be used, first by C.C. MacKenzie, then by Joseph P. Planta from 1889 to 1892. Efforts were made to have it preserved as a heritage building, like the Bastion, but it didn't have the same support and was demolished in 1893.

As the town grew, Isbister's skill as a stonemason was needed more and more, particularly for building house chimneys and lining furnace shafts. Anywhere there was a need for stonework, Isbister was there, and he built things to last. He also did other jobs as required. He laid the foundation for the HBC sawmill and built an oven for the village. In March 1856, he, Finlay and Ritch salted the herring that they had purchased from the Natives at the rate of one blanket for five barrels of fish.[36] In August of that year, he placed a beacon off Execution Point (Gallow's Point). He was helped in this by Mr. Shortly, the Native overseer, and several Snuneymuxw. When Shortly resigned two years later, Isbister was appointed to his position. He was so well regarded in the community that the

1887

In this 1887 photo, John Marwick is seated between his nephew, Colonel Slater, on the left and his son, William, on the right. John's wife, Jane (née Isbister) stands behind them. John was born in the parish of Rousay in the Orkney Islands in 1842.

Snuneymuxw thought of him as a friend and often sought his advice.

Isbister married his first wife, Jane, a Native woman, shortly after he moved to Nanaimo. They had two children: a daughter, also named Jane, born in 1858, and a son, William, born in 1861.

After Jane's death, Isbister married his second wife, Helen (Ellen), who was then aged 15. The marriage ceremony was in St. Paul's Anglican Church. The children from this marriage were Elizabeth, James, Mary Ann, Ellen and Robert. Son James was killed at age 17 in the Number One mine explosion of May 3, 1887.

After completing the foundations of the shaft for the Douglas Mine and building a square chimney of quarried stone, in 1860 Isbister resigned and turned his attention to building houses. At this time the management of the village and the coal mines was in flux as the HBC negotiated the sale of its holdings in Nanaimo to the Vancouver Coal Mining and Land Company.

The first home Isbister built was near the mouth of Millstone River, later the site of the Nanaimo Foundry and today part of Maffeo Sutton Park. This was sold to build another home "over the Ravine" on the knoll on Crace Street at Esplanade. City records show he built two others, on the northwest corner of Haliburton and Dixon streets in Block 7. One of these later became the Bow Kee Laundry and was across the street from the John Marwick residence. He also built three cottages in Block 7.[37]

Margaret Work mentioned Isbister in her letter to Christopher Finlay in 1857. In such a small community of Scots, they all knew each other, which may have been good, or bad. She wrote: "Give Isbister my compliments and tell him not to speak so free about me unless he know it to be the truth."[38] Whatever remark Isbister made about Margaret, it obviously found its way to her in Victoria.

Family members recalled Isbister's relationship with Robert Dunsmuir. At first it was a friendly one, with the two men sharing fishing trips together. What happened when Dunsmuir discovered a coal seam seems to have put a wedge between the two. There are several versions of the story, each told from a different point of view. Dunsmuir wrote about his discovery in a letter to the Honourable Hector-Louis Langevin, the federal minister of public works, and made no mention of the others involved in the discovery:

I found coal sticking on the upturned root, and digging a little under it, I saw that coal had been there... I then sent for two workmen, who brought picks and shovels, and in half-an-hour, we discovered a seam of coal... 9 feet in thickness.[39]

Another version of the story is that Jimmy Hamilton and Dunsmuir were fishing when Dunsmuir wandered off looking for coal, leaving Hamilton fishing. Dunsmuir told his wife, Joan, that evening that he had found coal at Diver Lake. Since Hamilton wasn't interested, he invited Isbister to come with him to confirm the find. Many people had found coal but few had done anything about it; Dunsmuir was different, and he saw an opportunity. Isbister drilled the test bores and expected to have his name on a claim, and probably expected to share in the rewards, but Dunsmuir staked a claim to the valuable seam of coal for himself. When Isbister learned later what had happened, it was too late. He never spoke to him again. Meanwhile Dunsmuir went ahead and developed the riches of the Wellington mine.[40]

Hamilton was hired to continue working the coal for Dunsmuir for several years. He was a hard worker, and a kind-hearted type of person who got along with everyone. He lived in a small cabin near Diver Lake, and was a neighbour of Mr. Smallbone, a bootlegger of some note. One day in September 1870, two young Natives visited Smallbone's for some grog, and, finding no one home, broke in, stole several items and drank all the beer. When Hamilton protested all the noise, they hit him on the head, cut his throat, dragged him from the cabin and set it on fire. A manhunt took place, and two Natives were arrested and brought to trial. One gave "Queen's Evidence" and was sentenced to a prison term. The other was hanged. The survivor died in prison.[41]

Tired of living in town, Isbister decided to move to a farm near the Nanaimo rapids in the Cedar District. In 1860 he cleared, plowed and planted a portion with turnips and potatoes. He soon discovered that getting his produce to market in Nanaimo was not easy; he grew tired of it and sold out. Mark Bate described Isbister's farm:

> Trees, 40 feet high, grew on part of the ground which had been cultivated, and were cut down by the next owner, Mr. T. O'Brien, for mine prop wood.[42]

Isbister's last move with his family was to the Chase River area, where he settled down to live out his remaining years with his wife, Ellen. He died on April 11, 1907, at age 87. Ellen died in 1922.

Isbister's daughter, Jane, married John Marwick on September 12, 1874. Marwick was also from the Orkney Islands, and had been a neighbour when the Isbisters lived on Haliburton Street. He was born in 1842 to Hugh Marwick and Catherine Craigie in the parish of Rousay, Orkney Islands. Family records show he came to Vancouver Island in May 1862 on the ship *Pacific* from San Francisco and worked for a time in the sheriff's office in Victoria. He farmed in Comox until the mid-1870s, before settling in Nanaimo.

As Robert Dunsmuir's Wellington mines expanded, Marwick operated a daily stage service between Nanaimo and Wellington in 1875. This business was sold to Robert Smith, a sale that included all his horses and wagons.[43] The following year he broke his leg in an accident in the Douglas Mine; he had been standing with one foot inside the rail when a run of boxes started and caught his leg, fracturing it between the ankle and knee. Dr. Loftus R. McInnes set the broken leg.

Over the years, John Marwick invested time and energy in many businesses. In the mid-1880s he purchased land in the Cranberry district, and in 1889 he bought the Red Lion Brewery on the southeast corner of the Nanaimo River Bridge in the village of Stovely, in Cedar. The brewery began operating in 1886 and produced 300 gallons a day. Two years later he sold the brewery to Walter Myles of the Union Brewing Company, then operated by the Reifel family. He was also in business with his friend Andrew Smith, who had a butcher shop at the foot of Nicol Street, and he was affiliated with the Keystone Wine Company. In the 1890 city directory, John lived on Haliburton Street; he was listed as one of the operators (Marwick & Hoflet) of the Britannia Hotel on Commercial Street.

Bill Marwick, his grandson, remembers John had "a white beard, steel blue eyes, and he wore a Panama hat in summer; he smoked a pipe, not much of a drinker or a talker."[44]

Before he retired in 1914, John Marwick took a trip back to the Orkney Islands. He sent a postcard on September 6, 1913, to his son William at 147 Haliburton St. in Nanaimo. On the card he wrote that he was leaving for Montreal that day and had had a good time visiting with Alexander Henderson. It was Henderson who built the Globe Hotel in Nanaimo in 1887.

Jane died in 1926 at age 68.[45] John died on November 21, 1929, at age 86. Many notables in the Nanaimo community attended his funeral, including his friend Andrew Smith. Others included Thomas Hodgson, mayor of Nanaimo in 1909, and Pete Maffeo, who operated the Davenport Ice Cream plant and became mayor in 1956. Also at the funeral were Mr. and Mrs. Con Riefel, and Mr. and Mrs. Henry Riefel, of the Union Brewery Company. The Marwicks had four children: William, John, Elizabeth Jane and James.

Today several generations can trace their ancestry back to pioneer William Isbister.

Village Pedagogue: Christopher Finlay

Christopher Finlay was 18 years old when he signed on with the Company at Orphir, Orkney Islands. Leaving behind his widowed mother and 14-year-old sister to farm the two acres the family owned, he left for Vancouver Island on the *Tory*, arriving at Fort Victoria in 1850. He was sent first to Fort Rupert, and then brought to Nanaimo to assist the first miners. The details of his personal life in Nanaimo are sketchy, with only his early work assignments briefly recorded.

On July 13, 1853, a number of canoes arrived from Fort Rupert, bringing a man "named Finlay who having been ill for some time back has been sent down for the benefit of medical advice." There is no indication as to the nature of his illness or how long he had been ill. The only doctor on the north Island at this time was Dr. George Johnstone, who had been moved to Nanaimo. The following year, Finlay must have recovered from his illness, for on March 4, 1854, he and Dunsmuir were on the sick list "in consequence of over indulgence in "spirituous liquor."

Finlay did not appear to have a designated job, but, like the other labourers, was required to do whatever work detail was asked of him. On September 18, 1854, he and Papley collected and quarried stones for house chimneys. This same year, he helped clear the area to build the Company sawmill and whitewashed houses, and then was ordered to work the coal.

His work assignments recorded in the Daybook give little indication of the man, or his schooling; however, he was well educated and adapted to any and all situations that arose. Among his many duties, he served as accountant in the Company store and office. According to Mark Bate, he was "well up in his mathematics" and considered "that of a village pedagoge [sic]," referring to the period of time when he served as schoolmaster in the pioneer school after Charles A. Bayley resigned and students were waiting for their next teacher, Cornelius C. Bryant, to arrive. Samuel Gough had first-hand knowledge of the interim schoolmaster; he knew him to be stern and known for "frequently administering physical punishment."[46] Gough became the city clerk after Nanaimo incorporated.

No further mention of Finlay is to be found until March 17, 1856, when he, Isbister and Ritch were salting herring to be traded with the Snuneymuxw at a rate of five barrels for one blanket. Nanaimo was fortunate to have a salt spring, located at the site

The coal wharf in Nanaimo, *circa* 1865.
IMAGE 1993 028 A-P63 COURTESY OF NANAIMO COMMUNITY ARCHIVES

of the present-day Howard Johnson Hotel on Comox Road. The salt was good quality and principally used for preserving fish and game. In the summer of 1853, the Company preserved 20 barrels of salmon, using the salt from the spring. Over the next 10 years, the Millstone brine springs supplied the salt required at Nanaimo for curing the post's annual salmon pack.[47] The spring was abandoned in 1862 when the Company holdings were sold to the Vancouver Coal Mining and Land Company.

The date of Finlay's marriage to a Native woman named Mary, from Rose Spit on the south end of Moresby Island, is unknown. Vital Statistics show a Mary Cartwright born in 1854 who was baptized in Nanaimo in 1871 at age 17. This may have been before she and Christopher Finlay married. The couple had a daughter named Mary, who married William Cartwright. The Cartwrights lived in East Sooke, where their two daughters, Sarah Ann and Mary Ann, were born. The latter died when she was only 23 years old.

Bate noted that Finlay was well respected in the community and "known as an upright man who would never wrong anyone."[48]

There is a note in the Nanaimo Community Archives that indicates Finlay's wife "returned to her home at Rose Spit to die."[49] Finlay died accidentally at age 46 after falling on the doorstep of his house on Mill Street, on August 23, 1879.

Cedar Farmer: James Stove

James Stove, 20, was also a passenger on the *Tory*, arriving in Fort Victoria in 1851. HBC passenger lists show he travelled in steerage with William Isbister, Adam Horne, Thomas Smith, John Malcolm and Robert Firth.[50] He signed on with the Company from the parish of Firth and Stenness, Orkney Islands, as a labourer, shipmaster, carpenter and builder. He served two years on the *Beaver* before settling down in Nanaimo.

Stove was one of the four men who sank the area's first coal shaft, and he also helped build the Bastion and the housing required for the miners along Front Street. He constructed chimneys, whitewashed buildings and did a variety of general chores required around the settlement. Of all the work assignments given to him, he only refused to do one, and that was work in the blacksmith shop as a hammer man, also known as a striker, working on the anvil.[51] The work would have been hot and strenuous. He preferred being at sea, and for two years, from 1854 to 1856, he worked on the *Cadboro,* a small Company schooner sent earlier from England for the coastal trade.[52] The ship was a frequent visitor to Nanaimo.

In 1860, Stove took up land in the Cedar District, south of Nanaimo, when agricultural land was advertised for sale in the area. Three years later he sold this land, then pre-empted other sections on the east side of the Nanaimo River. Stove married a Native woman, Margaret (Maggie), and they settled in Cedar, near the present crossing of the Nanaimo River, an area known historically as Stovely on old maps. It was located across the river from a reserve and a few hundred yards downstream from the

Cedar Bridge. James Stove also had a home on Esplanade near the No. 1 Reserve.[53]

The old Red Lion Brewery was located on a southeast corner in Stovely, and after it was sold to the Union Brewery of Nanaimo, the building became Mrs. Wilkinson's boarding house, a store and the Stovely post office. A village school opened in 1874 at the corner of Gordon and Stove, now Raines Road, run by teacher Emma Stark, the first black woman to hold such a position.

Two of the Stoves' children, Robert and John, died in the Number One mine explosion of May 3, 1887. John left a wife and child. Their other children were James, Margaret, Thomas, Jenny, William and David. Daughter Margaret's husband, Johan Westfeldt, was also killed in the mine explosion of 1887. Jenny married George S. Brown of Wesley Street. They had five children, all of them born between 1857 and 1864; all were baptized on May 26, 1867, in the Methodist Church, Nanaimo. James Stove died in 1908 at age 79; his wife, Margaret, died in 1897 at age 56.

Bate thought highly of James Stove. He wrote, "Stove was fairly prosperous, always a good citizen, industrious and frugal."[54] A good and kind comment from someone who knew him!

A "Faithful-reliable" Man: John Malcolm

John Malcolm seemed to have a close personal relationship with William Ritch, perhaps formed in their early years in the Orkney Islands. Sharing the long journey aboard the *Tory* bound for Fort Victoria may also have created a bond between them. The early records of the mining village show the two men working side by side in a variety of chores, doing whatever was required of them. Neither led an exciting life, made history or made headlines. They were just working men who served quietly and honestly in the founding of Nanaimo.

John Malcolm signed on with the Company at Stromness in the Orkney Islands. After a stay in Fort Rupert, he was assigned to

Nanaimo and was put to work doing a multitude of jobs required to make the village sustainable. He was among the first arrivals. The Daybook recorded his arrival on December 9, 1852, in one of two large canoes manned by 12 Kwakiutl and carrying 10 labourers, including James Stove and William Ritch.

The next day, John Malcolm and William Ritch were "employed with the mines," and, a week later, everyone worked at building house No. 4. Robert Dunsmuir and Adam French moved into this house in January 1853. Not everyone liked the accommodation. Adam's brother Archibald refused to work until provided with separate accommodation. The small log cabins built to house the first miners were built along what is now Front Street, facing the harbour. To distinguish one house from another, they were numbered house No. 1, No. 2, No. 3, etc.

On January 16, 1853, the miners went on strike over a long list of complaints. They met Douglas when he visited and outlined their concerns, and, according to him, he disposed of their complaints and "brought them to their senses." The angst was over wages that had been stopped at Fort Rupert because of a "disobedience of peaceful order," the first strike. The wages were to be returned.

At the end of January 1853, Malcolm again worked with Ritch and 12 Natives on the coal wharf. By this time the Muirs, Dunsmuir and McGregor were all mining. The mines in Nanaimo continued to have labour trouble. In May 1853, the miners and assistant miners were in another dispute over their pay. Arguments continued back and forth in correspondence between Douglas in Victoria, with McKay in Nanaimo relaying the miners' concerns:

> The present position of affairs at this place is certainly very discouraging. We have here two oversmen whose sole duty it is to superintend 5 miners and half a dozen labourers and though a very small task is expected from these worthies, who have a magnificent field of coal to work on, they cannot succeed in delivering even that small quantity in a marketable state.[55]

More men had arrived from Fort Rupert in April, including Dr. George Johnstone, the Company surgeon. Dr. Johnstone had taken over at Fort Rupert in 1851 after Dr. Helmcken left for Victoria. He continued as surgeon in Nanaimo until August 1854, when Dr. Alfred Robson Benson replaced him.

Dr. Johnstone's salary was 100 pounds sterling per year.[56] During his stay in Nanaimo, the doctor lived aboard a sailing ship anchored in the harbour, due to the shortage of housing. Douglas pressed McKay in August 1853 to find accommodation for the doctor as soon as possible. Douglas wrote about the doctor's working conditions:

> He spoke to me about the surgery, which leaks by the roof, and of his wish to live on shore, which he can do as soon as A. Hunter's house is finished. Knowing the many calls upon the time of the men under your charge, I cannot press you, but I wish that the roof of the surgery may be improved and Dr. Johnstone lodged on shore as soon as convenient.[57]

Dr. Johnstone was allocated No. 2 house. HBC records show that he returned home after his contract was completed in Nanaimo, but he still held an account with the Company until 1857.

In July 1853, John Malcolm used horses to haul logs from the forest to the small water-powered sawmill being built on the Millstone River. The Bastion was nearly completed, and three houses were already habitable. Four others were being built, and there were plans for three more. There was a dire need for lumber to build more houses, but there was no problem getting roof shingles; they came from Fort Rupert.

This same month, correspondence between McKay and Douglas, dated July 17, 1853, noted:

> Two births have occurred at this establishment since the *Cadboro* sailed in the cases of Mrs. Dunsmuir and the native wife of John Malcolm, labourer.

Malcolm's wife's name and that of the child are unknown. The Dunsmuir child was Alexander, the first white boy born in Nanaimo.

In September 1854, oxen were brought to the village to help with logging. Yoked together, they could haul logs from the forest along greased skid roads. The animals had to be fed, and John Malcolm and William Weston were sent up the Nanaimo River to cut hay for the cattle. In almost every job, Natives supplied the extra manpower.

It is not known when Malcolm began assisting Horne in the Company store; perhaps it was in the summer when Horne was ill, or when he was off exploring the Island in 1856. Mark Bate, Nanaimo's first mayor, wrote about Malcolm:

> Malcolm was the salesman at the store—a faithful-reliable man, inflexibly just, of impassive countenance. He was seldom seen to smile when in the performance of his duty—did everything in a sober, businesslike way. He served out rum at six shillings a gallon, or one shilling a bottle (but did not drink any himself); a twist of tobacco at two shillings and three pence per pound; flour, 100 pounds for twenty shillings; tea, one shilling and eleven pence per pound; molasses, two shillings and sixpence per gallon, dried salmon, two pence a pound, bed tick, one shilling and four pence, half penny per yard, and so on. He remained at the store until the stock of goods was sold to Mr. Thomas Cunningham in 1864.[58]

When the Vancouver Coal Mining and Land Company purchased all the Company holdings in 1862, Thomas Cunningham purchased the entire stock of goods remaining in the store.

Malcolm was then placed in charge of the powder magazine, the oil house and other mining requisites near the Douglas mine, which he gave out on written orders. In 1877 he left Nanaimo to work in Wellington and stayed there as long as there was work. He built a small house that stood on the lot where part of the Union

Brewery was erected on Mill Street, and later sold this to Samuel Brightman.

In the 1881 census, John Malcolm was 48 years old. His daughter, Ann, was 25, and he had four sons: John, 17, James, 16, William, 9, and Andrew, 7. The Nanaimo city directory of 1890 lists John Malcolm, William and Andrew living on Nicol Street.

Methodist minister Reverend Cornelius Bryant married John's son James, 18, and Eliza Jenner, 17, on January 15, 1884. Two children were later registered, John David, born 1885, and Louise Ann, born 1887.

The next census, in 1891, shows John Malcolm living with Charles Malcolm, 22, from Scotland, perhaps a visiting relative; Andrew, now 17; and two younger children, James, 7, and Louise, 4.

John Malcolm died in the Kamloops Old Men's Home in 1908.[59] According to Mark Bate, he was "broken down by the infirmities of age, and blind."

Blacksmith Striker: William Ritch

William Ritch was born on November 11, 1831, in the parish of Birsay, Orkney. He signed on with the HBC as a labourer, recruited by Edward Clouston. He left behind his parents, Magnus Ritch and Elizabeth Merryman; his sister, Elizabeth; two brothers, Magnus and Andrew; and his sweetheart, Margaret Swordie, from Stromness. Ritch sailed on the *Tory* in steerage with William Stockand, William Guthrie, William Garrioch, William Work and Christopher Finley (*sic*).[60] In 1851 he served in Fort Rupert as a "servant," and then was transferred to Nanaimo as a labourer.[61]

He arrived in Nanaimo with James Stove and John Malcolm on December 9, 1852, the same day as John Work arrived with Boyd Gilmour and the four miners and their families on the steamer *Beaver* from Fort Rupert. The families were housed in No. 1 and No. 2 houses.

Ritch worked as a "striker" in the blacksmith shop. When

"blowing the bellows," he at times moved very slowly, and, if heat was needed quickly, the smithy, who had a good strong voice, would yell, "Blow up, Willie, blow, blow, mon!" For a time he worked with Isbister as a "hod carrier," someone who assists a bricklayer or mason. (The "hod" is a V-shaped trough carried over the shoulder for transporting loads of bricks or mortar.) And he knew how to salt herring.[62] The fish were plentiful, and being able to salt and preserve fish was a bonus when fresh food was scarce.

Ritch lived in a hut on the peninsula, off Cameron Island. He was incapacitated from work a year before his death, which occurred on March 30, 1888, at age 60.[63]

Big-Island Settler: Magnus Edgar

Magnus Edgar was one of the first settlers on Vancouver Island who did not arrive by sea but came overland. He was born in the parish of Tingwall, Shetland Islands, on October 7, 1826. The Shetland Islands are usually shown on maps of Scotland as the small inset box at the top of the right-hand corner; they are farther north than the Orkney Islands. Shetland, which was Norse until 1468, is an archipelago of 100 islands and islets surprisingly closer to Bergen, Norway, than Aberdeen.

The sea dominates life on Shetland; fishing was and still is an economic factor, but when oil was discovered in the North Sea in the 1970s, the future of the islands changed. Oil is now piped ashore to the Sullom Voe oil terminal for transfer to tankers, bringing considerable prosperity to the islands. Tingwall is where the airport is today.

At the age of 25, Magnus Edgar sailed on the *Prince Albert* from Stromness, Orkney Islands, in June 1851. He then transferred to the *Prince of Wales* for the journey across the Atlantic, arriving at York Factory, Hudson's Bay, on August 13, 1851. There he worked as a labourer until the following year, when he was transferred to the Columbia District.[64] He made the trip across the Rocky

Mountains to Fort Simpson on the west coast, where he met his first wife, Susan. Susan died following the birth of their son George in 1852.

Edgar arrived in Nanaimo in 1853. His marriage to his second wife, Mary Ann, a Native woman, produced eight children: John, Mark, Ann, William, Catherine, Jane, Margaret and Agnes.[65]

On January 25, 1853, Magnus Edgar was appointed "hillsman" in Nanaimo, replacing George Henham, who refused to obey orders from mine manager Boyd Gilmour. This was considered a breach of duty, and it was judged that Henham should no longer be employed in that job.[66] The next day Henham was loading coal. What the position of hillsman involved is unknown.

Magnus Edgar, from the Shetland Islands, left the Nanaimo mines behind to farm on Gabriola Island. IMAGE 1995.002.023 COURTESY OF GABRIOLA HISTORICAL AND MUSEUM SOCIETY

Many of the Orcadians sent money home; others left advance notes on their pay, cashable with the HBC agent in Stromness. In August 1853, in a letter from McKay to Douglas, McKay advised that Edgar wanted to draw from his fur-trade account the amount of four pounds sterling, and asked that a draft in that amount be made to enable him to send money home to his friends in the Shetland Islands.[67]

On October 22, 1862, Edgar pre-empted 91 acres on Gabriola Island, on the southeast section, for one dollar. The property was

Crown-granted to him on August 11, 1879.[68] Located on the banks of False Narrows, it was known as The Maples.

It is unclear when Edgar left mining for farming on Gabriola Island; however, other settlers took up land on the south part of Gabriola in 1862. Thomas Degnen and Robert Gray were two Irishmen who had also worked in the Nanaimo mines and who became neighbours on the "Big Island," as Gabriola was then known. By 1875 the *Nanaimo Free Press* reported there were now 22 settlers on the island.

After the death of his second wife, Magnus Edgar returned home to the Shetland Islands, where he met Ann Swanson; she became wife number three when they married on October 8, 1891, in Vancouver. The *Nanaimo Free Press* of October 19 reported on the marriage:

> About a year ago, Mr. Magnus Edgar, one of the 40-year pioneers of this Province, and a prominent settler on Gabriola Island, paid a visit to his native home in the Shetland Isles. He must have made good use of his time, for on Thursday a lady by the name of Ann Swanson, arrived at Vancouver direct from the Shetland Isles. The expectant bridegroom Mr. Edgar was in waiting, and they were immediately united in holy bonds of wedlock by the Rev. R.R. Maitland. The newly married couple arrived by the SS Cutch last evening, and this morning proceeded in Mr. M. Edgar's beautiful home on Gabriola Island. The Free Press wishes our pioneer friend and his bride a full measure of connubial felicity.

The couple's life together was short, for Magnus died on January 4, 1894, only three years into their marriage. A large gathering paid its last respects to one of Gabriola Island's early pioneers. The Reverend R.R. Maitland, the minister who married the couple in Vancouver, officiated at a remembrance service and paid tribute to Magnus Edgar. Edgar was buried in the Gabriola cemetery. His wife Ann returned to Scotland.

Ill-fated Voyage

Back in Scotland, the Company continued to sign up more Ayrshire miners.

Most of the ship voyages to Fort Victoria were long and tedious and most without major incidents, the exception being the voyage of the *Colinda* that began on August 4, 1853, in London, bringing more miners with wives and children, from Ayrshire, Scotland, to work in the coal mines being developed in Nanaimo.

Expectations were high in Nanaimo in anticipation of the arrival of a new group of workers. Douglas had forewarned McKay of their arrival. In correspondence dated September 27, 1853, he noted:

> I have lately received letters from the HBC House announcing that the *Colinda* of 600 tons was to sail from Gravesend on the first day of August with 40 miners, 36 of whom are married and have altogether 87 children. With the working sons they are considered to be equal to 56 days or days work. This number of people are to be lodged and fed and employed and we must strive to meet their views in all these points.[69]

From the start of the voyage, the Scots were unhappy with the arrangements aboard and declared the food uneatable. A diary of the voyage kept by Dr. Henry Coleman, the doctor-in-charge on the ship, documented the unhappy circumstances. Coleman noted that as the ship rounded Cape Horn, Captain John Mills was too drunk to take the helm, and on several occasions, women complained that he was "loose and lewd" toward them. After running out of food, the passengers requested that the ship land to get provisions. Mills refused. When it did finally land, Mills accused the passengers of mutiny and piracy. On November 30, Admiral Moresby ordered a steamer to bring the ship to Valparaiso, Chile, to answer the accusations in court.

Coleman and one of the miners spoke for the passengers. After hearing evidence, the court found that allegations against Mills were true, that the food was unfit to eat and allowances were meagre. He was ordered to pay the costs of the inquiry. Unfortunately, Mills had no money and had mortgaged the ship and sold the cargo to make the voyage. He had even added 40 Norwegian craftsmen "as useful artisans" to the passenger list and had taken on some cabin passengers to help defray the costs of the voyage. The Norwegians were signed on from Christiana, Norway. By this time, the weary passengers had had enough and left the ship. The ship finally sailed for Fort Victoria without passengers in February 1853.

News of the fate of the ship and passengers took some time to reach Douglas; he was concerned the miners would arrive in the middle of winter. He made arrangements to take them directly to Nanaimo, where he expected there would be enough buildings ready to house them when they arrived. "I shall be relieved from much anxiety when we get them actively and cheerfully at work."[70]

A report finally reached Fort Victoria from Captain Mitchell of the SS *America* explaining that most of the passengers who had left the *Colinda* were wandering the streets of Valparaiso in a destitute state and declared that they would not go on the ship with Mills, but that they were quite willing to go to Vancouver's Island with any other captain. On the day Mitchell left that city, "80 men and women sailed from Valparaiso to work at the coal mines of Lota and that one of the owners of the mines, a Mr. Garland, had told him that he had secured the services of the whole of the Scottish miners and most of the Norwegians."[71] Coal mining at Lota in southern Chile was still in its infancy but would become a major enterprise. When the *Colinda* arrived in Fort Victoria, Mills was acquitted of embezzlement of cargo, but was sued for wages by the crew. A new captain was sent out from London to take charge of the ship.[72]

John McGregor and John Humphrey returned to Nanaimo from Victoria on April 18, 1854, by express canoe and reported of the arrival of the *Colinda* in Victoria.[73]

Some of the miners already in Nanaimo had previously signed on with the *Colinda* and were then assigned to a different ship. The Norwegians were the only group of passengers to reach Vancouver Island. Eighteen arrived at Fort Victoria, but stayed only briefly.

For the Lota coal company, the influx of the experienced Scottish miners was a godsend. The Nanaimo Coal Company would have also welcomed these newcomers; however, on November 27, 1854, a new group of miners arrived on the *Princess Royal* and filled the void.

EPILOGUE

The Scottish pioneers of Vancouver Island were a hardy lot, able to adapt to new and difficult conditions in the new colony. They worked hard, fulfilled their contracts with the HBC and set out to establish roots for their families. Their ability to assimilate new influences enabled them to maintain their culture and give it relevance for the next generation and those to come.

In the beginning, the HBC did not set out to establish a new British colony; it had only looked for a suitable location to establish another fort after the 1846 Oregon Treaty was signed, dividing the territory between Britain and the US. James Douglas was probably more interested in the fur trade than in settling a new colony, but he was a dutiful servant of the HBC and followed instructions from the London office. Somehow he managed to write and sign treaties with the Natives, organize the first government legislature, develop the coalfield in Nanaimo and put the Colony of Vancouver Island on a solid foundation that led to the formation of the province of British Columbia and its joining Confederation.

The first of the HBC ships brought a few Scottish miners with their families, and eight labourers who had signed on to work for Captain W. Colquhoun Grant, the first independent settler. Grant was a fine example of the type of people the Company hoped to attract; he was a big, braw Highlander, 26 years old and six foot two inches tall, with an engaging personality but little business sense. The company paid him a retainer fee as a surveyor, but

This statue by J. Mortimer, dated 1900, honours Scottish poet Robert Burns and is in Beacon Hill Park in Victoria. As in many other communities across Canada, the poet's birthday is celebrated here each year.

IMAGE COURTESY OF JAN PETERSON

when he got lost on his way to Fort Victoria, this sealed his fate in that regard.

John Tod, from Dumbarton, an old HBC fur trader, became the first retiree in Victoria, a city now well known for its retirement community. William John Macdonald, from Skye, became the first senator from Vancouver Island, appointed when British Columbia joined Confederation in 1871. Kenneth McKenzie, from Haddington, near Edinburgh, managed Craigflower, one of the PSAC farms, a subsidiary of the HBC. He brought out his own workers and their families, and established a small community around Craigflower. James Yates, from Linlithgow, came out with the first miners but hated working for the HBC, and had his contract terminated. He purchased one of the first lots sold by the HBC and established Victoria's first saloon.

The Muirs and the McGregors brought in the first mine in Nanaimo and proved the future of the coal industry on Vancouver Island. Robert Dunsmuir, an independent miner, found coal at Wellington, became rich, built the E & N Railway on the Island and built a castle for his Joan. The richness of the coal seam in Nanaimo kept thousands employed for decades.

In 1854, Douglas ordered an official census of the population of Vancouver Island. This census was meticulously conducted, and in July 1855, the results were submitted to the HBC head office in London. Statisticians today would be delighted with the thoroughness of the detail. It showed population, residence, age, and every house, shop, outhouse, church, school and sawmill. Farms had acreage recorded, and cash value of property and equipment, plus the number of horses, cows and other farm animals. W. Kaye Lamb in the *British Columbia Historical Quarterly* published the tables showing the progress of colonization on Vancouver Island.[1] Victoria's population was 232 and Nanaimo's 151, not including Natives. Almost half of the population were children who had not yet reached the age of 20. Douglas was pleased that colonization was well under way.

Today, Scottish and Caledonian societies are in most cities throughout Canada. Highland games and Burns suppers are celebrated, and Scottish pipe bands are established in almost every major city. The Scottish tradition remains strong.

In Nanaimo, McGregor Park on the waterfront is dedicated to the McGregor family and other Scottish pioneers who came to the city and made it their home. Every summer, Highland dancers perform and a piper plays Scottish music in front of the historic Bastion, keeping old traditions alive.

Hudson's Bay Company Ships, 1848-1854

Harpooner
Description:
Barque; three-masted vessel, square-rigged with mizzen-mast, fore-and-aft rigged.
History:
1848-1849: Chartered by the Hudson's Bay Company to carry labourers for the settlement on Vancouver Island.
May 31, 1849: Arrived in Fort Victoria with the Muirs and other miners, and labourers recruited by Walter Colquhon Grant, then proceeded to Fort Vancouver and Sandwich Islands.
Aug. 1850: Left for Fort Rupert.

Norman Morison
Master:
1849-1853: Master David Durham Wishart
Description:
1846: Built of teak from Burma for the East India Company.
History:
Nov. 1848: Purchased for 7,750 pounds from Finlay Hodgson & Co. in London to replace the *Vancouver*.
Oct. 20, 1849: Left Gravesend for the trip to the British Columbia coast with 250 tons of goods for the Russian American Company, 15 tons for the Hudson's Bay Company, and 65 passengers, 60 labourers "between decks" and four women.
Mar. 25, 1850: Arrived at Fort Victoria after only a five-month trip, one month shorter than the norm.
Sept. 23, 1850: Left the coast for London, arriving Feb. 20, 1851
May 24, 1851: Left London for the coast, arriving Oct. 30, 1851
Jan. 21, 1852: Left the coast for London, arriving June 12, 1852
Aug. 15, 1852: Left London, arriving in Esquimalt, Jan. 16, 1853
Mar. 16, 1853: Left the coast with furs, specie and gold dust, arriving Aug. 1, 1853.
Sold for 6,700 pounds sterling to Mr. George Bayley. She was afterwards owned by the firm of Teighe & Company of London, and sailed from London bound for India in 1860.
1865-1866: Disappeared between Australia and India. She was replaced by the *Princess Royal*.

Tory
Master:
1850-1851: Master Captain Edward Duncan
Description:
Three-masted vessel, square- rigged on the fore and main masts, and fore-and-aft rigged on the third aftermost mast.
History:
1850-1851: Chartered from F. W. Green by the Hudson's

Bay Company to carry labourers to the settlement on Vancouver Island.

May 14, 1851: Arrived in Fort Victoria with Captain James Cooper, his wife and family as supercargo.

June 4, 1851: Left for Fort Rupert, but "was unfortunately detained eight days outside before she got clear of the land in consequence of the weakness of her crew, four of whom deserted at this place, and made their escape to Nisqually."

June 28, 1851: Arrived in Fort Rupert and sailed the next day for Oahu and Shanghai to deliver furs and pick up a cargo of tea for England.

1853: Ship was wrecked off Sydney, Australia.

Colinda
Master:
1853-1854: Master John Powell Mills
Description:
Wooden, builder Southwick, County of Durham. Length 119.5 feet, breadth 26.4 feet, depth 19.9 feet. Two decks and a poop, three masts, sail, 581 tonnes, registered to James Tomlin and John Mills.
History:
June 9, 1853: Chartered to Hudson's Bay Company by John Bonus for the owner.

Aug. 4, 1853: Sailed for Fort Victoria with 40 Norwegian labourers, 1 Swede, 43 miners from Ayrshire with their families, a blacksmith and carpenter with families, and two cabin passengers, Miss Leigh and Miss Forsyth.

Nov. 3, 1853: The passengers requested that the ship approach land to get provisions.

Nov. 7, 1853: Landed at Valdivia, Chile.

Nov. 30, 1853: Admiral Moresby ordered a steamer to bring her to Valparaíso, Chile, to hold court on Captain's accusations of mutiny.

Dec. 13, 1853: Anchored at Valparaíso, Chile.

Dec. 19, 1853: Summons issued by W.H. Moorhead, Captain of the *Dido*, for a Naval Court.

Dec. 27, 1853: Report of the Naval Court held Dec. 21-27 by Henry Rouse, HM Consul at Valparaíso, Marcus Lowther, Lieutenant of *Portland*, Robert Cumming, Master of *Braganza*, and Robert Taylor, Clerk of the Court.

Feb. 19, 1854: Left Valparaíso, after Mills sold off cargo to pay expenses, and all but 16 passengers left ship.

Apr. 3, 1854: Capt. J. Middleton, appointed by the owners to replace Capt. Mills, left from London.

Apr. 17, 1854: *Colinda* arrived at Vancouver Island and was acquitted of embezzlement of cargo, then sued for wages in Admiralty by the crew.

List of passengers arriving at Fort Victoria on the *Harpooner*, May 31, 1849
(HBC a. 67/1 fo. 329)
Captain Grant's emigrants, 8 men*
James Yates & wife: ship's carpenter
John Flett: cooper
James Cathie: baker
Alfred Benson: surgeon and clerk

Miners:
John Muir & wife and 2 children
John Smith & wife and 1 child
John McGregor & wife and 2 children
Archibald Muir, nephew of John Sr.
Andrew Muir, son of John Sr.
John Muir, son of John Sr.
Robert Muir, son of John Sr.
Michael Muir, son of John Sr.

Capt. Grant's workers:
James Rose, blacksmith and engineer
William McDonald, joiner and house builder
Thomas Tolmie, carpenter and house builder
Thomas Munro, gardener
James Morrison, farmer and labourer
William Fraser, farmer and labourer
William McDonald, farmer and labourer
John McLeod, labourer

List of passengers arriving at Fort Victoria on the *Tory*, May 14, 1851
(HBC a. 67/1 fo. 639)
Colledge, Richard: apprentice clerk
Hunter, Andrew: engineer
Johnson (Johnstone), George: surgeon and clerk
Johnson, John Henry: engineer
McDonald, William (John): apprentice clerk
Mitchell, William: master mariner
Wark, John: apprentice clerk
Newton, William Henry: agricultural assistant
Langford, (Edward Edwards) and family: bailiff
Bayley, and family: bailiff
Dean(s), and family: bailiff

Labourers:
Atkinson, William
Burris, James and wife
Bayley, Charles
Barnes, Henry
Blinkhorn, Thomas and wife
Bond, Charles
Bond, George
Burden, John
Cluett, Joseph
Cole, Phillip
Cole, Thomas
Cooke, George
Cooper, James and wife
Crogham, William
Cross, William
Craigie, Thomas
Culley, George
Dean, Thomas Aubrey
Dean, George
Elliott, Jonathan

Francis, Matthew
Fiandez, Richard
Fish, Robert
Fish, James
Firth, Robert
Finlay, Christopher
Francis, James
Geal, George, and wife
Gorridge, Alvey
Grinham, Thos.
Geal, James
Guthrie, William L.
Garnich, William L.
Hutton, William
Humphreys, John
Harber, George
Hodge, Henry
Holland, Thos.
Hanham, George
Hayward, George
Jupp, James
Irvine, John and wife
Isbister, William
Lane, James
Longhurst, Jarvies
Lyons, Dennis
Linklater, James
Metcalf, Williaim (*sic*) and wife
Hall, Thomas
Hunt, William
Horne, Adam
Hollard, James
Malcolm, John
Northover, William
Pearson, John
Porter, Robert
Pike, Edward
Parsons, Thomas
Ritch, William
Sales, William and wife
Sratford, Joseph and wife
Staples, Richard
Smith, Richard
Salcomb, James
Shute, Edwin

Stone, Edward
Skea, David
Smith, Thomas
Stove, James
Stockland, William
Thornhill, Richard and wife
Thomas, George
William, Alfred
Wicks, George and wife
Wiles, Emanuel
Work, John
Work, William and wife

List of passengers arriving in Fort Victoria on the *Norman Morison* (October 20, 1849, to July 27, 1850)
(HBC Arch. Winnipeg, MB. HBCA SF: Ships)
Helmcken, John S.: Surgeon

Labourers:
Balls, George
Beachino, Edmund
Burgess, William, DD
Crittle, John
Cheeseman, Richard
Clarke, Robert
Edwards, Geroge
Field, Thomas
Fish, Charles
Foot, William
Guillion, Charles
Gray, Joseph
Gillespie, William
Hawkins, George
Heare, Edward
Horne, Henry
Horne, George
Hillier, William
Hunt, Robert
Jeal, Herbert
Kimber, Edward
Leach, Peter
Lag, William

Martin, Jonathan
Millar, George
Mills, George
Parsons, William
Payne, Charles
Phillips, John
Pearse, Edward
Paddock, James
Pike, William
Pike, Jonas
Pike, Caleb
Richardson, James
Richardson, George
Reid, Robert
Ross, William
Rickets, Samuel
Rowland, Mathais
Sampson, Henry
Sampson, William
Sabiston, John
Sinfield, William
Smart, George
Short, Eli
Sims, Walter
Wain, Henry
Williams, Charles
Willoughby, John
Wickham, Benjamin
Whiffen, Richard
Yellop, John
Young, William

List of passengers on the
Norman Morison, D.D.
**Wishart, Commander, on
a voyage from London to
Victoria, May 24, 1851, to
June 12, 1852**
(HBC Arch. C.I/614,fo. Id.)
Passengers
Cabin:
Miss Bernie
Mr. Benjn Pearce

Mr. Stephson Weynton
Steerage:
William Coray
William Harry
Jas. Marwick
Peter Merryman
David Gunn
Peter Sabiston
Robert Irvine
William Reid
Thos. Abernethy
Henry Wain
David Marwick
Peter Brown
Gideon Halcrow
George Mason
Alexr. Papley
Richd. Cheeseman
Hugh McDougall
John Horie
Has. Leisk
Peter Spence
Jas. Stockand, wife & child.

List of passengers on the
Norman Morison, August 15,
1852, to January 16, 1853, as
given in the vessel's log
(HBC Arch.C.I/615,fos.)
Those hired by Kenneth McKenzie
for Craigflower Farm*
Passengers
Cabin:
Hamilton, Gavin
McKenzie, Kenneth, wife and six
    children
Skinner, T.J., wife and five
    children

Intermediate:
Barr, John and wife
Stewart, James, wife Isabella and
    infant*
Weir, Robert and five children*

Steerage (Women Passengers):
Bell, Miss S.: Single Woman
Froud, Jane: Dairy Maid
Russell, Miss Isabella: Domestic
    Servant
Thomas Miss Amy: Single Woman
White, Miss Heriot: Domestic
    Servant

Steerage (Single Men):
Blaikie, John
Bell, John*
Cheeseman, William
Crittle, John
Deans, James*
Grout, John
Instant, John
Page, William
Page, William, Junior
Russell, Thomas*
Savage, Robert, Junior
Scudder, Thomas S.
Stockand, William
Stubbings, Robert
Thomas, Daniel
Weir, John
Weir, William*
Weston, William
Williams, Richard
Williams, William

Steerage (Families):
Anderson, Robert, wife Jessie
    with John, Robert and Eliza*
Bartleman, Peter and wife*
Casstleton, Richard and wife
Cheeseman, Richard and wife
Davey, John, wife and two
    children
Deans, George and wife Annie*
Deeks, George and wife
Dervint, John, wife, infant and
    two children
Flewin, Thomas and wife

Graham, John, wife and infant
Hume, Andrew, wife and infant*
Liddle, James, wife Ellen and son
    John*
Lidgate, Duncan, wife Helen and
    three children*
Melrose, Robert and wife Ellen*
Montgomery, Joseph, wife and
    infant*
Mullington, William, and wife
Parker, John and wife
Porter, James, wife Eliza, and two
    children
Reed, Thomas, wife, and one child
Russell, John and wife*
Savage, Walter, wife and infant
Sewell, James and wife
Shooter, Edward, wife and infant
Simpson, Henry and wife Adelaide
Simpson, John, wife Elizabeth and
    two children
Tait, James and wife
Veitch, William, wife and three
    children
White, James, wife Mary and
    infant*
Williams, Edmund, wife and two
    children
Williams, John, Senior, wife and
    two children
Williams, John, Junior and wife
Wilson, James and wife*

Craigflower employees of farm and school
Source: Craigflower Resources

Robert Anderson
Peter Bartleman
John Bell
Charles Clark
Henry Claypole
William Croghan (aka Crogan)
George Deans
James Downie
Charles, James & Robert Fish
George Greenwood
John Gregg (aka Greig)
William Harrison
William Hillier
Lynden Le Lievre
James Liddle
Duncan Lidgate
Robert Melrose
Joseph Montgomery
Caleb Pike
James Porter
Thomas Rabson (aka John Rabson)
Mathias Rowland
Thomas Russell
Jonathan & Henry Simpson
James Stewart
James Whyte

(This list may not be complete; six others are listed in the University of Victoria Craigflower resource: John Russell, Andrew Hume, Robert Weir, Joseph Thornton, James Wilson, David Wilson.)

South Wellington School class photo of 1914
Standing, at right:
Teacher Miss Agnes Waugh (later Mrs. Charles Mottishaw).

Front row, left to right:
Elizabeth Fearon, Eliza Louche, Louise Paterson, Marion (Pat) McGregor, Winnie Robson, Edith Cartwright, Amelia Foy, Agnes Wilson, Maggie Donnachie, Alvin Mayloert, Ed Carroll.

Second row, left to right:
Walter Head, Joe Laskovitch, Olive Richardson, Joyce Copeland and Joe Steele.

Third row, left to right:
Emma Krause, Alec Hunter, Jack Williams, Fernie Harrison, Harold English and Joe Hosko.

Fourth row, left to right:
Walter Richards, Harry Devlin, Tommy Cartier, George Tilley and John Richardson.

Fifth row, left to right:
Earl Jones, Jack Parker, George Sheppard, Clarence Godfrey and Ralph Masters.

Sixth row, left to right:
Jerrod McLaughlin, Bob Craig, Nellie Dobblin, Joe Fearon and Emil Breitcheca.

ENDNOTES

BCHQ: *British Columbia Historical Quarterly*

NCA: Nanaimo Community Archives

1: From Scotland to Vancouver Island

1 J. Cook and J. King, *A Voyage to the Pacific Ocean*, Vol. 2, p. 263.
2 D. Pethick, *First Approaches to the Northwest Coast.*, p. 54.
3 BC Archives, A/B/15/4.
4 P.C. Newman, *Caesars of the Wilderness*, p. 260.
5 J. Brown, "A Parcel of Upstart Scotchmen." Quote from HBC governor at York Fort, John Nixon, in 1682. Four recruits were signed on in March 1683 for an initial six pounds a year.
6 N.M.W.J. McKenzie, *The Men of the Hudson's Bay Company.*
7 T. Ball, "Company town," p. 43.
8 R. Glover, quoted in E.E. Rich and A.M. Johnson, *Cumberland House Journals,* p. xlviii.
9 Ball, "Company town," p. 43
10 Newman, *Company of Adventurers*, p.176.
11 Information on the Ayrshire Miners' Rows is from evidence submitted to the Royal Commission on Housing Scotland by Thomas McKerrell and James Brown for the Ayrshire Miners' Union.
12 R. Underhill, "A place to prosper, or just survive?"
13 Newman, *Company of Adventurers.* p. 2.
14 Newman, *Empire of the Bay*, p. 139.
15 File: Andrew Colville CO 2002 August, Hudson's Bay Company Archives.
16 Newman, *Caesars,* p. 232.
17 Newman, *Caesars,* p. 230.
18 Newman, *Caesars*, pp. 263-65
19 HBC Archives, biographical sketch.

2: The Scots of Fort Victoria

1 J. Adams, *Old Square-Toes and His Lady*, p. 3.
2 "Sir James Douglas: A New Portrait," *BCHQ*, 1943, p. 93.
3 F. Merk, ed., *Fur Trade and Empire*, p. 124.
4 W.K. Lamb, "Founding of Fort Victoria," *BCHQ*, Oct. 1937, pp. 71-92.
5 Douglas to Hargrave, the Hargrave correspondence, Feb. 5, 1843. *BCHQ*, p. 420.
6 W.K. Lamb, "Founding of Fort Victoria," pp. 76-77.
7 R. Mackie, *Trading Beyond the Mountains*, p. 281.
8 HBC Archives, SF Vancouver Island.
9 W.N. Sage, *Sir James Douglas and British Columbia*, p. 18.
10 G.P.V. and Helen B. Akrigg, *British Columbia/1847-1871*, p. 63.
11 Annie Deans, Correspondence Outward, BC Archives.
12 C. Lillard, "Douglas was an explorer, too."

13 Correspondence Outward, BC Archives. James Douglas, memorandum, Mar. 19, 1869. Governor Douglas, Miscellaneous Letters Nov. 30, 1859, to Dec. 8, 1863, pp. 130-31. (Also quoted in Ormsby, *British Columbia: A History*, pp. 82-83.)

14 C. Arnett, *Terror of the Coast*, p. 40.

15 J. Moresby, Admiral: *Two Admirals*, pp. 129-30

16 NCA, HBC Daybook, Dec. 6, 1852.

17 NCA, Sabiston family file.

18 J. Peterson, *Black Diamond City*, p. 46.

19 Arnett, *Terror of the Coast*, p. 45.

20 HBC Archives, E.31/2/1 fos. 26-28.

21 Adams, *Old Square-Toes*, p. 117.

22 Newman, *Caesars*, p. 361.

23 A.G. Dallas to H.H. Berens, Mar. 6, 1858, HBC Archives.

24 Correspondence Inward, BC Archives, H.H. Berens to James Douglas, Mar. 4, 1859.

25 *Colonist*, Apr. 10, 1861.

26 *Colonist*, Apr. 10, 1861.

27 J. LeDuc, ed., *Overland from Canada*, p. xxiii.

28 Letter from Charles Ross to his sister Elspat (Elizabeth) (Mrs. Joseph Macdonald) dated Apr. 24, 1843, *BCHQ*, 1943, pp. 103-18.

29 Letter to Donald Ross dated Jan. 10, 1844, *BCHQ* 1943, pp. 103-18

30 Ormsby, *British Columbia*, p. 85.

31 *BCHQ* 1943, pp. 103-18.

32 Letter from Charles Ross to Dr. W.F. Tolmie, Fort Nisqually, dated Jan. 11, 1844, *BCHQ*, 1943, pp. 103-18.

33 HBC Archives, biographical sketch, reference B.239. B.226. (1839-1862)

34 HBC Archives, SF Vancouver Island.

35 E. Stardom, *Dictionary of Canadian Biography Online*.

36 T. Reksten, *More English than the English*, p. 84.

37 Akrigg, *British Columbia Chronicle*, p. 63.

38 Reksten, *More English than the English*, p. 84.

39 Letter to Jos. Hardisty dated 11 May 1870, HBC Archives.

40 Obituary, *Daily Colonist*, Jan. 24, 1892.

41 S.F. Tolmie, "My father," pp. 227-40.

42 Tolmie, "My father," pp. 227-40.

43 W. Kaye Lamb, *Dictionary of Canadian Biography Online*, Vol. XI.

44 Akrigg, *BC Chronicle,* p. 63.

45 Akrigg, *BC Chronicle,* p. 63.

46 Reksten, *More English*, p. 83.

47 Biographical sketch, File DCB XI, HBC Archives.

48 Reksten, *More English*, p. 28.

49 Letter from Governor Simpson to C.T. John Tod, dated Norway House, June 20, 1850. Simpson's correspondence book No. 41, p. 189, HBC Archives, SF Vancouver Island.

50 Akrigg, *BC Chronicle,* p. 63.

51 Flora Hamilton Burns, "Victoria in the 1850s," p. 38.

52 W. Macdonald, "A Pioneer", p. 6.
53 T. Hunter, "Voyage of the Tory."
54 Macdonald, "A Pioneer", p. 6.
55 Burns, "Victoria 1850s," p. 38.

3: The Independent Settlers
1 J.S. Helmcken, "A Reminiscence of 1850."
2 W.E. Ireland, "Captain Walter Colquhoun Grant: Vancouver Island's first independent settler," pp. 87-125.
3 A.N. Mouat, "SF: Ships— Norman Morison."
4 Quoted in J. E. Hendrickson, "Two Letters from Walter Colquhoun Grant," p. 14.
5 Biographical sketch: James Rose, John McLeod, HBC Archives.
6 M.I. Helgesen, Footprints, p. 163.
7 J.K. Nesbitt, "The Diary of Martha Cheney Ella," p. 101.
8 Akrigg, British Columbia, p. 39.
9 Colonist, Apr. 28, 1935.
10 Biographical sketch, HBC Archives.
11 "Census of Vancouver Island, 1855," BCHQ, Jan. 1940.
12 W.R. Sampson, "Kenneth McKenzie," pp. 16-26
13 The New Statistical Account of Scotland: Linlithgow, Haddington, 1845, re: conditions at Rentonhall, Haddington.
14 "Kenneth McKenzie," UVic website.
15 James Deans, Rustic Rhymes, BC Archives.
16 Sampson, "Kenneth McKenzie," pp. 16-26.

17 Robert Melrose diary, BC Archives.
18 BCHQ VII, Robert Melrose diary, July 7, 1943, p. 209.
19 BCHQ VII, Robert Melrose diary, July 7, 1943. p. 199
20 BCHQ VII, Robert Melrose diary, July 7, 1943, pp. 119-34.
21 B.C. Coyle, "The Puget's Sound Agricultural Company," pp. 79-100.
22 Information on the workers comes from Craigflower Resources.
23 Colonist, Feb. 4, 1878, p. 5.
24 Maureen Duffus: Victoria families.
25 Biographical sketch, C.3/15, fo.42, HBC Archives.
26 Biographical sketch, B. 239/g/90, fo.90: B.239/g/91, fo.103, HBC Archives.
27 D.B. Smith, ed., The Reminiscences of Doctor John Sebastian Helmcken, p. 334.
28 Akrigg, British Columbia, p. 93.
29 Duffus: Yates family.
30 B.239/g/88, HBC Archives.
31 G. Barry, The History of the Orkney Islands.
32 C. Lyons, Salmon: Our Heritage, pp. 66, 70.
33 Correspondence: Clouston to Barclay, Oct. 28, 1848, HBC Archives. A 10/25 fo. 395.
34 V.E. Jaynes, "John and Janet Flett," (Wellington, NZ, Dec. 1, 1986). HBC Archives.
35 J. Gould, ed., Memories Never Lost.
36 BC Vital Statistics: Baptisms.
37 Gould, Memories Never Lost.
38 Jaynes, "John and Janet Flett," p. 5.

4: First Mining Families Arrive

1   Mouat, "SF Ships—*Norman Morison*", p. 203.
2   Archibald Barclay to James Douglas, Aug. 16, 1850, BC Archives.
3   Archibald Barclay to James Douglas, Aug. 30, 1850, BC Archives.
4   HBC Archives, B239/K/2, p. 488.
5   Smith, *Reminiscences*, pp. 108-9.
6   H.K. Ralston, "Miners and Managers," in Norcross, ed., *The Company,* p. 43.
7   P. Johnson, "Fort Rupert."
8   Ralston, "Miners and Managers," p. 45.
9   Biographical sketch, HBC Archives.
10 L. Bowen, "A man of contradictions."
11 *Victoria Gazette*: Jan. 13, 1859.
12 Muir family file, NCA.
13 D. Ashby, *John Muir*, p. 150.
14 Smith, *Reminiscences,* pp. 333-34.
15 "The Bevilockway descendants" in P. Nicholls, *From The Black Country.*

5: The Nanaimo Coalfield

1   NCA, HBC Daybook, Sept. 6, 1852.
2   NCA, HBC Letterbook, Aug. 26, 1852.
3   NCA, HBC Letterbook, May 31, 1853.
4   NCA, HBC Letterbook, Feb., 1853.
5   Charles Alfred Bayley, BC Archives.
6   NCA, HBC Daybook, May 1, 1854.

7   L.Bowen, *Three Dollar Dreams,* p. 86.
8   Helgesen, *Footprints,* 1983.
9   *British Colonist*, July 4, 1862.
10 J. Shaw, "The Clan Survives," p. 14.
11 Nicholls, *From the Black Country,* Vol. 5.
12 Obituary, McGregor family file. Also, untitled article, "Nanaimo mourns passing away of a hardy pioneer," NCA.
13 *Colonist*, July 10, 1894, p. 8.
14 E. Forbes, *Pioneer Women,* pp. 114-15.
15 Forbes, *Pioneer Women,* pp. 114-15

6: The Coal Baron: Robert Dunsmuir

1   Archibald McKay, *The History of Kilmarnock* (private printing, 1880), p. 195.
2   Kilmarnock Academy History (1808-1878) website.
3   Paisley Archives.
4   T. Reksten, *The Dunsmuir Saga*, pp. 4-6.
5   Riccarton Old Parochial Register, 1838, SGL, marriages and births, Kilmarnock Old Parish Register.
6   Douglas to McKay, May 6, 1853. McKay to Douglas, May 18, 1853. Nanaimo Correspondence, BC Archives.
7   NCA, HBC Letterbook, 1852-53 and Sept. 27, 1853.
8   Douglas to Barclay, Aug. 11, 1854, and Dec. 25, 1854, HBC Archives, PAM.
9   Reksten, *Dunsmuir Saga*, p. 15.

10 Obituary, *Kilmarnock Standard,* Apr. 3, 1869.
11 Nanaimo Memoranda 1855-1859, Oct. 12, 1855.
12 Norcross, "Birthday tapes tell story of Nanaimo," *Daily Colonist,* Feb. 4, 1979.
13 "Report on the Royal Commission on Chinese Immigration," Dominion Sessional Papers, Vol. xviii, No. 2, 1885, NCA.
14 Reksten, *Dunsmuir Saga,* p. 30. Also *Nanaimo Free Press,* Oct. 10, Nov. 11, Dec. 26, 1874, and Jan. 27, 1875.
15 J. Audain, *From Coalmine to Castle,* p. 56.
16 "Reminisces of Michael Manson," Mike Manson family file, p. 4, NCA.
17 Reksten, *Dunsmuir Saga,* p. 61.
18 *Nanaimo Free Press,* Apr. 13, 1889.

7: **Colony Population Doubles**
1 Ashby, *John Muir,* p. 111.
2 L. Bowen, *Three Dollar Dreams,* p. 50.
3 Hunter, "Voyage of the Tory."
4 McKay to Douglas, HBC correspondence, File 1, June 2, 1853, NCA:
5 Nanaimo City Directory, 1882-83, NCA.
6 Douglas to McKay, HBC correspondence, File 1: July 20, 1853, NCA.
7 NCA, HBC Daybook, Nov. 7, 1853.
8 Hunter family file, HBC McKay Day Journal 1852-54, NCA.
9 Hunter, "Gold rush made his fortune."

10 *Colonist,* Oct. 22, 1864, p. 3.
11 Nicholls, *From The Black Country,* "Richardson, John & Seadonal."
12 Nicholls, *From The Black Country.*
13 Minister of Mines Report 1879, p. 250.
14 Bowen, "Scots kept New Year's traditions," *Times Colonist Islander,* (n.d.).
15 Charles W. Dick, "The Dick Family," from South Wellington Historical Committee, *South Wellington: Stories from the Past,* p. 103.
16 M. Bate, "A Stroll around Nanaimo in 1874."
17 St. Andrew's Presbyterian Church 125 Anniversary booklet, p. 2.
18 Nanaimo Cemetery Records, NCA.
19 "Archibald Dick" in Scholefield and Howay, *British Columbia: From the Earliest Times to the Present,* Vol. IV, p. 792.
20 A. Leynard, "The Coal Mines of Nanaimo."
21 NCA, HBC Letterbook 1852-53, NCA.
22 NCA, HBC Daybook, Aug. 7, 1854.

8: **The Orcadians**
1 NCA, HBC Daybook, May 10, 1883.
2 NCA, HBC Daybook, Sept. 20, 1856.
3 Terry Simpson research on the Horne family.
4 O.B. Owen, "Biography of Adam Grant Horne."
5 *Daily British Colonist,* Dec. 18, 1877.

6 Adam Grant Horne file, Carry Brown Doney, Alberni District Historical Society Archives.

7 *Nanaimo Free Press,* Mar. 8 and Apr. 10, 1884.

8 R. Greene, *Personality Ships of British Columbia*, p. 20.

9 D.B. Smith, ed., *Lady Franklin visits the Pacific Northwest,* p. 126.

10 John Sabiston obituary, *Nanaimo Free Press*, Apr. 18, 1902.

11 Sabiston family file, NCA.

12 Underhill, "A place to prosper."

13 Letter from Alexander Papley, Orkney labourer, June 22, 1867, Nanaimo, to family. Correspondence Outward, BC Archives.

14 Adam Grant Horne, Sept. 10, 1856 diary entry, Adam Grant Horne file, Carry Brown Doney, Alberni District Historical Society Archives.

15 M. Bate, "A Story of Olden Days."

16 C. Davidson, *Historic Departure Bay—Looking Back,* p. 23.

17 Alexander Papley to family, Correspondence Outward, BC Archives.

18 Death certificate registered under the name Alexander Papley, BC Vital Statistics, Reg. #1884-09-042346, Reel B13084.

19 Bate, "A Story of Olden Days."

20 NCA, HBC Daybook, 1852-1854.

21 Davidson, *Historic Departure Bay*, pp. 24-25.

22 BC Vital Statistics, Reg. 1888-09042551, Reel B13084.

23 Davidson, *Historic Departure Bay*, p. 24.

24 B.226/z/1 fos. 2, 31, HBC Archives.

25 B.226/g/2 & 3, HBC Archives.

26 NCA, HBC Daybook, Dec. 9, 1852.

27 HBC Accounts book for Nanaimo A/C/20 n. John Work account, BC Archives.

28 McKay Journal, Aug. 11, 1854, NCA.

29 John Work family research, NCA, Information from HBC Archives, Nanaimo Memoranda 1855-1859. Apr. 18, 1856

30 Work family research, NCA.

31 Letter from Margaret Work in Victoria to Christopher Finlay, July 26, 1857, John Work family research, NCA.

32 *Wellington Enterprise*, Aug. 19, 1898.

33 Obituary for William Isbister, *Nanaimo Free Press*, Apr. 11, 1907.

34 NCA, HBC Daybook, Nov. 26, 1853.

35 *Nanaimo Free Press*, 1924 Jubilee Edition.

36 NCA, HBC Daybook, Mar. 17, 1856, and Aug. 26, 1856.

37 City of Nanaimo Tax Assessment, 1875, NCA.

38 Work family research, NCA.

39 Letter from Robert Dunsmuir to Hon. H.L. Langevin, Sept. 20, 1871. Bate, Box 3, 1997. Political Papers, series #4, NCA.

40 Isbister family file, NCA.

41 Isbister family file, NCA. *See also* Bowen, *Three Dollar Dreams,* p. 181.

42 Bate, "A Story of Olden Days."
43 *Nanaimo Free Press*, Sept. 22, 1875, and Nov. 24, 1875.
44 Alice L. Marwood research.
45 Obituary for Mrs. John Marwick, *Vancouver Province*, Dec. 5, 1926. Marwick family file, NCA.
46 Nicholls, *From the Black Country*, re: Samuel Gough.
47 Lyons, *Salmon*, p. 70.
48 Bate, "A Story of Olden Days."
49 Finlay file, NCA
50 B.226/z/1 fo. 1-2, 18d, 30-31; B.239/g/90, HBC Archives.
51 NCA, HBC Daybook, Aug. 10, 1854.
52 B.226/g/4, HBC Archives.
53 City of Nanaimo Tax Assessment of 1875, NCA.
54 Bate, "A Story of Olden Days."
55 James Douglas to Joseph McKay, June 4, 1853, HBC Correspondence, NCA.
56 B.239/g/32 fo.64, B.226/1/1 fo.22, HBC Archives.
57 NCA, HBC Letterbook 1852-53, July 30, 1853.
58 Bate, "A Story of Olden Days."
59 BC Vital Statistics, Reg. # 1908-09-200539, Reel B1311.
60 B.226/z/1 fos.1-2, 30-31, HBC Archives.
61 B.226/g/1; B.239/g/91, HBC Archives.
62 NCA, HBC Daybook, Mar. 17, 1856.
63 BC Vital Statistics: Reg. #1888-09-043019, Reel B13084.
64 C.1/693 & C.1/839: Also B.239/g/91, fo.13, HBC Archives.
65 Edgar family, Gabriola Museum Archives.
66 NCA, HBC Fonds 1852-1858.
67 NCA, HBC Letterbook 1852-53, Aug. 14, 1853.
68 J. Lewis-Harrison, *The People of Gabriola*, p. 34.
69 Douglas to McKay, Sept. 27, 1853, HBC Correspondence, NCA.
70 Letter from Douglas to Archibald Barclay from Fort Victoria, Nov. 4, 1853, B.226/b/11 fo. 8-9, HBC Archives.
71 Correspondence: David Cameron to Archibald Barclay dated San Francisco, Mar. 10, 1854, Ships: *Colinda*: Barclay, HBC, London, HBC Archives.
72 Speech by Pamela Mar to the Nanaimo Historical Society, Mar. 2006. Research from the HBC Archives.
73 NCA, HBC Daybook, Apr. 18, 1854.

Epilogue
1 *BCHQ* 4, 1940, pp. 52-58.

Books, Articles and Pamphlets

Adams, John. *Old Square-Toes and His Lady: The Life of James and Amelia Douglas.* Victoria: Horsdal & Schubart Publishers, 2001.

Akrigg, G.P.V. & Helen B. *British Columbia/1847-1871: Chronicle: Gold & Colonists.* Vancouver: Discovery Press, 1977.

———. *British Columbia Chronicle, 1778-1846.* Vancouver: Discovery Press, 1975.

Arnett, Chris. *Terror of the Coast: Land Alienation and Colonial War on Vancouver Island and the Gulf Islands, 1849-1863.* Burnaby: Talonbooks, 1999.

Ashby, Daryl. *John Muir: West Coast Pioneer.* Vancouver: Ronsdale Press, 2005.

Audain, James. *From Coalmine to Castle: The story of the Dunsmuirs of Vancouver Island.* New York: Pageant Press, 1955.

Ball, Tim. "Company town: Rugged Stromness in the Orkneys sent many men to the fur trade." *The Beaver,* June-July 1988.

Barry, George. *The History of the Orkney Islands.* London: British Library, Historical Print Editions, 1867. Originally published in 1805.

Bate, Mark. "A Story of Olden Days Graphically Told by One Who Knows." Nanaimo: *The Daily Herald,* 1907.

———. Speech: "A Stroll around Nanaimo in 1874." Mark Bate fonds, Nanaimo Community Archvies.

Bowen, Lynne. *Three Dollar Dreams.* Lantzville, BC: Oolichan Books, 1987.

———. "A man of contradictions." *Times Colonist Islander,* Sept. 28, 2003.

———. "Scots kept New Year's traditions." *Times Colonist Islander* (n.d.)

Brown, Jennifer S.H. "A Parcel of Upstart Scotchmen." *The Beaver,* Feb.-Mar. 1988.

Burns, Flora Hamilton. "Victoria in the 1850s." *The Beaver,* Dec. 1949.

Burrill, William J. "Class Conflict and Colonialism: The Coal Miners of Vancouver Island during the Hudson's Bay Company era, 1848-1862." MA thesis, University of Victoria, 1978.

Careless, J.M.S, ed. *The Pioneers: The Canadian Illustrated Library.* Toronto: McClelland and Stewart, 1968.

Campey, Lucille H. *After The Hector: The Scottish Pioneers of Nova Scotia and Cape Breton, 1773-1852.* Toronto: Natural Heritage Books, 2007.

Cook, James and James King. *A Voyage to the Pacific Ocean,* Vol. 2 of 3 vols. London: Printed by Champante and Whitrow, 1784.

Coyle, Brian Charles. "The Puget's Sound Agricultural Company of Vancouver's Island."

MA thesis, Simon Fraser University, 1977.

Craigflower Resources. Website: http://bcheritage.ca/craigflower/farmfolk/research.html

Davidson, Carole. *Historic Departure Bay—Looking Back.* Victoria: Rendezvous Historic Press, 2006.

Deans, James. Rustic Rhymes, BC Archives.

Forbes, Elizabeth. *Pioneer Women on Vancouver Island.* Vancouver: Evergreen Press. 1971.

Glover, Richard. Quoted in E.E. Rich and A.M. Johnson, *Cumberland House Journals, Second Series*, 1775-82. London: Hudson's Bay Record Society, 1951-52.

Gould, Jan. *Memories Never Lost: Stories of the Pioneer Women of the Cowichan Valley and a Brief History of the Valley, 1850-1920.* Compiled by the Pioneer Researchers (Friesen & Sons), 1986.

Greene, Ruth. *Personality Ships of British Columbia.* Vancouver: Marine Tapestry Publications, 1969.

Helgesen, Marion I., ed. *Footprints, Pioneer Families of the Metchosin District Southern Vancouver Island, 1851-1900.* Victoria: Metchosin School Museum Society, 1983.

Helmcken, Dr. John Sebastian. "A Reminiscence of 1850." *Daily Colonist*, Dec. 1887, p. 4.

Hendrickson, James E. "Two Letters from Walter Colquhoun Grant." *BC Studies,* No. 26, summer 1975.

Hunter, Terry. "Voyage of the Tory: A grisly tale." *Times Colonist Islander,* June 10, 2001.

———. "Gold rush made his fortune." *Times Colonist Islander,* Aug. 5, 2001.

Ireland, Willard E. "Captain Walter Colquhoun Grant: Vancouver Island's first independent settler." *BCHQ,* Vol. XVII, Nos. 1 and 2, Jan.–Apr. 1953.

Jaynes, V.E. "John and Janet Flett: Early Settlers of Vancouver Island." Wellington, NZ: Dec. 1, 1986. HBC Archives.

Johnson, Patricia. "Fort Rupert." *The Beaver,* spring 1972.

Lamb, W.K. "Founding of Fort Victoria." *BCHQ,* Oct. 1937, 1943.

———. *Dictionary of Canadian Biography Online*, Vol. XI. Website: http://www.biographi.ca/009004-02-11-e.html. University of Toronto, 2000.

LeDuc, Joanne, ed. *Overland from Canada to British Columbia by Mr. Thomas McMicking of Queenston, Canada West.* Vancouver: UBC Press, 1981.

Lewis-Harrison, June. *The People of Gabriola: A History of our Pioneers.* Cloverdale, BC: D.W. Friesen, 1982.

Leynard, Arthur. "The Coal Mines of Nanaimo." [n.p.]. NCA, Apr. 20, 1982.

Lillard, Charles. "Douglas was an explorer, too." *Times Colonist Islander,* Apr. 24, 1988.

Lyons, Cicely. *Salmon: Our Heritage.* Vancouver: Mitchell Press, 1969.

Macdonald, William John. "A Pioneer, 1851." Private printing, 1914.

Mackie, Richard Somerset. *Trading Beyond the Mountains: The British fur trade on the Pacific, 1793-1843*. Vancouver: UBC Press, 1997.

McColl, William. "Papers Connected with the Indian Land Question, 1850-1875." Victoria: May 16, 1864.

McKay, Archibald. *The History of Kilmarnock*. Scotland: Private printing, 1880.

McKenzie, N.M.W.J. *The Men of the Hudson's Bay Company*. Fort William, ON: 1921. Fort William *Times-Journal* presses. University of Toronto Robarts Library website.

Merk, Frederick, ed. *Fur Trade and Empire: George Simpson's Journal 1824-1825*. Cambridge, MA: Harvard Historical Studies, No. 31, 1931.

Moresby, Admiral John. *Two Admirals: Sir Fairfax Moresby, John Moresby: a record of a hundred years*. London: Methuen, 1913.

Mouat, A.N. "SF: Ships—*Norman Morison*," July 1939. HBC Archives, reprinted from *BCHQ*, Vol. III, No. 3, notes on the *Norman Morison*, July 1939, pp. 203-14.

Nesbitt, James K. "The diary of Martha Cheney Ella 1853-1856." *BCHQ* 13, 1949.

Newman, Peter C. *Caesars of the Wilderness*. Markham, ON: Penguin Books Canada, 1987.

———. *Company of Adventurers*. Markham, ON: Penguin Books Canada, 1985.

———. *Empire of the Bay*. Markham, ON: Penguin Books Canada, 1989.

Nicholls, Peggy. *From The Black Country to Nanaimo 1854*, Vols. 1-5. Nanaimo: Nanaimo Historical Society and Peggy Nicholls, 1991 to 1995.

Norcross, E. Blanche, ed. *The Company on the Coast*. Nanaimo Historical Society, 1983.

———. "Birthday tapes tell story of Nanaimo." *Daily Colonist*, Feb. 4, 1979.

Ormsby, Margaret A. *British Columbia: A History*. Toronto: Macmillan Publishers, 1958.

Owen, Olga Blanche. "Biography of Adam Grant Horne." Unpublished manuscript, Feb. 1980, courtesy of Terry Simpson.

Peterson, Jan. *Black Diamond City: Nanaimo–The Victorian Era*. Surrey, BC: Heritage House, 2002.

Pethick, Derek. *First Approaches to the Northwest Coast*. Vancouver: J.J. Douglas, 1976.

Reksten, Terry. *More English than the English*. Victoria: Orca Book Publishers, 1989.

———. *The Dunsmuir Saga*. Vancouver: Douglas & McIntyre, 1991.

Rich, E.E and A.M. Johnson. *Cumberland House Journals, Second Series*, 1779-82. London: Hudson's Bay Record Society, 1951-52.

Sage, Walter N. *Sir James Douglas and British Columbia.* Toronto: University of Toronto Press, 1930.

Sampson, William R. "Kenneth McKenzie and the Origins of British Columbia Agriculture." *BC Historical News* 7.4, June 1973.

Scholefield, Ethelbert and F.W. Howay. *British Colmbia from the earliest times to the present (1914),* Vol. IV. Vancouver: S.J. Clarke Publishing Co., 1914.

Shaw, John. "The Clan Survives." *Daily Colonist Islander,* May 12, 1957. p. 14.

Smith, Dorothy Blakely, ed. *The Reminiscences of Doctor John Sebastian Helmcken.* Vancouver: UBC Press, 1975.

———. ed., *Lady Franklin visits the Pacific Northwest.* Provincial Archives of BC (PABC) Memoir No. XI, 1974.

South Wellington Historical Committee. *"South Wellington: Stories from the Past: 1880s–1950s."* Nanaimo: South Wellington Historical Committee, 2010.

St. Andrew's Presbyterian Church 125 Anniversary booklet: 1865-1990. Published in 1990.

Stardom, Eleanor. *Dictionary of Canadian Biography Online,* Vol. XII. Website: http://www.biographi. ca/009004-02-12-e.html. University of Toronto, 2000.

Tolmie, Simon Fraser. "My father: William Fraser Tolmie 1812-1886." *BCHQ,* Oct. 1937.

Underhill, Ruth. "A place to prosper, or just survive?

Motivations for the emigration of Scottish labourers to Vancouver Island, 1848-1852." M.Litt. thesis, School of Modern History, University of St. Andrews, Scotland, 1997.

University of Victoria: "Kenneth McKenzie of the PSAC Farm at Craigflower." Website: uvic. ca/vv/student/craigflower/ mckenzie/kmckenzie-left.html

Newspapers, Periodicals and Magazines

BC Studies
Beaver, The (now called *Canada's History*)
British Colonist
British Columbia Historical News
British Columbia Historical Quarterly (BCHQ)
Colonist
Daily Colonist
Daily Herald
Kilmarnock Standard
Nanaimo Free Press
Times Colonist
Times-Journal (Fort William)
Vancouver Province
Victoria Colonist
Victoria Gazette
Wellington Enterprise

Government Records

BC Archives (including Vital Statistics)
City of Nanaimo Tax Assessment of 1875 [NCA]
Minister of Mines Reports
Nanaimo City Directory 1882-83

Letters, Minute Books, Diaries, Notes and Research

Alberni District Historical Society Archives

Cowichan Valley Museum and Archives
Gabriola Museum Archives
Hudson's Bay Company Archives:
Biographical sketches
Ship passenger lists Vancouver Island
Nanaimo Community Archives (NCA):
Family history files
Hudson's Bay Company Correspondence
Hudson's Bay Company Letterbook
Nanaimo Cemetery Records
Nanaimo Daybook 1852-1854
Nanaimo Memoranda 1855-1859
Nanaimo Museum Archival Collection
Nanaimo Museum
Provincial Archives of British Columbia (PABC)
Scotland:
Kilmarnock Academy History (1808-1878) website
Kilmarnock Old Parish Register
Paisley Archives
Riccarton Old Parochial Register
The New Statistical Account of Scotland: Linlithgow, Haddington, 1845.

Family Research
Maureen Duffus: Yates
Dr. Charles W. Dick: Archibald Dick
Arlene Galloway: Dick, Galloway
Alice L. Marwood: Isbister, Marwick
Cathy Payne: Sabiston
Gary Seriani: Isbister

Bill Sikonia: Stove
Terry Simpson: Horne
Ronald J. Weir: McGregor
John Work: Work

Scottish Assistance
Robert Currie, Scottish historian
Anne Geddes, Community Librarian, Heritage Services, East Ayrshire
Ian H. Macdonald, Chairman of Trustees, Stewarton & District Museum
Bruce Morgan, Museums Officer, Dick Institute, Kilmarnock
David Roberts, Paisley Museum

INDEX

Anderson, Robert, 94, 103–104,
253, 254
Ayrshire, 11, 13, 25–28, 117–120, 158,
192, 242

Barclay, Dr. Archibald, 101, 111, 117,
118, 120, 262, 263, 264, 266
Barr, Robert, 94, 96, 252
Bartleman, Peter, 94, 102–103, 253,
254
Bate, Mark, 190, 201, 212, 229, 232,
234, 255
Bayley, Charles, 76, 144, 145, 183,
184, 231
Blanshard, Richard, 107, 108, 130
Blenkinsop, George, 125, 128, 130,
131
Brown, Peter, 45–46, 50, 100, 252
Bryant, Cornelius, 202, 215, 225,
231, 238
Bryden, John, 149, 164, 166, 167,
169, 170, 172, 187, 188, 190, 222

Cameron, Chief Justice David, 41,
71, 72–73, 108, 266
Cape Horn, 14, 17, 64, 75, 77, 86,
121, 209, 242
cholera epidemic in Scotland, 63,
64, 87, 154, 155
Churches, Nanaimo: St. Andrew's
Presbyterian, 149, 166, 186,
190, 213, 258, 264; St. Paul's
Anglican Church, 212, 227, 237;
Wesleyan Methodist, 186, 234
Churches, Victoria: Christ Church
Cathedral, 103, 113–134
Clark, Charles, 97, 254
Clouston, Edward, 25, 111, 195, 217,
238, 262
Colony of Vancouver Island, 40,
70, 73, 76, 82, 83, 94, 137;
electoral districts, 136; House

of Assembly, 38, 42, 68, 71, 108,
136
Colville, Andrew, 21, 28, 31–32, 72,
92, 96, 100, 140, 141, 260
Comox, 16, 187, 204, 229
Cooper, Captain James, 75, 76, 83
Cowichan: Cowichan Bay,
46; Maple Bay, 114, 115;
Quamichan Lake, 113

Dallas, Alexander Grant, 45, 50–55,
141, 196, 261
Deans family: Annie, 40, 95, 104,
108, 253, 260; George, 40, 94,
105, 253, 254; James, 95, 104,
256, 262
Departure Bay, 162, 166, 173,
216
Dick, Archibald, 190–191
Dick, John, 185–189, 206
Douglas, Amelia, 34, 35, 39, 40,
107, 182
Douglas, Sir James, 33–45;
description, 44; education, 34;
governor of British Columbia,
42, 51; governor of Vancouver
Island, 38; knighthood, 45
Douglas Mine, 158, 184, 192, 215,
227, 229, 237
Dunsmuir, Alexander, 11, 163, 237
Dunsmuir, James, 11, 163, 175, 176,
177, 223
Dunsmuir, Robert, 154, 156,
159, 206, 220, 227–228, 247;
castle 170; coal discovery 161;
death 172; E & N Railway, 166;
family, 163

East Wellington, 187, 191, 197.
See also South Wellington,
Wellington
Edgar, Magnus, 239–242

Esquimalt, 46, 61, 92, 95, 97, 103,
106, 136, 137, 166, 171, 176, 249
Esquimalt and Nanaimo Railway
(E & N), 167, 170, 173, 176, 206

Flett, Alf, 114–115
Flett, John, 110–115, 220, 250
Finlay, Christopher, 220, 225, 251
Finlayson, Roderick, 57, 60, 61–63,
76, 196, 200; chief factor,
63, 77; council of Vancouver
Island, 62; mayor of Victoria,
63
Fort Rupert, 16, 25, 105, 117, 123,
124–131, 140, 143, 146, 179–180,
182, 196, 217, 223–224, 238;
coal discovery, 66; first labour
strike, 127–128; first recorded
shipment of coal, 126; fort
management, 125
French brothers (Adam,
Archibald), 157, 192–194, 235

Gilmour, Boyd, 143, 146, 155–160,
192, 193, 194, 238, 240
Grant, Captain Walter
Colquhoun, 83–91, 117, 120, 131,
134–135, 245, 249, 250

Helmcken, Dr. John Sebastian, 42,
85, 107–108, 125, 129, 130, 137,
236, 251
Horne, Adam Grant, 179, 183,
195–207, 251; Comox, 204;
expeditions, 196, 201
Hudson's Bay Company (HBC),
18–21; farms, 91, 183; Fur Trade
Reserve, 88; Oregon Boundary
Treaty, 20, 37, 245; Royal Grant
of Vancouver Island, 18, 37, 52;
Rupert's Land, 28, 32, 53
HBC Forts: Astoria, 64, 131;
Babine, 56; Garry, 31, 53, 54,
55; George, 35, 56; Langley, 19,
73, 118, 141; McLeod, 19, 56,

57; McLoughlin, 20, 57, 58,
64, 65; Nisqually, 36, 37, 59, 61,
64, 65, 66, 86, 209; Simpson,
20, 80, 127, 131–132, 204, 211,
213, 240; St. James, 34, 35,
40; Vancouver, 20, 35, 36, 37,
61, 66. See also Fort Rupert,
Victoria.
Hunter, Andrew, 75, 179–185

Isbister, William, 224–230, 231,
239, 251

Johnstone, Dr. George, 75, 231,
236, 250

Langford, Captain Edward
Edwards, 75, 92, 108, 137, 250
Legislative Assembly, 198;
Nanaimo, 140–145, 196; Sooke,
133–137, 145

Macdonald, William John, 74–81,
220, 250; mayor 74; senator, 80
Malcolm, John, 143, 178, 195, 233,
234–238, 251
Marwick, John, 226, 228–230
McGregor, John Sr.: Fort Rupert,
124–130; gold find, 131–133;
Jack (grandson), 149–152;
James (son), 150–151; Margaret
(daughter), 152; Mary (wife),
147–153, 192, 196, 235, 244,
247, 250; Nanaimo, 143–147;
Oakwood, 147; William (son),
147–149
McKay, Joseph William, 47,
77–78, 91, 108; Fort Simpson,
204; House of Assembly, 137;
officer-in-charge Nanaimo,
140, 142–144, 146, 158, 180, 182,
185, 193, 235–236, 240, 242
McKenzie, Kenneth, 91–100, 252;
Craigflower Farm, 40, 92, 99,
103, 133; Lakehill Farm, 99, 100;

Born and educated in Scotland, Jan Peterson immigrated with her family in 1957 to Kingston, Ontario. She moved to Port Alberni with her husband, Ray, and their three children in 1972. With a lifelong interest in painting, writing and history, she is recognized for her many years of involvement in the arts and community service. As a reporter for the *Alberni Valley Times*, she won a Jack Wasserman Award for investigative journalism. Jan was honoured with a Canada 125 medal for community service, and has received a Heritage Award from the Alberni Valley Museum & Heritage Commission.

Jan and Ray retired to Nanaimo in 1996, where she continues to research and write. She is the author of nine books: *The Albernis: 1860-1922; Twin Cities: Alberni-Port Alberni; Cathedral Grove: MacMillan Park; Journeys down the Alberni Canal to Barkley Sound; Black Diamond City: Nanaimo—The Victorian Era; Hub City: Nanaimo 1886-1920; Harbour City: Nanaimo in Transition 1920-1967; Listen tae yer Granny; A Place in Time: Nanaimo Chronicles.*